EVIDENCE AND COMMENTARY
Historical Source Books

SERIES EDITORS:
C.M.D. Crowder, M.A., D.Phil.
L. Kochan, M.A., Ph.D.

SOCIETY AT WAR

Society at War

The Experience of England and France During the Hundred Years War

EDITED BY

C. T. ALLMAND
University of Liverpool

BARNES & NOBLE
BOOKS
10 East 53d St., New York 10022
(a division of Harper & Row Publishers, Inc.)

Published in the U.S.A. 1973 by
HARPER & ROW PUBLISHERS, INC.
Barnes & Noble Import Division

Published 1973 by
OLIVER & BOYD
Croythorn House,
23 Ravelston Terrace,
Edinburgh, EH4 3TJ
A division of Longman Group Limited

Introduction, text as printed, final comments, bibliography
© Christopher T. Allmand

ISBN 0 06 – 490161 – 0 (paperback)
      0 06 – 490160 – 2 (hardback)

Printed in Great Britain by
Cox & Wyman Ltd, London, Fakenham and Reading

CONTENTS

GENERAL EDITORS' PREFACE

HISTORICAL WRITING IS based on the control of evidence and commentary. Everything that has happened in the past is potentially historical evidence, and it therefore follows that the historian must apply rigorous selection if his story is to have intelligible form. The inroads of time and common sense greatly reduce the quantity of evidence that is effectively available; but what is left still demands discernment, if its presentation is not to be self-defeating in volume and variety. Even the residue left from this process of irrational and rational refinement does not tell its own story. Documents may speak for themselves, but they say different things to different listeners. The historian's second task is commentary, by means of which he completes the interpretation of the evidence which he has previously selected. Here he makes explicit the insights which have guided his choice of what to include and what to omit. Here he may go beyond what have hitherto been accepted as the common-sense limits of historical territory; the history of public events is extended to the history of private thoughts and beyond this to the historical analysis of instinctive, unreasoned attitudes, and to the gradations of man's experience between these extremes. By this extension of its range, history as a discipline has moved some way to meet sociology, borrowing some of the sociologist's methods to do so.

As a result of the processes by which the historian has become increasingly self-conscious and self-critical, students are introduced nowadays not only to the conclusions drawn from new historical exploration, but to the foundations on which these conclusions rest. This has led in turn to the proliferation of collections of historical evidence for senior students, mainly documentary evidence of a familiar kind rather than the visual and aural records which are made available to younger age-groups.

The question has already been asked whether any further series of this kind is needed. The volumes to be included in this series will effectively prompt an affirmative answer by their choice of significant subjects which, as they accumulate, will provide the basis for comparative study. Each title will authoritatively present sufficient material to excite but not exhaust the curiosity of the serious student. The passages chosen for inclusion must often abbreviate the original documents; but the aim has been to avoid a collection of unconnected snippets. The necessary framework of interpretation is provided, but the student still has the opportunity to form his own judgements and pursue his own insights. A modest critical apparatus and bibliography and an editorial conclusion will, we hope, direct readers beyond these selections to seek further evidence for use in constructing their own commentary.

CHRISTOPHER CROWDER
LIONEL KOCHAN

EDITOR'S PREFACE

I HAVE INCURRED a number of debts while preparing this book. My thanks are due to Professor Christopher Crowder for his patient over-seeing and for much good advice; to Professor D. W. Lomax, of the University of Birmingham, for translating a document from the Spanish (IV.4.c); and to Professor N. F. Blake, of the University of Sheffield, for assisting me with problems of Middle English vocabulary. To my wife, for her encouragement over a considerable period of time, my debt is greatest of all. I, alone, am responsible for any errors and imperfections which this book contains.

C.T.A.
1972

Unless otherwise acknowledged, all translations are by the Editor.
For the convenience of the reader certain
words and phrases (which are printed in italics),
in the untranslated (Middle English) texts are explained as they occur.

ACKNOWLEDGEMENTS

THE EDITOR WISHES to thank the following for permission to use material in their possession, or originally published by them:

The City Librarian, Guildhall Library, London (*The Great Chronicle of London*, ed. A. H. Thomas and I. D. Thornley, London, 1938); G. W. Coopland and the Cambridge University Press (*Le Songe du Vieil Pèlerin*, Cambridge, 1969); G. W. Coopland and the Liverpool University Press (*The Tree of Battles of Honoré Bonet*, Liverpool, 1949); the Council of the Borough of Beverley (the Town Chartulary); the Council of the Early English Text Society (*The Book of Fayttes of Armes and of Chyualrye*, ed. A. T. P. Byles, London, 1932, 1937: *The Book of the Ordre of Chyualry*, ed. A. T. P. Byles, London, 1926: *The Brut*, ed. F. W. D. Brie, II, London, 1908: *The Coventry Leet Book*, ed. M. D. Harris, I, London, 1907: *Hoccleve's Works: III. The Regement of Princes*, ed. F. J. Furnivall, London, 1897); the Council of the Scottish Text Society (*The Bruce*, ed. W. W. Skeat, Edinburgh-London, 1894); the Custodian of the Bishop's Archives and Registers for the Diocese of Hereford (*The Register of John Trefnant*, ed. W. W. Capes, Hereford, 1914: *The Register of Thomas Spofford*, ed. A. T. Bannister, Hereford, 1917); the Editor of the *English Historical Review* and Messrs Longmans (C. G. Crump and C. Johnson, 'The Powers of Justices of the Peace', *English Historical Review*, 27 (1912)); the Editor of *Romania* [Professor Lecoy] (C. J. Liebman, 'Un Sermon de Philippe de Villette, abbé de Saint-Denis, pour la levée de l'Oriflamme (1414)', *Romania*, 68 (1944–5)); N. B. Lewis and the Council of the Royal Historical Society ('Indentures of Retinue with John of Gaunt, duke of Lancaster, enrolled in Chancery, 1367–1399', ed. N. B. Lewis, *Camden Miscellany XXII*, London, 1964); the Oxford University Press (*The Essential Portions of Nicholas Upton's De Studio Militari, before 1446*, ed. F. P. Barnard, Oxford, 1931); the Trustees of the British Museum (Additional Charters 4, 10); Dr Helena Wright [executrix of the late K. B. McFarlane], the Editor of the *English Historical Review* and Messrs Longmans ('A Business-partnership in War and Administration, 1421–1445', *English Historical Review*, 78 (1963)); the Columbia University Press (*The Chronicle of Jean de Venette*, trans. J. Birdsall, ed.

R. A. Newhall, Columbia University Press, New York, 1953); Crown Copyright documents (P.R.O., E101/55/7) are reproduced with the permission of the Controller of Her Majesty's Stationery Office.

INTRODUCTION

SINCE THE EARLY years of the nineteenth century, the period of inter-
mittent war between England and France in the late Middle Ages has
been known as the Hundred Years' War, although it lasted somewhat
longer.[1] The unity which the name recognises is not something which
has been imposed upon it by a later age, all too anxious to attach labels
to movements or events, however misleading these may be: men in the
fifteenth century fully recognised that the war which had broken out
between the two countries in the late thirteen thirties was fundamentally
the same war over a century later. While additional issues emerged, in
the course of time, to those which had originally brought the two
greatest powers of western Christendom into conflict, the very initial
issues were never settled peaceably. The English failed to get what they
sought by force of arms; in the end the French won the war because, by
expelling the English, they were able to frustrate their enemies' ambition.

The causes of the War have been debated at length.[2] Some, seeing
the matter in the perspective of history, have regarded it as stemming
from an almost inevitable conflict between two systems of government
which had grown up in the course of earlier centuries. Others, looking
for more immediate causes, have seen the struggle chiefly in terms of a
dispute between a feudal sovereign, the king of France, and his recalcitrant vassal, the duke of Aquitaine (or Gascony), none other, by an
historic trick of fate, than the king of England. To these may be added a
third cause, the most immediate of all. In 1328, the last Capetian king
of France, Charles IV, died, leaving no direct heir. Edward III, who
had become king of England only a year before, claimed the French
throne by right of being the nearest in line to the succession, since his
mother, Isabelle, was Charles' sister. The throne, however, was seized
by another: the war with France broke out when Philip [VI] of Valois,
the man whom the English regarded all along as an intruder, denied
Edward his rightful inheritance. According to this view of events, the
Anglo-French struggle was brought about by a disputed succession

[1] K. A. Fowler, *The Age of Plantagenet and Valois*, pp. 13–15.
[2] For some of the literature relating to the causes of the war, see the select
bibliography.

1

which, according to English thinking, could only be resolved by the
French 'king' according the English king his just demands. If he refused
to do so, war could be legitimately used to make him change his mind.

The war which ensued, a dominant and seemingly ever-present factor
in the history of Europe of the period, forms the basic study of the
present book. For the historian, it is a war which may be usefully
studied in isolation: it possessed sufficient unity of purpose, involved
much the same territories from beginning to end, and lasted long
enough for it to be regarded, in its own right, as a 'period'. At the same
time the social and military organisation of the two societies at war
changed sufficiently to make them worth studying.

The fortunes of war, which sometimes reflected the domestic politics
of the participants, were forever changing in the course of the long conflict. For the first twenty years or so of its duration (up to 1360), the
turn of events favoured the English. They greatly embarrassed the
French by landing in Flanders (IV.2.B) and then by defeating them in
the important naval battle of Sluys in June 1340 (IV.4.B); they landed
in Brittany in 1342 (IV.3.I) in an attempt to involve themselves in the
events of the war of the Breton succession, and thereby cause more
trouble for the king of France. In 1346 Edward III met and defeated the
French army at Crécy, and in the following year, after a prolonged
siege, he captured Calais. In 1356 his son Edward, the Black Prince,
won another victory at Poitiers, in the course of which the king of
France, John II, was made a prisoner. In these years, too, long raids, or
chevauchées, deep into the enemy's territories were organised, by the
king from Normandy and Calais, by the Black Prince from Bordeaux
and Gascony, and by Henry of Lancaster from both north and south.
These raids were much feared by the French populations: the English
armies did untold harm on these occasions, not merely killing, but looting, burning and bringing destruction in other ways to goods and
property alike. The intention, and sometimes the effect as well, was to
achieve an element of demoralisation and a spirit of criticism of the
administration among the French king's subjects; this was the way by
which the war was to be won. The regular battle on a major scale was
seen to be only the death-blow at the end of the process.

In 1360, after a settlement negotiated at Brétigny, a village near
Chartres, there began a period of peace—or, at least, what was intended
to be peace. Before long, however, the problems of the absence of war
forced themselves upon societies which had come, by now, to accept a
state of war as normal and, in the eyes of some, as even desirable
(VI.2.B), and in the middle thirteen sixties a further period of war
began, this time in Spain. In 1369, the war in France was renewed, and
almost immediately the French, inspired by the able Charles V, began
to regain the upper hand. Under the active command of the Constable

of France, Bertrand du Guesclin, they narrowed the effective sphere of English influence in Gascony: they won an important naval battle off La Rochelle in 1372: and in 1376 and 1377, within a short space of time, England witnessed the death first of the Black Prince and then of his father, Edward III, followed by the accession of the minor, Richard II, to the throne of England. This gloomy period for England, during which she suffered much both from the divided counsels of her nobility and from a series of successful attacks upon her coastline by the Franco-Castilian fleet of galleys, was only finally ended in 1393 when Richard II made peace with Charles VI, whose daughter he was to marry in 1396. At the end of the century, military honours were about even, and the war lay stalemated.

This official, if uneasy and unstable peace remained in force until Henry V ascended the English throne in 1413. Motivated, as some would have it, by ambition, but perhaps, more accurately, by a desire to ensure that the crown which he had inherited should suffer no diminution of the rights which he and his immediate predecessors claimed to hold in France, Henry renewed the war, and twice invaded his adversary. On the first occasion, in 1415, he established an important foothold at Harfleur (IV.3.E) and went on to defeat the French and their allies at Agincourt (IV.3.B): in 1417 he returned to begin what may perhaps be seen as an attempt to obtain the French kingdom *de facto*, by systematic conquest. Overambitious this plan, if it was the plan, undoubtedly was; less ambitious, quite logical and most important for the future was the settlement of Englishmen in Normandy and other areas over which Henry had established control.[3] In 1420, at Troyes, he was able to compel Charles VI to accept peace on conditions humiliating for France: a dual kingdom with England was to be created, and Henry, rather than the true heir, the Dauphin Charles, was to inherit the French throne when Charles VI died.

In its last phase, the war was to be prolonged for about another thirty years. The Dauphin refused to take the sentence of the treaty of Troyes lying down. At first passively, and then with greater initiative, he became the symbol and the rallying-point for those who wished to resist the English invader. After suffering initial reverses, for example at Verneuil in August 1424, he was reinforced by the energy of Joan of Arc, whose impact both upon morale and on the military conduct of the war was considerable. The fourteen thirties, therefore, witnessed the beginnings of a revival in French fortunes, and this process was carried further during the years to come. More actively and positively led than they had been for many decades, the French set about achieving the effective expulsion and defeat of the English who, once more, were

[3] C. T. Allmand, 'The Lancastrian Land Settlement in Normandy, 1417–50', *Economic History Review*, 2nd series, 21 (1968), pp. 461–79.

suffering from divided leadership and falling morale. Diplomatic negotiations and military reforms (II.1.E, F) had their part to play in this transformation of French fortunes. By 1449, France was ready for a decisive effort. Given a pretext to ignore the terms of a truce negotiated at Tours in 1444 which, it was claimed, the English had already broken, she began a series of rapid campaigns which achieved the expulsion of the English first from Normandy in 1450, and then from Gascony, temporarily in 1451, and finally in 1453 (IV.3.C)—a military, administrative and moral triumph for which the French king, Charles VII, was given due credit by his subjects (V.4.B). With these events, the Hundred Years' War was virtually over.[4]

Men regarded war in different ways, ways which may be illustrated from the manner in which the Hundred Years' War began or, later on, was renewed. The theory of the 'just war', which Thomas Aquinas had expounded in the thirteenth century, taught that war was not always wrong, as some maintained. Nevertheless, in Thomas' view there were conditions which had to be satisfied if war was to be justifiable at all: it must be fought to achieve the ends of justice, and it must be declared in due form. That this teaching was, at least outwardly and for official purposes, normally accepted, appears fairly clear. When Edward III challenged Philip VI (IV.2.B) he gave as his reason the French king's failure to do him justice by continuing to withhold from him what Edward considered to be his legitimate inheritance in France. Since there was no other course open to him, Edward declared war upon the French king. Philip's reply was not unreasonable. He chose to regard the English king as a recalcitrant vassal against whom he had no option but to take the strongest measures known to man, an obligation of which Charles VI was to be reminded in the early fifteenth century when threatened with invasion by Henry V (I.1.E). War, however unpleasant, was thus a way of achieving justice and, consequently, peace; it was also seen as a manner of chastising those who broke that peace. In both cases it was regarded not only as permitted by God, but also as a means by which God providentially intervened in human affairs, using men as his instruments to act in his name. This conviction that Divine Providence was on the side of right was a source of great confidence, for even if victory did not come immediately and quickly, God would ultimately provide it. He would never abandon the righteous.

Important as it is to appreciate men's reasoning about war, it should never be forgotten that the realities of war are more forcibly impressive than theories can ever be. Fighting implied armies, and armies involved organisation which, if not already in existence, had to be improvised. In

---

[4] None knew, of course, that it was over, and all English monarchs during the next century undertook some form of military activity in France.

both countries, the long conflict between England and France led to change and development, some of it quite radical. In France, a country growing ever larger and more centralised, the emphasis was chiefly upon the creation of a national army under the national leader—the king—which could meet not only the challenge occasioned by the presence of the English and their armies in the country, but also the threat to security, order and discipline which the unofficial forces roaming around France, the *routiers* and *écorcheurs*, undoubtedly constituted. The presence of the English and of the unofficial forces certainly was a challenge: the country itself was weakened; the royal authority was undermined; and any sense of nationhood which may have existed was attacked. The creation of an effective French army (II.1.) was a slow process which continued for about a century. But by organisation, determination and some courage, the process was completed. The English were expelled from France. Only Calais remained to them after 1453. The activities of the *écorcheurs* were virtually stamped out; the country developed a normal existence and became more prosperous; and the monarchy's authority was restored, its credit greatly strengthened (V.4.B). The army had brought peace: this much, in a narrow context, may be asserted. But the results of war, now successfully concluded, went deeper. The peace which descended upon France was to be both the background and the foundation of a period of greatness which began in the second half of the fifteenth century. The military successes of the late Hundred Years' War, based upon solid military organisation, did more than simply defeat the English. For much of French society, these developments and achievements were to have a profound effect which extended far beyond the expulsion of the English from France. Upon them, at least part of the future was to be built.

In England, too, there was change, in some measure provoked by the needs and demands of a new situation. The foreign ambitions of English kings had led, in the course of the thirteenth century, to an ever-increasing demand for soldiers who had to be paid for their service, whether in France or in Wales, a tendency which was accompanied by the decline of the feudal army, in which recruitment had been based largely upon the fulfilment of the military obligation which was an essential part of the tenurial system. The need for bigger armies, ready to serve outside England and for longer than the forty days specified in the feudal agreement, meant that an army whose existence and cohesion depended largely upon financial reward was coming into being by the time the Hundred Years' War began. This tendency was accentuated, too, by an increasingly fluid society and by a greater flexibility in the use and employment of man-power, which helped those who wished to make a more or less permanent profession of arms. If king John, at the beginning of the thirteenth century and Edward I, at the end of it, had

B

both been faced with a refusal to fulfil feudal obligation by fighting abroad, Edward III scarcely experienced the same problem. By the fourteenth century, both the noble and the non-noble were ready to serve under the king's command because he was able and willing to pay them. It is the ever-increasing emphasis upon financial and material reward which characterises the period with which we are concerned.

In both England and France the objective came to be an efficient military force, properly armed, paid and, consequently, disciplined, rather than the less-well trained but perhaps numerically superior armies which the application of the call to arms, based upon feudal obligation, might have produced. Order, in an age of disorder, was preferable to, and more likely to produce the desired results, than size alone. Discipline had two outstanding merits to commend it: order might be maintained in a place or area where a properly organised army happened to be; it helped, too, as the English came to prove at Agincourt, in the defeat of the enemy in battle. For these two excellent reasons it was highly desirable that discipline be maintained. To achieve it, however, was not always easy. Certain military leaders, but by no means all, might rule their men by force of character or sheer ability. But even great leaders sometimes found this difficult; Henry V himself could not guarantee that all his men obeyed orders. The problem, as many contemporaries realised, lay in the existence of war's material gains which were there for the taking. An army which went unpaid would seek its rewards from other sources, often from those least able to afford them or to protect themselves. The lure of material gain, or the enticements of war, presented not only war leaders, but society at large, with one of its greatest problems: how could might be prevented from always imposing itself? It was in order to achieve some measure of control that the laws of war were frequently reiterated to the soldiers. The courts, especially the newly-constituted military courts, could deal with cases of military indiscipline; but a case in the courts was, in a sense, a confession of failure on behalf of those whose task it was to keep the activities of soldiers within reasonable bounds (III.7.B). And all the while, when steps were either not taken or taken ineffectually, society continued to suffer at the hands of the soldiery.

This kind of activity, as Alain Chartier complained with bitterness, passed off as war. There was always the danger, he went on, that those who were the victims of the pillagers might feel compelled to take refuge by joining in their nefarious activities.[5] The career of a man like Jean Guérard would suggest that this was so (V.5.B). The fact remains however, that in spite of the murmuring of critics and chroniclers, the war was not always and invariably directed against those who lacked the means necessary to defend themselves and their property. If battles

[5] Alain Chartier, *Le Quadrilogue Invectif*, p. 20.

were relatively infrequent, that was partly due to the fact that only on a few occasions were there at least two large forces in the same part of France at the same time. When, however, one side or the other was firmly intent upon a major trial of strength, it could, if it set about matters in the right way, catch the other army whose commander would be hard put to it to refuse the challenge of a battle. In 1356 the French king was determined to meet the Black Prince's army; to have failed to do so would, in a sense, have been to acquiesce too readily in the Prince's destruction of French property, indeed in his very presence with a sizeable army in France, itself a challenge to the French king's authority. Much the same may be said of the decision which led to the barring of Henry V's road to Calais. At both Poitiers and at Agincourt, however, it was the challengers, confident of victory, who suffered defeat. Perhaps we may seek here a reason why the number of great battles was small. For the battle was the supreme test which required, in addition to confidence, a measure of skill and a commander's control of himself as well as of his soldiers, as Thomas, duke of Clarence, discovered to his great cost at Baugé in 1421, if victory was to be achieved.[6]

The war, therefore, was not typified, and certainly not decided by the outcome of battles, the only exceptions being those fought at Formigny in 1450 and at Castillon in 1453 (IV.3.C) which enabled the French to complete the process of the expulsion of the English from France. Feats of arms, both for a strictly military purpose as well as for show and the personal gratification of the participants, were performed on many other occasions (IV.3.J). However, the emphasis was now moving away from the battle fought on open ground, carefully chosen beforehand to give the mounted nobility the maximum of opportunity to exercise the traditional skills. The age was to witness the decline of the dominance of the cavalry, and the shift in tactical superiority to the dismounted soldier, as the English victory at Agincourt plainly showed (IV.3.B). But the English did not have things all their own way. However superior their archers might prove to be in battle, the English came to realise, late in the day and to their cost, that war was characterised more by sieges than by any other form of martial exercise (IV.3.D, G), a fact which led to an increased use of artillery in both siege and battle, and to the appreciation that technical developments now had a contribution to make towards the achievement of victory, an historical development which is revealed in the career of the French master-gunner, Jean Bureau (IV.3.C, H).

If greater military and technical inventiveness were given their opportunity in siege warfare, sieges themselves resulted from the dictates of French geography. The open countryside (*plat pays*) looked to

[6] '... the Duke of Clarence was slayne ... be-cause he wold not be gouerned ...' (*The Brut*, II, 447.)

the castle or fortified town to which it was 'attached'. In military terms, in the event of an attempted conquest, it became necessary to capture the town or castle in order to establish control over the country round-about; at the same time, the town or castle served as refuges not only to which the rural population fled in time of invasion, as men, women and children fled to Falaise and Rouen during Henry V's campaign for the conquest of Normandy in 1417–19, but also within which the force or army which controlled the region sought shelter from the enemy. No conquest, therefore, could claim to be complete unless it included the capture of towns, castles and other fortified places. To the matter of siege warfare, the military theorists devoted considerable attention: the best means of attack, the surest means of defence, the weapons to be used and the ruses to be employed were all described.[7] On this form of military activity the influence of the writers of earlier times, and especially that of the early fifth-century authority, Vegetius, was very considerable. In a military context in which relatively 'open' fighting, based upon the use of cavalry, had predominated, Vegetius' writings had been ignored; but with the increased use of other means of fighting, he rapidly came into his own, being frequently and extensively cited, with relatively little adaptation or critical spirit, by the majority of those who wrote on war, notably by Christine de Pisan, extracts of whose works appear in the pages which follow (IV.3.D, F).

The decline of the pre-eminence previously accorded to cavalry (essentially the preserve of the noble caste) is reflected in a number of ways. Chivalric combat, as Caxton lamented (I.2.E), was fast becomng anachronistic and faintly ridiculous. The Fight of the Thirty of 1351 (IV.3.J), or the great tournament of Saint-Inglevert of 1390, were characteristic of ideas and practices now becoming outmoded. In their place a new form of war was coming to the fore, certainly no less pro-fessional than that which had prevailed earlier, imbued with new ideas and employing new techniques. The importance accorded to the siege perforce obliged the cavalry to seek other employment; gunpowder, and the weapons which used it, could achieve more trouble and destruction in a matter of seconds than earlier weapons had been able to do in hours or days, as when the wall was breached at Limoges in 1370 (V.1.A); the attitude of those who fought for financial reward contrasted sharply with that of their more blue-blooded counterparts, to the point where the mercenary would desert for reasons which would never have pro-voked the same reaction on the part of one imbued with the chivalric ideal (I.3.D); while the active seeking after, and use made of, intelligence

---

[7] On this aspect of human inventiveness see *Conrad Kyeser aus Eichstätt: Bellifortis* ed. Göte Quarg, passim; and Sotheby's sale catalogue, *Bibliotheca Phillippica. Medieval Manuscripts: New Series: Part VII. 21 November, 1972*, pp. 58–60.

gathered by spies working for money was significant of a changing out-
look to war (IV.3.I). If Thomas Aquinas had thought it necessary, in the
mid-thirteenth century, to discuss whether trickery could be used to
bring about an enemy's defeat,[8] few would have had such scruples a
century or so later, once they had been conditioned by the practices of
the leaders of the bands (*routiers*) who seldom held back if their advantage was threatened.

The military means employed to defeat the enemy were thus changing
with the times. But perhaps one of the biggest changes in warfare which
occurred at this period was the way in which, as the scale of war continued
to expand, this expansion was made to embrace larger proportions of
the populations of both England and France than ever before. Consider
France first. It was her unhappy fate to provide the battleground for
much of the war; few of her regions were spared the visitations of even
supposedly friendly armies or the depredations of the unofficial bands;
some, including a substantial part of the country north of the river
Loire, experienced occupation by the English for up to thirty or more
years of the fifteenth century. The result was that most Frenchmen
came, at one time or other in their lives, to learn of war at first hand,
sometimes even at very close quarters if their city was in disputed territory or their village near a battlefield. The slightest acquaintance with
the historical literature of, say, the fourteenth century makes one
appreciate how demoralising this could be for the population—as,
indeed, it was intended to be—and how dispirited those could become
who had nothing to do with the fighting of the war, but who only grew
their crops and asked to be left in peace (III.2.A).

The most scrupulous were in a dilemma when it came to deciding
whether the conventions of law protected the ploughman or the merchant if they could be demonstrated as making a positive contribution
to the war, however small or indirect (I.4.C). Nor was this dilemma
posed by a purely theoretical question, of interest only to the academic
lawyer. On the contrary, the available evidence shows quite clearly that
war was not fought by men-at-arms alone, but that many others, whom
we would today call civilians, had an important part to play in it, too.[9]
The more that we learn about the background and the organisation of
war, the more we come to appreciate that without the active effort of
civilian personnel, war could never have been extended to such large
dimensions. For men were being asked, with greater and greater frequency, to pay for war, a tendency which made war increasingly
national rather than simply a conflict between princes; civilians

[8] *Summa Theologiae*, II, ii, q. 40, 3.
[9] H. J. Hewitt, *The Organization of War under Edward III*, passim; C. T.
Allmand, 'The War and the Non-Combatant', *The Hundred Years' War*, ed.
K. A. Fowler, pp. 163–83.

provided ships for both fighting and transportation (II.7.A, B); they performed many other services, such as growing crops to feed the army,
brewing beer for it to drink (II.6), as well as making uniforms for it to
wear,[10] weapons for it to use, and gathering feathers to help make the
arrows fly (II.5.A). In brief, surnames which survive to this day, names
such as Bowyer, Arrowsmith and Fletcher are more than symbolic of
the civilian population's real involvement in war, which was now
including all branches of society in its manifold activities.

Thus war was undergoing transformation. The more people were
called upon to contribute in different ways towards the defeat of the
enemy, the more they wanted to know and to be kept informed about
the state of the war. Any successful national war leader, therefore, saw
that it was to his advantage to keep his people informed of what was
happening, and to ask for their support, in prayer as well as in material
things (V.3). Similarly, and in complementary fashion, propaganda
came to be used on an increasingly large scale in an attempt, in circumstances in which loyalties could be less rigid than today, to prevent
the enemy's civilian population from giving him their active support. If,
by way of reaction, treason came to be defined in stricter and narrower
terms than before,[11] this was partly to counter attempts of hostile
propaganda to sow doubts about loyalties, for even doubt should not be
allowed to prey upon men's minds, especially in time of war. Hence the
attempts made to prevent men from yielding to written and oral
propaganda by ensuring that they neither saw nor heard it (V.3.E).

A further aspect of war which requires notice is the war fought at
sea.[12] This must not, as has recently been strongly emphasised, be
regarded in modern terms of the control of the sea, but rather in terms
of 'zones of control' which would be maintained for a particular time in
order to enable an army, or merchandise, to be conveyed from one place
to another.[13] It was sufficient to deter the enemy from attacking by
making him feel that he had more to lose than to gain by so doing.
The manner of raising ships to serve at sea is the most persuasive
evidence of this fundamental principle of late-medieval maritime warfare. It has been stated that 'in England private shipowners bore by far
the greatest part of the contribution to the naval war effort',[14] an
opinion which emphasises the important fact that ships were not kept

[10] See E. M. Carus-Wilson, 'Evidences of Industrial Growth on some Fifteenth-Century Manors', *Economic History Review*, 2nd series, 12 (1959–60),
pp. 190–205, and especially pp. 197 ff.

[11] On treason, see J. G. Bellamy, *The Law of Treason in England in the Late
Middle Ages*.

[12] On this subject, see the select bibliography.

[13] See C. F. Richmond, 'The War at Sea', *The Hundred Years' War*, ed.
K. A. Fowler, pp. 98–9. The essay is a valuable contribution to the subject.

[14] Richmond, 'The War at Sea', p. 108.

permanently at the ready but were raised for military service at sea only as and when they were needed. However much Englishmen might deplore the lack of any permanent naval force which might be called a navy (and the fourteenth century witnessed complaints of this sort in Parliament) none was called into permanent existence, partly because of the expense, but chiefly because war was not understood in terms of the constant control of the sea. In a sense, this was not dissimilar from war on land, in which permanent control of territory was the exception rather than the ruling objective. It is, perhaps, no coincidence that only under Henry V, when England's aim and achievement, the more lasting occupation of parts of northern France, came to dominate naval policy, was there any real attempt on the English side to build something like a permanent navy of king's ships, ever ready for war at sea.

The French attitude towards the provision of a navy was a little more professional. It is scarcely an exaggeration to suggest that in the four-teenth century their most successful ventures against the English resulted directly from the steps which they had taken to provide them-selves with, or at least to have access to, a naval force. The French appreciated, rather better than did the English, the value of the galley, with its shallow draught, manoeuvrability and independence of wind conditions, all of which made it into a truly versatile vessel of war. The Castilians and Genoese were peoples with great experience in the use of galleys; both came to provide the French with valuable aid in the war against the English. But the French did much, too, to help them-selves. At Rouen, on the river Seine, they built the famous *Clos des Galées*, where galleys were built and repaired, thereby providing the French with the basis of their naval strength, especially during the reign of Charles V, who personally inspired much of this programme. The results were worthwhile and soon observed. In 1372, the Franco-Castilian fleet attacked and largely destroyed an English fleet of sailing ships becalmed off La Rochelle; and in the years which followed, the southern maritime counties of England suffered a good deal from the attacks and depredations of the galleys, which transported men to carry out swift surprise attacks upon harbours and villages, large and small (IV.4.c). In spite of many requests to the central government for help, there was very little which could be done to counter such raids. Like their counterparts in France, some Englishmen came to learn about war the hard way.

In spite of what contemporaries, at times somewhat despairingly, might think, war could not, and did not, go on for ever. The Hundred Years' War was punctuated by periods of peace, or truce,[15] periods during which the cessation of hostilities might be more apparent than real, but

[15] K A. Fowler, 'Truces', *The Hundred Years' War*, ed. K. A. Fowler, pp. 184–215.

officially periods of peace nonetheless. Diplomacy and negotiation
should, therefore, be seen as an integral part of the study of war in a
period which was to witness the growth in importance and scale of international diplomacy, and an increasing sense of 'specialism' among those
who carried it out.[16] Diplomacy, as has long been realised, was an aspect
of the widening of men's horizons, just as war itself was to be. It involved
not only those parties which confronted one another; others, too, kings,
princes and, most important of all, the Papacy, in spite of deep English
suspicions concerning its neutrality, came to act as arbitrators and
peace-makers between those at war (VI.1). If, for different reasons, their
efforts were not always rewarded, it may none the less be said that peace-
making was looked upon, in a sense, as an effort of the whole community.

Whatever settlement peace might bring, problems were sure to arise,
for peace (or the absence of war) could not hope to solve immediately all
the problems which war had created. Many were the difficulties bound
to remain, of which the hardest to resolve equitably were the social and
human ones. What should happen to populations which had moved as a
result of war? What was to happen to their property? How was the
economy of a region or country, perhaps severely disrupted by military
activity, to be revived and reinvigorated? And in what ways could the
chosen methods best be applied?

These were important problems, and the solutions which were
brought to bear upon them are, therefore, revealing. But of even greater
historical significance is the fact that these problems should have arisen
at all. For their very existence is evidence that war often touched men
other than those directly concerned in the fighting. That famous soldier
of the fifteenth century, Sir John Fastolf, could advocate, in 1435, that
from then on war should be fought strictly 'betwixt men of werre and
men of werre', soldier against soldier (I.3.c), an important and revealing
expression of opinion, not the least for its assumption that civilians were
looked upon as fair game in times of war. Men went to war for many
reasons; the military defeat of the enemy was not always their first aim.

What needs to be emphasised is that the implications of war spread
far beyond the fighting and skirmishing which took place. One may be
horrified by what seem to be the brutal and callous acts of violence and
destruction of which all armies, even the most disciplined, were guilty.
But moral judgements should not be allowed to obscure our appreciation that such methods were an essential part of war, whose aim
was not only to bring the enemy to his knees but to win the allegiance of
his subjects as well.[17] There was a gulf between those who criticised the

---

[16] C. T. Allmand, 'Diplomacy in Late-Medieval England', *History Today*,
17 (1967), pp. 546–53.
[17] H. J. Hewitt, 'The Organisation of War', *The Hundred Years' War*, ed.
K. A. Fowler, pp. 88–9.

admittedly callous methods of the soldiers and the war aims of many of the war's participants, a gap which it would be almost impossible to bridge. They had, however, one factor in common. For better or worse, critics and soldiers recognised that war was a form of human activity which had by now come to pervade all the ranks of those societies in or between which it was being fought.

The manner of viewing war by placing it in the wider context of societies in conflict, and considering its broader human implications, has not always been appreciated. In the past, rather too much has been written concerning the Hundred Years' War in political or military terms which allow for too little else besides. These are valid and important approaches, for war has always been an aspect of what we may, perhaps somewhat loosely, call politics, and its history may be written largely in terms of political situations and political decisions. Likewise, the military approach is clearly relevant and appropriate, and the study of military techniques and weapons is important. But in both cases the field is a narrow, special-ised one, which only too easily becomes an end in itself, without including or appreciating the wider implications of its own study.

In recent times, however, rather different approaches have been adopted. If the laws and conventions of war appear, at first sight, as a daunting and seemingly specialised way of approaching the study of war, the student should persevere.[18] For what he is being offered is an analysis of the conflict between the exigencies of war and conquest, the motives and interests of the soldier and, in many cases, the rights of those who, in spite of themselves, are caught up in war. What results is a thorough 'humanisation' of war, not always pleasant, frequently unedifying, but always intensely interesting as a study of men at war, of their aims, both public and private, their underlying assumptions, and their reactions to particular circumstances as these occur.

Even more recent, and perhaps of even greater importance, is a study of the background to overseas military enterprise in the England of Edward III.[19] Although it is about events which took place 600 years ago, the basic assumptions of Hewitt's book are very modern. For the author, having already written a fine piece of history on the military activities of the Black Prince,[20] has put aside the study of how the sword was used in order to ask how men organised themselves for war in the fourteenth century. The emphasis is no longer upon the activities of the soldier on campaign, but rather upon seeking to find out who he was; how he was enrolled and conveyed to the theatre of war; how he was equipped and at whose expense; what steps were taken to replace a

[18] M. H. Keen, *The Laws of War in the Late Middle Ages.*
[19] H. J. Hewitt, *The Organization of War under Edward III.*
[20] H. J. Hewitt, *The Black Prince's Expedition of 1355–1357.*

horse which might be killed underneath him, and so on. In such a study, the armourer, purveyor and quartermaster are caught in the spotlight, while the captains only appear up-stage—if at all. To repeat, we have here a work of the very greatest importance, which adds a whole dimension to our understanding of war and its background, a book which will certainly influence the way in which the history of war is written for many years to come.

It is in the knowledge of being influenced in this way that the present editor has assembled the collection of documents which follow. An attempt has been made to cast the net of selection fairly widely, and thereby to illustrate from what variety of documents and sources the historian of war may derive not only the detail which he needs for a close study of a particular aspect of war, but also those required for the more general impressions which must be behind any valid generalisation.

Not every act committed, not every attitude adopted during the period of the Hundred Years' War was necessarily or invariably typical of war as men fought and thought of it in the late middle ages. Notwithstanding this warning, one may with justice say that there were ways in which things were generally done, or practices and ideas which found a sufficiently wide acceptance for them to be regarded as fairly typical of the age. Many of the documents which follow reflect what people thought; a certain number from the writings of theorists, moralists and social commentators have therefore been included, chiefly to ensure that the reader shall clearly understand that war was a form of human activity about which men thought and, as will be clear from some of the documents, about which they worried, too. A conscious effort has therefore been made to allow the past to express its own opinions, whether concerning the morality of war, the best method to defend a beleaguered castle, or how a king should take steps to organise his army in one way rather than in another. Similarly, the historians of the past—the chroniclers—have been cited for their descriptions of events and their opinions concerning the significance of those same events. Administrative ordinances, such as those regarding the formation of the French army, have their place, too, for it is important to see not only what was done, but also how it was done. Finally, documents from archives have a most important role to play: these are chiefly the routine administrative papers of government—correspondence, indentures, letters of remission, letters bequeathing grants of land—which tell us so much of what happened, and in what circumstances.

The result may be like a jigsaw but, it is hoped, not too confusing a one. What should result is an appreciation of the breadth of the history of war as a subject, together with its complexity. Clearly, no one kind of source can hope, on its own, to tell us anything approaching the whole truth concerning what men did at war, why, and with what results. The subject is too large for that. What is evident is that to understand his chosen period, and then a particular subject—war—within it, the historian must be prepared to look to many and diverse sources for information and opinion. Only in this way can he study war, the thoughts as well as the actions of the men who, in one or more of a number of ways, became involved in it.

I

LATE MEDIEVAL ATTITUDES TO
WAR

WAR MEANT DIFFERENT things to different people. Those who agreed with Thomas Aquinas (d. 1274) conceived of it on an elevated plane so long as it was fought for the highest end, the achievement of that peace which men equated with justice. In such conditions, when war was fought openly and honourably, it was better for men to suffer hardship, if peace could thereby be achieved. Rulers, it was argued, had a moral obligation to fight in the cause of right. This concept was firmly entrenched in the chivalric code of honour which called upon the strong to defend the weak so that justice and harmony might be maintained.

Chivalry had led to the development of a code of conduct which not only influenced men's conduct in war, but also actively encouraged them to seek glory and fame through the practice of martial acts carried out in the spirit, as well as according to the letter, of that code. In earlier centuries feudalism had produced a military caste—the nobility—associated with war and largely dependent upon it for the justification of its privileges. In the late middle ages many members of that caste, which included the noble, the knight and his squire, became more than ever committed to war both as a way of life and as a means of achieving advancement and honour. The fact is clearly reflected in the creation of a number of chivalric orders, the best known being probably that of the Garter, an order which, through its membership, openly recognised the international character of chivalry.

War, however, was not the preserve of the knightly class alone. Many, far from nobly-born, came to make a business of war, showing less concern for the methods which they employed than for the ends which they achieved. Such men were involved in war for what they could get out of it, and it was they who, in no small measure, were responsible for some of war's more horrific aspects. To the suffering populations, bands of free-lance soldiers became the scourge of God, to be accepted humbly as a purge before better days could come to pass. War was thus often regarded as an instrument of God, by the use of which He showed his hand, the victor being the recipient of his favour, the conquered receiving his reproach. War, and above all its outcome, as the frequent use of

16

biblical texts was intended to show, represented the will of God manifested from the seat of judgement.

The ethic and values of chivalry, expressed in moderation, might well find considerable support. Many, however (and not surprisingly the most outspoken came from among the clergy), found the excesses of certain bellicose practices not only distasteful but a veritable damnation in more than one sense—the cause of death to the body and a danger to the eternal salvation of the soul. Consequently, in spite of its glorious aspects and the positive good which it might achieve, in the eyes of many war was wrong, and ought to be curtailed.

I.1 THE JUSTIFICATIONS FOR WAR

The aim of all war, as St Augustine and many others following him explained, was peace. While Thomas Aquinas condemned those who made war solely for the sake of achieving ambition or of bringing renown upon themselves, he cited Augustine's teaching with approval. War fought with the right motives in mind, and properly declared, was a justified war, and merited support.

I.1.A   The long tradition of Christian thinking on war is reflected in St Thomas Aquinas' use of biblical and patristic authorities in his classic statement on the conditions to be fulfilled in the declaration of a just war. (Latin text in *Summa Theologiae*, II, ii, q. 40, 1; also translated in *Aquinas: Selected Political Writings*, ed. A. P. D'Entrèves, trans. J. G. Dawson, pp. 159–61.)

Concerning War

Article 1

Whether to wage war is always wrong.

In reply to this I say that in order that a war shall be considered just, three conditions must be fulfilled. First, [there must be] the authority of a ruler by whose order war is declared; for no private individual may declare war, since he may seek justice at the hands of a superior. Nor may he summon an army, which must be done in [times of] war, since the well-being of the state is given over to rulers, and to them belongs [responsibility for] the safety of the city-state, or kingdom or province subject to them for their protection. And just as when they punish criminals they are rightfully defending the state against its internal enemies by the exercise of their civil power (so the Apostle [Paul] tells us [Rom. 13: 4]: 'He beareth not the sword in vain. For he is the minister of God, a revenger to execute wrath upon him that doeth evil'), so must they also protect the state against its exterior foes by using the sword of war. Thus rulers are instructed [Ps. 82: 4; Vulg. 81: 4]:

'Deliver the poor and needy: rid them out of the hand of the wicked.'
And Augustine comments [*Contra Faustum*, XXII, 75] that 'the natural
order amongst men, so that it may work in harmony, requires that the
authority and decision to make war should rest with the rulers.'

Secondly, there must be a just cause for war, so that those who are
attacked because of some fault will have really deserved the attack.
Augustine comments [*Quaest. in Heptat.*, lib. VI, qu. 10: *Super Iosue*
VIII] that 'wars are usually said to be just if they redress some wrong;
[for example] if a people or a state is punished for failing to remedy
wrong done by its members, or for neglecting to restore what has been
unjustly stolen.'

Thirdly, the belligerents must have the proper intention in mind:
either some good must be sought, or some evil avoided. Thus Augustine
comments [see *De Civit. Dei*, XIX, 12]: 'For those who really follow
God, wars may themselves be peaceful, since they are not fought out of a
desire for gain or cruelty, but out of a longing for peace, so as to correct
the wicked and relieve the good.' It is therefore possible for war to be
declared by the properly constituted authority, and for a just cause; yet
it may be rendered unjust because the motive for fighting has made it
base. On this Augustine says [*Contra Faustum*, XXII, 74]: 'The desire
to [cause] harm, the cruelty of revenge, the unforgiving and inflexible
spirit, the arrogance of the contestant, the desire to dominate, and all
such motives, are rightly to be condemned when it comes to war.'

I.1.B   War fought in the pursuance of a legal claim was also approved
         by the early fifteenth-century Frenchwoman, Christine de Pisan,
         whose popular book on warfare was rendered into English and
         printed by William Caxton in 1489. (Text in Christine de Pisan,
         The Book of Fayttes of Armes and of Chyualrye, ed. A. T. P. Byles,
         pp. 9–10.)

Chapter II.

. . . that this present werke by somm *enuyous* [envious (person)] myght
be reproched sayeng that it is but ydlenes & losse of tyme as to treate of
thynges not lawfull. First it is to *wyte* [know] yf warres & batuylles,
chyualrye & faytes of armes, of whiche thynge we hope to speke, it is or
not *o* [a] thynge iuste, for as in excersysing of armes ben doon many grete
euyllis [evils], extorcyons and *grieues* [hurts], lyke as *occisions* [killings],
rauuayne [destruction] by forces, to *brenne* [burn] by fyre, & infenyte
harmes may seme to somme that warres & batuylles shold be acursed
thyng, & not *due* [right]. And therfore to ansuere to this question, it is
to wete, that it appiereth manyfestly that warres *emprysed* [undertaken]
by iuste cause be *permysed* [permitted] and *suffred* [allowed] of god, lyke
as we haue founden in the holy scrypture in many places, how our lord

him self ordeyned to captaynes of *hostes* [armies] that whiche they shold doo ayenst theyre enemyes, lyke as it is wreton of one that was called Ihesus, to whom he saide that he shold *ordeyne* [make ready] him to bataylle ayenst his enemyes, & made an *enbusshe* [ambush] for the better to vaynquisshe theym. And of other *ynowe semblably* [much the same] is recyted. And also the holy escripture saith of god that he is *fiers* [strong] & *gouernour* [master] of hoostis & bataylles. And warre & bataill whiche is made by iuste quarell is none other thing but right execucion of iustyce, for to gyue the right there as it *apperteyneth* [belongs]; and to this accordeth the lawe *deuyne* [divine], & semblably the lawes ordeyned of men for to represse the *arrogaunts* [presumptuous] & malefactours; & as touchyng the harmes & euyllis that ben doon aboue the right & *droyt* [law] of warre, lyke as other *auctours* [authors] sayen, that cometh nothyng of the right of warre, but by *euylnes* [wicked-ness] of the peple that vsen it. . . .

I.1.c   A letter, written in the summer of 1373, by John IV, duke of Brittany, to Charles V, king of France, in which he asserts his right and determination to resist with force the French king's unwarranted aggression. (French text in Froissart, *Chroniques*, VIII, 451–2.)

To my well-beloved lord, the king of France. My lord, Charles of France, you who claim sovereignty over my duchy of Brittany: it is indisputable that, since I took the oath of fealty and gave homage to the crown of France, I have always done my duty to it, to you and to those to whom it belonged. In spite of this, you and your servants, quite arbitrarily and without giving reason, have ordered and abetted your Constable[1] and armies, all ready for war, to enter my duchy of Brittany with hostile intent. They have seized many of my towns, castles and fortresses and have taken prisoners, some of whom have been ransomed while others have been put to death; in addition they have committed, and are still committing, outrages, wrongs, damages and other foul deeds against me for which compensation is impossible. In this way you have knowingly, freely and quite openly shown yourself to be my enemy, planning to defeat and destroy me and my lordship. And because you have refused to return to me the lands whose restoration you had promised me by a certain date, such a promise having been made in diverse ways, including by letters sealed by you, as I requested of you on many occasions at considerable trouble and expense to myself, but have rather banished me from my faith, homage and obedience to the said crown of France, although without good reason, since neither I nor any of my people had done anything wrong. Now I, filled with

---

[1] The Constable of France was the chief leader of the king's army. Since 1370 the office had been held by Bertrand du Guesclin.

displeasure and moved by the above-mentioned grievances and a great
number of others which cause me to act, formally notify you that, if you
persist, I shall consider myself quit, free of, and discharged from the faith
and homage which I gave both to you and to the said Crown of France;
free, too, of all duty to obey or to subject myself to you or to the said
crown, or to any cause of yours or even of the crown itself, but will rather
consider and hold you to be my enemy, so that you should be in no way
surprised if I order reprisals upon your supporters so as to avenge
myself of the great outrages, wrongs, damages and deeds which are
mentioned above.

The duke of Brittany and count of Montfort and Richmond, written
with our own hand.

I.1.D   Arguments in defence of war put forward, in 1393, by certain
        Cambridge theologians deputed to refute the pacifist views of
        William Swynderby, a Lollard. (Latin text in *The Register of
        John Trefnant, Bishop of Hereford (A.D. 1389–1404)*, ed.
        W. W. Capes, pp. 377–8; *Registrum Johannis Trefnant, Episcopi
        Herefordensis, A.D. MCCCLXXXIX–MCCCCIV*, ed. W. W.
        Capes, p. 377–8.)

To fight in the defence of justice, against both unbelievers and
Christians, is in itself holy and permissible: to hold the opposite is to be
in error. Such opinion has it that it is not permitted to Christians to
fight against unbelievers, pagans or others, so as to bring about their
forcible conversion to the Christian faith: it [also] claims that no
Christian may fight other Christians for the defence of justice.

This opinion is false and erroneous, for the following reasons. First it
would not permit any Christian king to defend his kingdom against
invaders or false intruders, so that, for example, it would not be right
for the king of England to defend his lands against the French or the
Scots, nor against anybody else, etc. Secondly, the teachings of the holy
Fathers have approved and vindicated just wars as being permissible
and righteous when fought by Christians, if their end is the defence of
justice or the protection of the Church and the catholic faith. Thus
saints approved by the Church have granted indulgences to men going
to war for these purposes: God Himself has vindicated just wars of this
kind, and, indeed, often ordered his chosen people to fight, as is made
plain by a reading of almost the whole of the Old Testament. Thus it
may be accepted that this is true and catholic doctrine, the contrary of
which, propounded by the above-mentioned opinion, is an error.

As for the suggestion that a Christian is forbidden to defend himself
and to resist attack by the use of force, that, too, is an error. This
opinion holds that Christians cannot freely and forcefully defend themselves against injuries aimed at them, nor against bodily attacks, nor

against violence of other kinds. Such an opinion is against the good of the general peace, against all order of government and against all reason. It is an error to uphold it, and the opposite must be maintained, namely that Christians may defend themselves with force, above all against injuries which they suffer unjustly, and may oppose force with force, especially when the hand of correction is not readily available.

I.1.E In a sermon preached before Charles VI, probably in April 1414, the abbot of Saint-Denis urges his monarch to bring his recalcitrant feudal vassal, the duke of Aquitaine, alias Henry V, king of England, to heel by the use of force. The emphasis placed by the preacher upon supporting texts from the Old Testament should be noted. (French text in C. J. Liebman, 'Un Sermon de Philippe de Villette, abbé de Saint-Denis, pour la levée de l'Oriflamme (1414)', *Romania*, 68 (1944–5), 460.)

... And as for the cause for which you are now preparing, I say that you should order it to be fully publicised throughout your kingdom, for it is so evidently righteous that no man may deny the justice of it. For a subject who is unfaithful to his lord must be brought back to subjection by the use of arms and force [2 Kings: 3; Vulg. 4 Kings: 3]. Just so, he who rebels against his prince, and encourages the common people to wrongful doing and to treason, must be brought to heel by the use of force [2 Samuel: 20; Vulg. 2 Kings: 20]. He who publicly insults his lord and his envoys must be punished by force of arms if he will not return to right-doing [2 Samuel: 10; Vulg. 2 Kings: 10]. The vassal who seizes his lord's lands, and refuses to restore them to him, must be brought back to reason through the use of force [2 Samuel: 3; Vulg. 2 Kings: 3]. He who, in any manner, protects, helps and assists the enemies of the king who have committed the crime of treason against their lord, must be punished by force of arms if he refuses to do right [2 Samuel: 8; Vulg. 2 Kings: 8]. When a notorious and open act of disobedience is justified and obdurately defended, the king, as God's lieutenant, must avenge himself of the sin [Judges, 20 and 21]. ...

I.2 WAR AND CHIVALRY

War, as was generally admitted, had its inhumane and less pleasing aspects. On the other hand to the man who embraced the chivalric code, the glory of war and the manner of fighting it could easily mitigate this. Fighting, if carried out in the true spirit of prowess and valour, became in itself a glorious activity, even in the moment of defeat conceded to a yet more skilful opponent; while the *camaraderie* of those who, imbued with this spirit, fought either against or alongside one another, received considerable emphasis in the writings of the period.

I.2.A   Part of Froissart's account of the battle of Crécy, fought in
August 1346, in which he emphasised the opportunity which
war gave to a young man of sixteen, eager to win fame for himself in battle. (French text in Froissart, *Chroniques*, V, 61–3.)

The battle, fought on that Saturday between Broie and Crécy, was
indeed deadly and very bloody; yet, there were done many fine deeds
of arms which were never recognised, for it was already very late when the
battle began. This fact hindered the French more than anything, for
many of their men-at-arms, knights and esquires, because of the dusk,
lost their lords and masters; they wandered about the fields, often
coming across the English whom they fought and by whom they were
at once killed, for the enemy took no prisoners and spared the lives of
none; they had decided to act in this way only that very morning, when
they had heard of the great number of French who were pursuing them.

Count Louis of Blois, nephew to king Philip [VI] of France and to the
count of Alençon, came with his people, bearing his banner to fight
the English, and the count bore himself in a very valiant fashion, as did the
duke of Lorraine. Many said that if the battle had begun in the morning,
rather than in the late afternoon, the French would have been able to
demonstrate great feats of arms, which in fact they did not. Yet certain
lords and knights and esquires on the French side, in addition to certain
Germans and Savoyards, did actually break through the archers in the
Prince of Wales' division, and came up against his men-at-arms, whom
they attacked with swords, man to man, with great valour, and in this
fighting many fine deeds of arms were done, for there were on the
English side those splendid knights, Sir Reginald Cobham and Sir
John Chandos,[2] and many others, too, not all of whom I can name; for
all the flower of English chivalry was there around the Prince. Thereupon the earls of Northampton and Arundel, who had charge of the
second division and were holding themselves in the wings, came to
bring help to the Prince, who was having to fight very hard; and those
who had charge of the Prince, seeing the danger, sent one of their
knights to the king, who was further up the slope on the mound of a
windmill, in order to seek his help. He approached the king and said:
'Sire, the earls of Warwick and Oxford, and Sir Reginald Cobham, who
are in the Prince's company, are heavily engaged, and are fighting the
French very fiercely. They seek your help, and that of your division, to get
out of danger, for they fear that if the pressure is maintained much longer,
your son may have too much to do.' The king, in reply, asked the
knight (whose name was Sir Thomas Norwich): 'Sir Thomas, is my
son dead, fallen or so wounded that he cannot help himself?' 'No,'
replied the knight, 'if it is God's will, but he is in the thick of the fighting, and may need your assistance.' 'Sir Thomas,' replied the king, 'go

_____
[2] See I.2.E and III.5.A.

back to him and to those who sent you, and tell them, on my behalf, not to seek my aid again for fear of what could happen so long as my son is alive; and tell them, too, that I order that the lad be allowed to earn his spurs, for it is my wish, if God so allows it, that the day be his, and that the glory of it belong to him and to those in whose charge I have entrusted him.' Having heard these words, the knight went back and reported to his commander what you have heard. They were all greatly encouraged and reproached themselves for having sent [Sir Thomas]; they now fought more manfully than before, performing many fine deeds of arms, as is recounted, so that the field remained in their hands with honour.

I.2.B By contrasting Edward III's disapproving attitude towards Sir Godfroy de Charny, a highly respected French knight who had allowed himself to be persuaded to attempt the recapture of Calais from the English by underhand means in a period of truce, with the same king's very positive response to the outstanding fighting qualities of Sir Eustache de Ribemont, Froissart is able to emphasise the generous and upright attitude of the true knight to the business of war [1348]. (French text in Froissart, *Chroniques*, V, 246–8.)

When this task was completed, the king of England retired to Calais, going directly to the castle and ordering that all the knights who had been captured should be brought there. Then the French learnt that the king of England had been present in person [at the encounters], and had served under the banner of Sir Walter Manny; and all the prisoners were pleased about this, hoping that they would be better treated as a result. The king then ordered that they should be told, on his behalf, that he wished to give them dinner in his castle at Calais that very evening, the first of the year, which, again, they were glad to hear. And the moment came when the tables had been prepared for dinner, and the king and his knights were ready and richly dressed in fresh, new robes, as was fitting for them; and all the French, too, although prisoners, made good cheer since the king wished it so. And when dinner was prepared the king washed, and all the French did likewise; then he seated himself at table, and made them sit all around him in a very honourable way. And the gallant Prince of Wales and the knights of England served the first course, while for the second, they sat down at another table, where they were served in a quiet and leisurely fashion.

When they had dined, the tables were removed, and the king, who was bare-headed except for a diadem of fine pearls on his head, remained in the hall among the French and English knights. He began to go from one to another, entering into conversation with them. He came up to Sir Godfroy de Charny but, while he was addressing him, the expression on his face changed a little, for he looked at him out of the corner of his eye, saying: 'Sir Godfroy, Sir Godfroy, I think that I owe you but little love, since you wished to steal from me by night what I obtained at very great expense. I was very pleased when I put you to the test; you wanted to have it at a cheaper price than I did, when you thought to win it for 20,000 crowns. But God has helped me by making you fail in your intention. If it is his will, he will aid me to fulfil my entire plans.' Having said this the king moved on, leaving Sir Godfroy unable to say a word in reply.

Then the king approached Sir Eustache de Ribemont, and cheerfully said to him: 'Sir Eustache, you, of all the knights of the world, are the one whom I have seen attack his enemies and defend his own body with the greatest skill and valour. I have never found, in any battle in which I have taken part, a man who gave me so much to do in close fighting as you have done today. I therefore award you the prize, and all the knights of my court agree with me in this decision.' Thereupon the king removed the fine and valuable diadem which he was wearing upon his head, and placed it firmly on the head of Sir Eustache, adding these words: 'Sir Eustache, I award you this diadem for having been the best fighter of the day on either side, and I ask you that you should wear it during the coming year for love of me. I know well that you are lively and fall in love, and that you are always happy to be in the company of ladies and damsels. Tell them, therefore, wherever you go, that I gave it to you. And although you are one of my many prisoners, I release you from your detention. You may depart tomorrow, if you so choose.'

You may well imagine how very happy Sir Eustache de Ribemont was when he heard the noble king of England speak in this way: one reason was that the king had done him a great honour when he had awarded him the prize of the day by placing upon his head his very own diadem of silver and pearls, which was very fine and valuable, all this being done in the presence of so many fine knights who were there; and the other reason [for his pleasure] was that the valiant king had released him from captivity. Sir Eustache, bowing very low before the king, replied thus: 'Noble sire, you do me greater honour than I am worthy of, and may God reward you the courtesy which you do me. I am a poor man who desires to improve himself, and you give me cause and example to strive after willingly. I shall carry out, sire, both loyally and openly all that you have instructed me to do for, after the service which I owe to my much-loved and much-revered lord the king [of France], I know of no other king whom I would more willingly serve, nor with so much love, than I would you.'

Immediately wine and spices were brought, and then the king said farewell to a great many people, and retired to his quarters. The following morning he ordered that two horses and twenty crowns be given to

Sir Eustache de Ribemont, in order to get him home. Taking leave of the French knights who were there and who were going to England as the king's prisoners, [Sir Eustache] went back to France. And everywhere that he went, he spoke of the things which he had been ordered and instructed to speak of; and he wore the diadem which had been given to him for the entire year.

I.2.c   The influence of chivalric ideals upon the practice of war was considerable. The constitutions of a small military order, or brotherhood, in which the founders, the duke of Bourbon and others, undertook to maintain their intention of fighting for and with honour, illustrates the influence of chivalry upon the manner of proceeding with hostilities [1415]. (French text in *Choix de pièces inédites relatives au règne de Charles VI*, ed. L. Douët-d'Arcq, I, 370–4.)

We John, duke of Bourbon, count of Clermont, Forez and the Isle, lord of Beaujeu, peer and chamberlain of France, desirous of avoiding idleness and wishing to employ our person to advance our good name by the profession of arms, hopeful of thus acquiring personal fame and the favour of that most beautiful person, whose servant we are, have sworn and undertaken that we, in the company of sixteen other knights and esquires of worth and ability, that is to say the Admiral of France, the lord Jean of Châlon, the lord of Barbasen, the lord of Chastel, the lord of Gaucourt, the lord of la Huse, the lord of Gamaches, the lord of Saint-Rémy, the lord of Moussures, Sir Guillaume Bataille, Sir Drouet d'Asnières, the lord of La Fayette, and the lord of Poulargues, knights, together with Carmalet, Louis Cochet and Jean du Pont, esquires, will wear on their left leg a prisoner's iron hanging from a chain, emblems which will be made of gold for the knights, and of silver for the esquires, every Sunday for two whole years, beginning on the Sunday following the issue of these letters, in the expectation that, within that period, we may find an equal number of knights and esquires, of worth and ability, all of them men without reproach, who will wish to fight us all together on foot to the end, each to be armed with what armour he will, together with a lance, axe, sword and dagger at least, and with clubs of whatever length he may choose; and that those who are defeated and taken prisoner may be freed on the following conditions: namely, that those among us who are defeated may be released on the giving of an iron and chain similar to those which we ourselves wear, while those of the other party may seek release on the payment of a gold bracelet to the knights, and a silver one to the esquires, these to be given away as seems good. For this reason we, duke of Bourbon and all those above-named, of a common will and accord, have today, in the name of the Blessed Trinity, of the glorious Virgin Mary and of Saint Michael the Angel, again promised to fulfil the undertaking outlined above. And in order to make its fulfilment more certain, and to bind us together all the more in loyal and fraternal love, and above all in order that God and his blessed Mother may grant us their grace in this, as in every matter, and that the honour due to each and everyone of us may increase, we have sworn and promised, and now swear and promise, to carry out, hold and accomplish the articles which follow below:

Namely, that we shall cause to be painted a picture of Our Lady of Paris, before which image we shall have deposited a golden iron, such as the one which we ourselves wear, to serve as a candle holder, in which shall be placed a burning candle to burn, night and day, for two years; and all our arms shall also be painted in the said chapel.

Item, we shall have celebrated daily, for the next two years, in the said chapel, one sung Mass of Our Lady and one low Mass, and we shall donate the chalice, chasuble and other ornaments which are required for the altar of the said chapel. And the Mass will be celebrated every day at nine o'clock.

Item, if it be God's will that we fulfil this enterprise for our own honour, we will endow the candle in perpetuity, and order that the said Mass be celebrated daily in perpetuity. And each of us will have himself painted in the chapel wearing the armour which he wore on the day [of the fulfilment of the enterprise]. And each of us will present to the chapel the bracelet which God shall have given him to wear on that day, or another of the same value. And the said chapel will be dedicated as a thank-offering to Our Lady.

Item, were it to happen that, by forgetfulness or other reason, one of us should fail to wear the iron on Sunday (on which he has undertaken to wear it), he who thus fails shall be obliged to offer to charity 400 shillings for each occasion that he shall forget.

Item, we, duke of Bourbon, shall pay a larger part than the others of the expenses mentioned above, as we are the leader of the enterprise.

Item, if one of us should die within the period in which we are wearing the iron, he shall be obliged to donate and cause his own iron to be sent to the chapel to be placed before the image of Our Lady.

Item, if one of us should die or should be killed before the said day (which God forbid), none shall replace him except by the common consent and agreement of us all.

Item, if any of us goes from life to death, all the others of our company shall have prayers recited for him in the said chapel, each having seventeen Masses celebrated for him, and shall be present at these services, if possible dressed in black. Those who cannot be present shall each contribute their share to the expenses of the obsequies, and shall have the seventeen Masses celebrated wherever they may be at the time.

Item, each and every one of us shall undertake to do everything possible to maintain the honour of all ladies and women of good birth; and if we find ourselves in company where evil or wicked things are said of ladies, then shall we be held to maintain the honour of womanhood, as we would our own, and to do this with our bodies, if need be.

Item, whenever widows, virgins and ladies have need of our aid and assistance, each of us shall be compelled to give it.

Item, we, duke of Bourbon, when we go to England or before the judge who shall have been agreed upon, shall promise to inform all the members of our company who are not on this side of the sea, and to give all our companions such letters from the king granting them the permission and leave required.

Item, all our company shall swear and promise that, within the next two years, none shall undertake any voyage or like venture which could prevent him from being at the engagement to take part in and further our enterprise, except by express licence and leave from us, duke of Bourbon.

Item, for any fault which any of our company may commit, we, duke of Bourbon, shall not be able to replace the recalcitrant except with the agreement of all, or at least of the majority of those named above.

Item, we swear, promise and undertake to respect one another, and to act with all love and loyalty, to guard the honour, seek the good and prevent the dishonour of one another with all our power, and, during the period of the undertaking, to be loyal and fraternal to one another as brothers and companions should be.

In witness thereof we, duke of Bourbon, and the others above named, have all sealed this instrument with our seals. Done at Paris, on the 1st day of January, in the year of grace, 1415.

I.2.D   In *Le Jouvencel*, a fifteenth-century war story based largely on fact while containing elements of fiction, the hero, in a famous passage, elevates the proper pursuit of warlike activities to the realm of the sublime. (French text in Jean de Bueil, *Le Jouvencel*, ed. L. Lecestre, II, 20–2.)

Supper and indeed the whole evening, with Jouvencel and the company being present, passed by in merry-making.

Then Jouvencel spoke cheerfully in these words:

'What a gratifying thing war is, for many are the splendid things heard and seen in the course of it, and many are the good lessons to be learnt from it. When war is fought in a good cause, then it is fought for justice and for the defence of right. And I believe that God favours those who risk their bodies by their willingness to make war to bring the wicked, the oppressors, the conquerors, the proud and all who act against true equity, to justice. Those who go to much trouble to repress such as these are worthy of praise. When war is carried out for this purpose, it is a good and worthwhile occupation for young men, for which they are esteemed by both God and the world. People respect one another in war. One thinks to oneself: 'Shall I let that tyrant abuse his power to take away the goods of another, so that he will be left empty-handed?' When one feels that one's cause is just, and one's blood is ready for the fight, tears come to the eye. A warm feeling of loyalty and pity comes into the heart on seeing one's friend expose his body with such courage to carry out and to accomplish the will of our Creator; and one makes up one's mind to go and die or live with him, and, out of love, not to abandon him. No man who has not experienced it knows how to speak of the satisfaction which comes from this sort of action. Do you think that a man who acts in this way will fear death? Not at all; for he is so comforted, so much carried away that he doesn't realise where he is. He simply does not fear anything. I think that he who serves in arms in this way as the true agent of God is equally blessed both in this world and in the next.

For this [reason] I beg you all, my brothers, friends and companions, that you should always wish it thus, and that you should never go to war in support of an unjust quarrel; nor that you should use this gift of grace given to you by God so as to be noble and valiant in the service of the devil, by helping persons pursue their unjust causes, or by assisting the proud, the grasping, or those who are filled with hatred, so that, if God should so will it, we shall achieve our salvation by the exercise of arms just as we would by contemplation or by only eating roots.

I say, further, that those to whom God has given the grace of a healthy body should gladly offer it for the faith of Our Lord Jesus Christ in order to give aid to the just cause, rather than to drinking or committing dissolute, unreasonable and excessive acts without reason, none of which they are asked to do, and by which, disregarding the consequences, they bring advantage neither to themselves nor to others. They could just as well be a horse or stag which, to show its independence, jumps over a hedge, or a ditch or a rock, impaling a stake into its belly or breaking neck or limb, simply from jumping from high up without reflecting on the possible dangers in store. For this reason I tell you that he who uses his body and destroys it without good reason is worse than a dumb beast. For God has given men their natural gifts to use for good purposes, namely, to those in religion in order to worship our Creator and to pray for the whole world; to others in order to plough and to cause the earth to yield her fruits, from which they and others may live; and to men of war, in order to defend those who pray and those who till, as well as the public good and those to whom wrong is done; and they should use their skills to these ends, not to useless ones which may bring about their untimely deaths. I pray you, therefore, not to use your bodies in such exploits and excesses, nor in any [activity] which is not of advantage to God, to your neighbour, to the public good or to yourselves.'

It was of such things that Jouvencel and his companions spoke that evening; and frequently, when he had leisure, he willingly told them some good tale.

I.2.E   At the end of his translation of Ramon Lull's work on chivalry, William Caxton complains of the decline of chivalric practices in the England of his day, and suggests positive methods to encourage their revival [c. 1483–5]. (Text in William Caxton, *The Book of the Ordre of Chyualry*, ed. A. T. P. Byles, pp. 121–5.)

Here endeth the book of thordre of chyualry, whiche book is translated oute of Frensshe in to Englysshe, at a requeste of a gentyl and noble esquyer, by me, William Caxton, dwellynge at Westmynstre besyde London, in the most best wyse that God had *suffred* [allowed] me, and accordynge to the copye that the sayd squyer delyuerd to me; whiche book is not requysyte to euery *comyn* [common] man to haue, but to noble gentylmen that by their vertu entende to come & entre in to the noble ordre of chyualry, the whiche in these late dayes hath ben vsed accordyng to this booke here to fore wreton but forgeten, and *thexersytees* [the practices] of chyualry not vsed, honoured ne excercysed as hit hath ben in auncyent tyme; at whiche tyme the noble actes of the knyghtes of Englond that vsed chyualry were *renomed* [renowned] thurgh the vnyuersal world, as for to speke to fore thyncarnacion of Jhesu Cryste, where were there euer ony lyke to Brenius and Belynus,[3] that from the grete Brytayne, now called Englond, vnto Rome & *ferre* [far] beyonde conquered many *Royammes* [kingdoms] and londes, whos noble actes remayne in thold hystoryes of the Romayns. And *syth* [since] the Incarnacion of Oure Lord, byhold that noble kyng of Brytayne, kyng Arthur, with al the noble knyghtes of the round table, whos noble actes & noble chyualry of his knyghtes occupye so many large volumes, that is a world or as thyng incredyble to byleue.

O, ye knyghtes of Englond, where is the custome and vsage of noble chyualry that was vsed in tho dayes? What do ye now but go to the *baynes* [baths] & playe att dyse? And some, not wel aduysed, vse not honest and good rule ageyn alle ordre of knyghthode. Leue this, leue it and rede the noble volumes of *saynt graal* [The Holy Grail], of Lancelot,[4] of Galaad,[5] of Trystram,[6] of Perse Forest,[7] of Percyual,[8] of Gawayn[9]

---

[3] Brennius and Belinus, the sons of a British ruler, Dunvallo Molmutius, were well-known for their conquests and military exploits. They appear in many medieval histories of early Britain.

[4] Lancelot of the Lake.   [7] Perys Forest, an evil knight.
[5] Galahad, a Grail knight.   [8] Perceval, a Grail knight.
[6] Tristram.   [9] Gawain, nephew of King Arthur.

& many mo. Ther shalle ye see manhode, curtosye & gentylnesse. And loke, in latter dayes, of the noble actes syth the conquest, as in kyng Rychard dayes *cuer du lyon* [Lion heart]; Edward the fyrste and the thyrd, and his noble sones; Syre Robert Knolles; Syr Iohan Hawkwode; Syr Iohan Chaundos; & Syre Gaultier Manny,[10] rede Froissart. And also behold that vyctoryous and noble kynge, Harry the fyfthe, and the capytayns vnder hym, his noble bretheren, therle of Salysbury Montagu,[11] and many other whoos names shyne gloryously by their vertuous noblesse & actes that they did in thonour of thordre of chyualry. Allas, what doo ye, but slepe & take ease, and ar al *disordred* [degraded] fro chyualry. I wold demaunde a question, yf I shold not displease: how many knyghtes ben ther now in Englond that haue thuse and thexcercyse of a knyghte, that is to wete, that he knoweth his hors, & his hors hym; that is to saye, he beynge redy at a poynt to haue al thyng that longeth to a knight, an hors that is *accordyng* [compliant] and broken after his hand, his armures and harnoys *mete* [decent] and *syttyng* [fitting] & so forth, et cetera. I suppose and a due serche shold be made, ther shold be many founden that lacke, the more pyte is. I wold it pleasyd oure souerayne lord that twyes or thryes in a yere, or at the lest *ones* [once], he wold do crye *Iustes* [jousts] of pees, to thende that euery knyght shold haue hors and harneys, and also the vse and craft of a knyght, and also to tornoye one ageynste one, or ii ageynst ii, and the best to haue a prys, a dyamond or Iewel, suche as shold please the prynce. This shold cause gentylmen to resorte to thauncyent customes of chyualry, to grete fame and *renomee* [renown], and also to be alwey redy to serue theyr prynce whan he shalle calle them, or haue nede. Thenne *late* [let] euery man that is come of noble blood and entendeth to come to the noble ordre of chyualry rede this lytyl book, and doo therafter in kepyng the lore and commaundements therein comprysed. And thenne I doubte not he shall atteyne to thordre of chyualry, et cetera. And thus thys lytyl book I presente to my redoubted, naturel and most *dradde* [dread] souerayne lord, kyng Rychard, [III] kyng of Englond and of Fraunce, to thende that he commaunde this book to be had and redde vnto other yong lordes, knyghtes and gentylmen within this royame, that the noble ordre of chyualrye be herafter better vsed & honoured than hit hath ben in late dayes passed. And herin he shalle do a noble & vertuouse dede. And I shalle pray almyghty God for his long lyf & prosperous welfare, & that he may haue victory of al his enemyes; and, after this short & transitory lyf, to haue euerlastyng lyf in heuen, where as is Ioye and blysse, world without ende, Amen.

[10] Knolles, Hawkwood, Chandos and Manny were well-known soldiers of the fourteenth century. For other references to Chandos, see I.2.A and III.5.A.

[11] Thomas de Montacute, earl of Salisbury, a famous English captain of the fifteenth century.

I.3 THE PROFESSIONAL ATTITUDE

Not all soldiers viewed warfare with the eyes of the chivalric knight. For many, probably for the majority, war was a business like any other, whose rewards compensated for its dangers. To such as these, the prospects of profit and self-improvement were in the forefront of their minds. But the military aims of war were not forgotten; it is useful to be reminded that some looked upon war as soldiers should, their intention being the military defeat of the enemy.

I.3.A   In this passage, Froissart underlines the difficulties faced by the peace-maker in late fourteenth-century England, while illustrating the feelings of some of the soldiery towards the prospect of peace [1390]. (French text in Froissart, *Chroniques*, XIV, 314–5.)

You will recall what has already been recounted, namely that Sir Thomas Percy was sent to the French kingdom on behalf of king Richard [II] of England who, as he showed then and has again shown since, greatly desired that a final peace should be arranged between France and England. In this aim two of his uncles, John, duke of Lancaster, and Edmund, duke of York, were very much in agreement with him; but his other uncle, their brother, Thomas, duke of Gloucester, earl of Essex and of Buckingham, and Constable of England, did not nor would not in any way agree, secretly maintaining that he would never concur in any peace made between the French and themselves, whatever the demands or offers might be, if it were not to their honour and did not lead to the return of all the lands, cities, towns, castles and lordships which had come to the king of England and his heirs by right of succession, and which the French, fraudulently and without any right whatever, had taken back. In addition the French should pay the sum of 1,400,000 francs which they still owed when they had renewed the wars.

Several English barons were of this opinion, too, especially the earl of Arundel, who declared that he would not change his opinion as long as he lived; but the other barons of England who agreed that the duke of Gloucester had right and reason for his point of view, kept their opinions to themselves when they saw that the English king earnestly wished for the peace which he had so much at heart. Others, too, who favoured the [continuation of the] war were the less well-off knights, esquires and archers of England, who appreciated its comforts and, indeed, maintained their status through war.

You should understand that by no manner of means whatever could love, peace or concord exist or be brought about between these parties.

For the French, in their demands, required that Calais should be demolished, and that Guînes, Hames, Marck and Oye, all the lands around Fréthun, and all the dependencies of Guînes up to the river at Gravelines should be held by them.[12] It is true that the king of France and those who were consulted about it were willing to restore to the English king and to his heirs as much land or more (to be taken from lands won in Aquitaine) than the towns, castles and lands above-named were worth annually to the crown of England. But the duke of Gloucester argued very strongly against this proposal, saying:

'The French want to pay us out of what is already ours. They know this: we hold charters, sealed by king John [II] and all his children, that all Aquitaine was given over to us to hold in sovereignty, so that what they have since retaken, they have obtained by fraud and trickery; for they are constantly plotting, both day and night, so as to deceive us. If Calais and the other lands which they are demanding were given back to them, they would be masters of all their maritime frontiers, and all our conquests would be lost. So I shall never agree to peace for as long as I live.'

I.3.B   In this agreement, made in 1421, two English esquires look to the future, and in so doing reveal something of their attitude towards Henry V's wars in France. (French text in K. B. McFarlane, 'A Business-partnership in War and Administration, 1421–1445', *English Historical Review*, 78 (1963), 309–10.)

The agreement made between Nicholas Molyneux and John Wynter, esquires, to maintain and preserve, point for point, the articles in the form and manner which follows:

[1] First, to increase and augment the respect and brotherhood which has for long existed between the said Molyneux and Wynter, so that it may henceforth be even stronger and more enduring, the said persons have personally sworn to become brothers in arms;[13] that is to say, that each shall be loyal to the other without fraud or deceit. And should it happen (which God forbid) that one should be taken prisoner by the king's enemies, the other, who shall not have been so taken, shall then ransom him, free of expense, provided that the money required for this does not altogether exceed 6,000 golden *salus*. And if this sum of 6,000 golden *salus* were to be surpassed, the brother in arms still in possession of his freedom shall give himself up as a hostage for the other, if need be for eight or nine months, so that the brother in arms who has been captured may have the means of seeking aid among his friends to raise the difference for the ransom demanded.

[2] Item, it is agreed between the said Molyneux and Wynter that any

[12] All these places are not far from Calais.
[13] See M. H. Keen, 'Brotherhood in Arms', *History*, 47 (1962), pp. 1–17.

money required above the said ransom of 6,000 golden *salus* shall be paid at the expense and from the fortune of the prisoner and his other friends.

[3] Item, all expenses to be incurred as a hostage, as for the raising of the total ransom demanded, shall be shared equally between the said Molyneux and Wynter, until he who is a prisoner is fully free.

[4] Item, were it to happen (which God forbid) that both Molyneux and Wynter be captured together, one shall remain as a hostage for the two, if this is necessary and possible. If not, a reliable man shall be chosen by both to collect the ransom and work for the release of them both, as will be agreed and ordained by them.

[5] Item, if there were not sufficient means to pay for their full ransom, then a way shall be found of obtaining the release of one of them, so that he may negotiate their joint ransom; and he shall sell their movable and immovable property, at their joint expense, until the full release of both of them shall have been achieved.

[6] Item, it is agreed between the said Molyneux and Wynter that all the profits which, by God's grace, they shall gain between them, and which can be saved, shall be sent to the city of London for safe-keeping in a coffer at Saint Thomas Acon,[14] for which coffer there shall be two keys, one for Molyneux, the other for Wynter, and in which coffer shall be kept such gold, silver and plate as each or both of them may wish to keep to purchase lands in the realm of England.

[7] Item, as soon as is conveniently possible, either Molyneux or Wynter shall be sent to England to stay there, so as to enquire about and purchase land at the most advantageous rates for them both and for the survivor and for their heirs.

[8] Item, if the said Molyneux and Wynter were to be married, and they were both to live in the realm of England, the said lands would be divided into two portions, one half for Molyneux, the other for Wynter.

[9] Item, it is agreed that the survivor, be it Molyneux or Wynter, shall have for himself and for his heirs all the lands which the said brothers in arms shall have bought separately or together, provided however that the wife of the deceased shall have possession of a third part of the inheritance as her dower (for the space of her lifetime only), of which her husband shall be the owner.

[10] Item, the survivor shall be held to feed the children of the deceased, if he has any, to send them to school while they are of age for it, and then to give them £20 sterling of revenue a year between them for their livelihood. And after the death of the said wife and the children, and of their heirs, the said dower and the annuity of £20 sterling shall revert and belong to the survivor of the said Molyneux or Wynter and to the heirs of his body in perpetuity.

[14] St. Thomas Acon was a hospital with a church.

[11] Item, if both Molyneux and Wynter die without leaving heirs, the survivor of them, or his executors, may sell all their lands to have Masses sung and prayers said for their souls, and for the souls of their fathers and mothers.

The whole has been agreed, without deception, dispute or intent to defraud, in the church of St. Martin at Harfleur. In witness whereof we have sealed this agreement with our seals, on the 12th day of July, in the year of grace 1421.

Thus signed: Molyneux and Wynter.

I.3.c   A few years later, the exigencies of the situation obliged the veteran soldier, Sir John Fastolf, to advocate a tough and realistic campaign against the French, in which the military needs of the English were to take precedence over any other consideration, personal or material [1435]. (Text in *Letters and Papers*, ed. J. Stevenson, II, ii, 579–81.)

Item, and in cas the king *conclude* [decide] to the werre, yt is thoughte expedient, undere the noble correccion abovesaide, that aftere that the case stondithe now, that the werre shulde be *demened* [managed] and continued in the manere that folowethe for the avauncement of his conquest and distruccion of his ennemies.

First, it semythe, undere the noble correccion abovesaid, that the king shuld doo ley no sieges nor make no conquest oute of Normandie, or to conquest *be* [by] way of siege as yet; for the sieges hathe gretely hindered his conquest in tyme passed, and distruyd his peple, as welle lordis, capetaines and chieftaines, as his othere peple, and wasted and consumed innumerable good of his finaunces, bothe in England, and in Fraunce and of Normandie. For there may no king conquere a grete *reaume* [kingdom] be continuelle sieges, and specially seing the *habillementis* [equipment] and *ordinaunces* [weapons] that bethe this day used for the werre, and the knoulege and experience that the ennemyes have theryn, bothe in keping of there placis and otherwise; and also the favoure that thei fynde in many that shulde be the kingis true *sugettis* [subjects].

Wherefor, under the noble correccion abovesaide, it is thoughte righte expedient, for the spede and the avauncement of the kingis conquest and *distruyng* [defeat] of his ennemies, to ordeyn two notable chieftains, discrete and of one accorde, havyng eithere of theme *vij c.l* [750] speris of welle chosen men, and thei to holde the felde contynuelly, and *oostay* [go on expedition] and goo vj, viij or x *lekis asondre* [leagues apart] in *brede* [breadth], or more or less aftere there discrecion; and iche of hem may answere to othere and joigne togithers in cas of necessite. And that thei begyn to oostay frome the firste day of Juyne contynuelly unto the first day of Novembre, landing for the first tyme at

Cales [Calais] or at *Crotay* [Le Crotoy], or the *tone* [one] at Caleis and the *tothere* [other] at Crotay, as shalbe thoughte expedient; and so holding forthe there way thoroughe Artois and Picardie, and so thoroughe Vermandoys, *Lannoys* [Laonnois], Champaigne, and *Bourgoyne* [Burgundy], *brennyng* [burning] and distruynge alle the lande as thei pas, bothe hous, corne, veignes, and alle treis that beren fruyte for mannys sustenaunce, and alle *bestaile* [cattle] that may not be dryven, to be distroiede; and that that may be welle dryven and spared *over* [in addition to] the sustenaunce and *advictailling of the ostis* [provisioning of the army], to be dryven into Normandie, to Paris, and to othere placis of the kingis obeissaunce, and if goodely them think it to be done. For it is thoughte that the traitours and rebellis must nedis have anothere manere of werre, and more sharpe and more cruelle werre than a naturelle and *anoien* [known] ennemye; or els be liklines in proces of tyme no manere of man, ner tounes, ner countries shalle rekenene shame to be traitours nere to rebelle causeles *ayens* [against] theire souvereyn lorde and ligeaunce at alle tymes aftere theire owne wilfulle disobediens.

. . . Item, it is thought, undere the noble correccion abovesaide, that none of the chieftains shuld in no wise raunsone, appatise,[15] ner favour no contre nor place that thei pass thoroughe for no singuler lucre nor profite of them silfe; but that dei doo and execute duely that that thei come fore. And it semethe veraly that be these weies and governaunce, the king shalle conquere his reaume of Fraunce, and *greve* [harm] and distruye his ennemyes and save his peple and his soldiours, and *yeve* [give] theme grete courage to the werre; and shalle cause the cities, tounes and countreis that be rebellid causeles fayne to seche unto his grace; and shalle yeve also grete exsample to alle thayme that *bithe* [remain] this day in his obeissaunce to kepe alleweies of theire trouthis.

Item, it is thoughte, undere the noble correccion abovesaide, that the kinge may, and aughte resonablye, make alle this cruelle werre withoute any noote of tirannye, seing that he hathe offered unto his adversaries, as a goode Cristen prince, that alle menne of Holy Chirche, and also the comyns and labourers of the reaume of Fraunce, *duelling* [living] or being oute of forteresse, shuld duelle in *seuerte pesible* [peaceful safety], without werre or prince, but that the werre in eithere partie shuld be [and] rest alonly betwixt men of werre and men of werre, the whiche offre the said adversarie have utterly refused, and be concluded to make theire werre cruelle and sharpe, without sparing of any parsone.

I.3.D As these Commons' petitions indicate, the captain, entrusted with the wages of his men whom he did not pay, and the soldier who deserted, might both be among those under arms to whom the activity of war apparently had but little appeal [1439]. (Text in *Rotuli Parliamentorum*, V, 32–3.)

[15] For ransom and *appatis*, see III.3 and III.4.

Deceats of Warr

For as much as the kyng is and hath *be* [been] wele *lerned* [informed]
of menyfold and gret disceitz and untrouthes that have be *doo* [done]
unto hym and to his *Roialme* [kingdom] by some of the Capptaines that
have afore this *endented* [contracted] with the King, to serve hym in the
feet [pursuance] of *Werre* [war], som on that other side of the See, and
to diversez partes as they ben ordeyned and bound by their Indentures,
and somme in his Marchez on this side [of] the See, and of the Kyng for
their wages have been treuly paid and content, accordyng to their said
Indentures, for hem and for all their retenues, *after their degres*
[according to their ranks]; of the which Wages many of the said Capptaines have abused, and taken uppon hem to *rebate* [deduct] upon their
Souldeours, of some more, of some lesse, so that such as thei have
rebated upon have not been of myght to continue their service, *ne* [nor]
perfourme it as of trouth and reason them ought for to have doo, and
peraventure wold have doo if their hadde ben ful paied, the which hath
caused thes to falle to Roberie and Pilage, als welle before their goyng
on this side the See as in that other side of the See whan thei come
thider, among other hath be a gretter cause of the long continuance of
the Werre, and greter hurt and losse that have fallen to the Kyngs
Lordships and Contres in his obeisaunce of that other side of the See;
and not that oonly, but leose also of gret good which hath ben graunted
to the King, and paied in the wise above-said for the defense of his
land.

[The Commons petition that steps shall be taken to prevent this
practice].

Item, for so moch also as diversez and many Souldeours afore this
tyme, the which have taken their Wages, some or half, of their Capptaines, and so have mustred and entred in of record the Kyngs Souldeours, afore his Commissioners, for such termes as their Maisters have
endented fore, have somme tyme anoon aftre their mustre and the receit
of their wages, partie or all, departed away and goon *whedir* [whither]
hem *lust* [desired], and not *past* [over] the See with their said Captaines,
and some past the See, and long within their termes departed away fro
their Capitaines, and fro the Kyngs service, without licence appering
graunted to them by their said Cappitaines, wherof hath growen so gret
hurt unto the Kyng and to his Roialme, and so many inconvenientz that
couth nogh [could not] lightly be expressed, as of long tyme thexperience
hath shewed; and the which Souldiours so doyng, in as much as in hem
was, *juperded* [jeopardized] the King oure Soveraine Lords honour and
worship, and have been many gret causers of hurt that has fallen in his
Landes and Lordshipps over the See, and the jupard also of the persones
of the Lordes and Cappitaines that ledde hem.

[The petition asks that strong measures shall be taken against such deserters].

I.4 THE OPPONENTS OF WAR

Not unexpectedly, those who criticised the practice of war and, more fundamentally, the very notion of war itself, were to be found among the clergy; the passages printed below form the expression of opinion of members of that group. Their criticisms fall into two broad categories: those who criticised war for the manner in which it was fought, bringing unnecessary material destruction upon innocent people; and those who saw its moral dangers, as well as its material ones, to both the soldier and to those whom he caused to suffer. To a man such as Wyclif, ever ready with his biblical text, it was difficult to justify war as he saw it being fought in his time.

I.4.A   Wyclif appeals to the spirit of Christ's teaching to show that war is wrong, and that men must settle their differences by toleration and understanding [second half of the fourteenth century]. (Text from 'On the Seven Deadly Sins', *Select English Works of John Wyclif*, ed. T. Arnold, III, 137–8.)

Bot yitte, argues Anticrist, to mayntene mennis feghtyng, that *kynde* [nature] techis that men schulden by strenght ageynstonde *hor* [their] enmyes. Sith a *nedder* [adder] by hir kynde stynges a mon that tredes on her, why schulde we not feght ageynes oure enmyes? For elles thei wolden destrye us, and dampne *hor* [their] owne soules. And thus, for luf, we chastisen hom, as Gods lawe techis us. And so, sith oure enmyes wolden assayle us, bot if we sayliden hom byfore, sith we loven better oureself, we schulden first assayle hom, and thus we schal haf pees.

Here me thenkes that *tho fende* [the devil] disseyves mony men by falsenes of his resouns, and by his fals principlis. Ffor what mon that hafs witte connot se this *fallas* [deceit]? If hit be *leveful* [lawful] by strenght to ageynstonde violence, then hit is leveful to feght with men that ageynstonden us. *Wil* [well] I *wot* [know] that aungels ageynstode fendes, and mony men by strenght of lawe ageynstonden hor enmyes; and yitte thei killen hom not, ne feghten not with hom. And wise men of tho worlde holden hor strenghtes, and thus *vencuschen* [vanquish] hor enmyes withouten any strok, and men of tho gospel vencuschen by pacience, and comen to reste and to pees by suffryng of deth. Right so may we do, if we kepen charite; *thof* [though] men *ravischen* [seize] oure lordschipp, or elles oure *meblis* [movables], we schulden suffre in pacience, ye, thof thei diden us more. These ben tho counseils of Crist. But here tho world *grucches* [complains] and seis that by this *wise* [manner] weren *rewmes* [realms] destryed. Bot here byleve techis us, sith Crist is oure God, that thus schulden rewmes be *stablid* [established] and oure enmyes vencusched. Bot peraventure mony men schulden lese hor worldly richessis. Bot what harm were thereof, sith in tho state of innocense alle men schulden comynly wante suche lordschipp. Bot tho fende takes *ensaunple* [examples] at wormes of venyme, and by a naked *propurte* [characteristic] teches men to feght; bot mony other ensaunples of pacience of bestis schulden teche us to suffre, for myche more gode. And a fendis conscience *reulis* [rules] hym that bringes of this, that if he were thus pacient his enmyes wolde kille hym. As if a mon wolde sey, that if he keppid Cristis counseil, tho fende wolde *fordo* [destroy] hym, for he is more then Crist. And if we feghten thus for luf, hit is not luf of charite; ffor charite sekes not propur gode in this lif, bot *comyne* [common] gode in heven by virtuouse pacience. And wil I wot that worldly men wil scorne this sentense; bot men that wolden be martirs for tho love of God wil holde with this sentense; and thei ben more to *trow* [believe], for thei have more charite and better ben with God. And disseyt of love is with men that feghten, as with fendes of helle is feyned fals luf. Bot at Domesday schal men *witte* [know] who feghtis thus for charite; ffor hit semes no charite to ride ageyne *thin* [thine] enemye wil armed with a scharpe spere, upon a strong courser; ffor yitte tho *cosse* [kiss] of *Scariot* [(Judas) Iscariot] was more token of charite. And so Gods lawe techis men to cum bifore in dedes of charite and werkes of worschip; bot I rede not in Gods lawe that Cristen men schulden cum byfore in feghting or batel, bot in meke pacience. And this were tho mene whereby we shulden have Gods pees.

I.4.B   Wyclif's contemporary, the orthodox English Dominican friar, John Bromyard, although more temperate in his opinions, plainly disapproved of both the manner and the spirit in which his fellow men went off to fight one another [c. 1390]. (Latin text in John Bromyard, *Summa Predicantium*, under 'Bellum', chapters 23 and 24.)

As to the taking of advice: much help can be sought from God by means of prayer, and much good advice can be obtained from men of experience before a prince takes part in a war. . . . Thus Judas Macca- bees fasted and prayed before the battle, and he overcame his enemies. . . . Thus, too, the noble king Edward [III] had the habit of going on a personal pilgrimage before a war, and of taking advice from persons experienced in both the law of God and of the world. As Seneca points out, force of arms is of little value unless it is backed by wisdom: and even if relevant examples do not come to hand, man should act reason- ably, since the greater the danger, the more cautiously men should act. For in war is the occasion of the greatest danger to be found: danger to bodies as well as to souls, for not only may men's bodies die, but their souls may, too; and not only men, but kingdoms as well. . . . History therefore teaches that those who have been successful have generally been persons who have prayed, and have taken and heeded advice. Thus we read in a chronicle written about his life that the most noble emperor, Charlemagne, when about to go to battle, would make a clean breast of all his sins and receive the Sacrament in Communion, being thus prepared, in both body and soul, to set out to fight when the time came. And it is said of another who, having partaken of Communion, when asked whether he had eaten, replied that he had eaten only the Sacrament; [whereupon he was mocked by his opponent]. But he struck down the blasphemer with divine assistance, as was right and just; yet having achieved victory, he took no credit for it, but rendered thanks to God in the words of psalm CXIII: Not unto us, O Lord, not unto us [Ps. 115: 1; Vulg. Ps. 113: 1]. . . . For victory in battle is not achieved by the size of one's army, but by the help of God. Yet nowadays, alas, princes and knights and soldiers go to war in a different spirit; with their cruel actions and desire for gain, they incline themselves more to the ways of the devil than to those of God; for they set out for war not with prayers, but rather with oaths and curses in their mouths; nor do they fight at the expense of the king or of themselves, but at that of the Church and of the poor, despoiling both. . . . Recently, a certain knight, noticing an English army going forth with such pride, commented that it looked more as if it were going to a wedding than going to war. . . . And if they obtain victory, it is more frequently because of their opponents' lack of ability than because of their own merits, although they attribute it more to themselves than to God.

I.4.c   At about the same time a French cleric, Honoré Bonet, was making a defence of the non-combatant against the activities of the soldiery who, he claimed, carried out pillage and robbery while purporting to wage war [1387]. (Text in *The Tree of Battles of Honoré Bonet*, trans. G. W. Coopland, p. 189.)

Whether in time of war the oxdriver's man should have the privilege of the oxdriver.

Some of our masters put forward another doubt or question. They ask what opinion we shall give on the oxdriver's man. Since the ox-driver has privilege, as I said, to go in safety, then if he has a man to carry the corn and other seed to the fields, the point is whether this man should have the same privilege as his master of passing in safety.

It would seem that he should not have it, for no one has the privilege except the oxdriver; but for my part I hold the contrary, for if a man commit a crime or other offence, and some other man help him to commit the crime, the latter will be punished for the deed like the principal agent. And hence, for what reasons should a man helping in a

virtuous work not have his share of the merit? Certainly the contrary
would not be right reason. I argue still more strongly. Suppose it were
customary to imprison women, and a cultivator's wife was carrying seed
to her husband as the women do in Provence, I say that, according to
justice, she should not be imprisoned. If I were king or judge, I should
decide quickly that she might go free, for, since her husband, by reason
of his occupation, has this privilege, his good wife must have it similarly,
for the law says that a knight's wife has the privileges of her husband.

But although in law this business of cultivating corn and land confers
privileges on those who do it, God well knows how far the soldiery of
to-day pay heed to it; and in faith, this is an evil thing, for neither
emperor, king, duke nor count, nor any person whatsoever can excuse
himself from keeping this law, for these privileges were given by the
Holy Father of Rome, who by his decretals compels and binds all the
Christians in the world; and those who do the contrary, sin by sin of
disobedience, and the bishops, if they wished, could excommunicate
them. May it please God to put into the hearts of Kings to command
that in all wars poor labourers should be left secure and in peace, for in
these days all wars are directed against the poor labouring people and
against their goods and chattels. I do not call that war, but it seems to
me to be pillage and robbery. Further, that way of warfare does not
follow the ordinances of worthy chivalry or of the ancient custom of
noble warriors who upheld justice, the widow, the orphan and the poor.
And nowadays it is the opposite that they do everywhere, and the man
who does not know how to set places on fire, to rob churches and usurp
their rights and to imprison the priests, is not fit to carry on war. And
for these reasons the knights of to-day have not the glory and the praise
of the old champions of former times, and their deeds can never come to
great perfection of virtue.

I.5 THE JUDGEMENT OF GOD

War, it was widely thought, could be, both in its effects and its outcome,
a direct manifestation of the divine will. The English who marauded in
France were frequently accepted as the physical expression of God's
wrath being inflicted upon the French: 'The English, as the flail of God,
would waste and destroy the kingdom of France.'[16] Similarly, a battle
was a test not only of human skill and endurance, but of God's intention, too, an evident manifestation of his justice. This may, in part,
account for the reluctance of large armies to come to blows, for battles
could be risky affairs in more senses than one. Victory, however, gave

16 '... les Anglois tamquam flagellum Dei gasteroient et destruiroient le
royaume de France. ...' ('Documents relating to the Anglo-French Negotiations of 1439', ed. C. T. Allmand, *Camden Miscellany*, XXIV, p. 116).

confidence, as the divine will had been seen to be done; hence it was that Edward IV of England, in a semi-official history, emphasised that the defeat of his Lancastrian opponents showed up the hollowness of his enemies' claim to the English throne.

I.5.A 'Victories come from Heaven.'[17] Such is the clear message conveyed to Charles VI by Philippe de Villette, abbot of Saint-Denis in a sermon preached before the king in April 1414, when he was preparing hostilities against the English. (French text in C. J. Liebman, 'Un Sermon de Philippe de Villette, abbé de Saint-Denis, pour la levée de l'Oriflamme (1414)', *Romania*, 68 (1944–5), 463–5.)

. . .

As for the second point, I was saying that those princes who offer themselves to the perils of war must rely more upon the devout prayers and supplications of holy Church than upon their strength or their arms, for humanity is very weak and frail, and men's provision is unreliable and insufficient to bring rescue in time of peril, and above all when it occurs in the emergencies of war. It is for this reason that the noble princes and most christian kings of France, whenever they have decided to expose their bodies in war for the public good, having taken every care which human reason and sense demand, have been accustomed to come to their apostle, their father and patron, Saint Denis, to commit their cause into the hands of God and to the protection of their patron, thereby showing their complete confidence in the devout prayers of the clergy, who are ordained to be the mediators between God and man, and who can reconcile sinners to Him: for the clergy is ordained to seek peace and victory from God by devout prayers, just as the chivalry is cast to fight.

In this context the stories of holy scripture, as of pagan peoples, are full [of evidence] that by means of the prayers of holy men, princes have on many occasions achieved victory over their enemies . . . for, as we read in the book of Ezra, the emperors Cyrus, Darius and Artaxerxes, who were not of the people of God, used to give provisions and other necessities from their lands to the sons of Israel so that they might pray for them, that God should not turn in anger against their rule and the government of their children. For many are the well-known cases to be found in holy scripture of people who, without hope in war, but turning with devout prayers to God, have seen Him confounding their enemies by sending upon them some divisions, discord or disaster to the very extent, as we learn from the devout king Jehoshaphat [II Chron. 20; Vulg. II Par. 20], that they have even killed themselves. In another story, too, we read

[17] 'Les victoires viennent du ciel' (Philippe de Mézières, *Le Songe du Vieil Pèlerin*, ed. G. W. Coopland, II, 382).

that Samuel prayed to God devoutly for the people of Israel who feared
the outcome of a battle against the Philistines, and that God duly sent a
great thunderstorm, accompanied by hail and stones, from Heaven, so
that the Philistines were so frightened that they had neither the determination nor the will to resist, but only to take to flight, during which
time they were overcome. And he who would reflect diligently upon the
history of battles will learn that even a large host, containing many well-
versed in the art of fighting and experienced in battle, is all too easily
overawed and dismayed by the evidence of God's power; so, according
to holy scripture, he sometimes gives victory to the good, sometimes to
the wicked, not by chance or hazard, but for reasons and causes which
are very good, even though they may not seem constant or intelligible to
men. For great hosts are less alarming to God than is an army of flies to
a man: for as Isaiah says in the fortieth chapter of his book [Is. 40: 17]
'All nations before him are as nothing and they are counted to him less
than nothing, and vanity.' And just as men terrify flies without difficulty,
so God resolves wars according to His will.

  Thus christian princes must not rely on their plans, on the size of
their armies, on force, or strength, or on experience or wisdom alone,
but must humble themselves before God, recognizing that they can do
in battle none other than what God ordains and decides should be
achieved by them, and that they are but the instruments and ministers
of God, the true swords of God, a sword which, if God thrusts it out of
his hand, from his protection and defence, has no power to cleave nor
strength to strike. Then, in all battles where the outcome is in any way
in doubt, or uncertain, you should fight fearing lest God wishes to
punish you for anything else than the cause at issue. 'He delighteth not
in the strength of the horse: he taketh not pleasure in the legs of a man.
The Lord taketh pleasure in them that fear Him.' [Ps. 147: 10–11:
Vulg. 146: 10–11.]

I.5.B   The compiler of the account of king Edward IV's return to
         England from exile in 1471 was at pains to emphasise that the
         king's victory over his enemies, achieved at Barnet, north of
         London, on Easter Day, was a sign of the divine favour, and
         proof of the efficacy of prayer. (Text in the *Historie of the Arrivall
         of Edward IV in England*, ed. J. Bruce, pp. 20–1.)

This battayle *duryd* [lasted], fightynge and skirmishinge, some tyme in
one place and some tyme in an othar, ryght dowbtefully, becawse of the
myste, by the space of thre howrs, or it was fully achivyd; and the
victory is gyven to hym by God, by the mediacion of the moaste
blessyd virgen and *modre* [mother], owr lady Seint Mary; the glorious
martire Seint George, and all the saynts of heven, mayntaynynge his
qwarell to be trew and rightwys, with many-fold good and contynuall

prayers, whiche many devout persons, religiows and othar, ceasyd not to yelde unto God for his good spede, and, in especiall, that same day and season, whan it pleasyd God t'accepte the prayers of people being confessyd and in clene lyfe, whiche was the Estare mornynge, the tyme of the servyce-doynge of the resurection, comonly, by all the churches of England. And, *albe hit* [albeit] the vyctorye remayned to the Kynge, yet was it not without grete danger and hurt, for ther were slayne in the filde the Lorde Cromwell, the Lord Say, the Lord Mountjoies sonne and heyre, and many othar good Knyghts, and squiers, gode yemen, and many othar meniall servaunts of the Kyngs. And it is to *wete* [know] that it *cowthe* [could] not be judged that the Kyngs hoste passyd in nombar *ix*m [9,000] men; but, suche a great and gracious Lorde is Almyghty God, that it plesythe hym gyvythe the victory as well to fewe as to many,[18] wherefore, to hym be the *lawde* [praise] and the thanks. And so the Kynge gave him speciall *lovinge* [thanks], and all that were with hym. This thus done, the Kynge, the same day, aftar that he had a little refresshed hym and his hoste, at Barnette, he gathered his felow-shipe togethars, and, with them, returned to his Citie of London, where into he was welcomyd and receyvyd with moche ioy and gladnesse. And so rode he forthe streyght unto *Powles* [(St) Paul's (cathedral)] at London, and there was receyvyd with my Lorde Cardinall of England,[19] and many othar bysshops, prelates, lords spirituall, and temporall, and othar, in grete nombar, whiche all humbly thanked and lovyd God of his grace, that it plesyd hym that day to gyve to theyr prynce, and sove-raygne lord, so *prosperous* [successful] a *iowrney* [encounter], whereby he had supprised them that, of so great malice, had procured and laboryd *at theyr powers* [to their utmost] his uttar destruction, contrary to God, and to theyr faythes and liegeances.

[18] The same idea is expressed by Philippe de Mézières, in II.1.D.
[19] Thomas Bourchier, archbishop of Canterbury.

II

ARMIES AND THEIR
ORGANISATION

THE LATE MIDDLE ages were to witness very considerable changes both in the form of armies and in the manner of raising them. In England, the decline of the feudal levy, whose service had been based largely upon obligation, was almost complete, and the growth of the system of indenture, whereby men would choose to serve in return for a promise of pay and/or reward, was becoming generally accepted. In France, a country distraught by dissension within and invasion without, development was to depend upon the ability of the monarchy, the nation's symbol of unity, to create the kind of army which the times demanded and to impose new practices upon those who benefited from the lack of social stability and order. At a time when the Hundred Years' War was emphasising society's need for men ready and committed to fight in the monarchy's name, it was but a short step to the evolution of a national, professional army, a process which, although slow to get under way, came to be developed with increasing enthusiasm and energy, and with consequences which were to be political as well as military.

In both countries, the success of the new armies would lie largely in the methods used to achieve control over them. Hence the historical importance of the indenture, or the commitment to serve and to receive pay in return, and of the system of muster and review, which ensured that control was preserved by the threat, easily put into practice, of witholding pay if the service were not fulfilled.

The manner of raising an army, and who should serve in it, were both important matters, with social and political connotations. In many respects equally important, but now all too easily forgotten or ignored, were the every-day problems which faced any military commander in this, as in any, age: how to convey an army—and not merely its soldiers —from one place to another; how to arm it, and to secure weapons in sufficient quantity for it to fight effectively; how to provide it with the essential non-military skills which it would need in war; how, too, it should be provided with sufficient provisions to prevent it having to seek these basic necessities from the population of the place in which it found itself, since such a need might rapidly lead to indiscipline. Some of the documents which follow illustrate these important aspects of military organisation.

Finally, there were naval factors to be considered. Both the French and the English relied heavily for assistance upon merchant vessels, often converted for war, when they came to face each other on the seas. But ships were needed, too, for purposes other than fighting: the protection of fleets, both military and commercial, and the transportation of troops and equipment for war on land were among the important tasks carried out by the masters and sailors of ships specially requisitioned for such purposes.

II.1 THE FRENCH ARMY[1]

In France, the century 1350–1450 was to witness a progressively more successful attempt to establish an army which not only came to look to the king as its chief source of authority and effectiveness (thereby contributing substantially to the growth of the monarchy's powers during the period), but which was also a better trained and more reliable force than any known before, an achievement which owed much to a series of royal ordinances, the chief of which are printed below.

II.1.A   Part of an ordinance, issued by John II in April 1351, the emphasis of which was upon an ordered force, properly led and paid, giving service in return for its wages, the withholding of which was to be used as a disciplinary measure by the king. It marked the first, tentative step towards the creation of the royal army which was to evolve during the next century or so. (French text in *Ordonnances des Roys de France de la Troisième Race*, ed. D. F. Secousse, IV, 67–70.)

(1) ... One banneret will receive in wages forty shillings *tournois*[2] a day; a knight, twenty shillings *tournois*; an esquire, bearing his own arms, ten shillings *tournois*; a varlet accompanying him and armed with a [short] coat of mail, basinet with mail,[3] gorget,[4] gauntlet, and a tunic above the coat of mail, five shillings *tournois*.[5]

(2) We have given orders and [now] order that all men-at-arms be brought together in large companies, there being at least twenty-five, thirty, forty, fifty, sixty, seventy, seventy-five or eighty men-at-arms in

[1] The fundamental book on the French army is now P. Contamine, *Guerre, État et Société à la fin du Moyen Age, passim.*
[2] Money of Tours.
[3] A form of helmet, with mail side-pieces protecting the neck.
[4] A piece of armour for the throat.
[5] The value of the shilling *tournois* and the shilling sterling should not be confused. How to convert one currency into the other bothered contemporaries no less than it does historians today.

a company, according to the importance of the leaders and lords of those companies. And we have ordered and [now] order that our Constable, Marshals, Master of the Crossbowmen, Masters of the Household, or others whom it may concern, shall take the musters: and if they may not do so [personally], they shall nominate for this [task] proper and reliable persons who will be sufficiently informed to appreciate if anything is amiss; and they shall oblige them to swear to take the musters loyally, and to do favour to none. And when the men-at-arms arrive to be counted, the person will carry out this task individually for each company, the leader of the company being there in person with his men, each knight, esquire and varlet being armed and riding his warhorse. And he will summon each of them to appear before those who have been instructed to take the muster; and the name and family name of the leader and of each of his companions shall be noted down, as well as the colour, distinguishing marks and price of the horses being ridden; and there and then, before departing, the said horses will be taken and branded on the thigh with a hot iron, the sign being decided upon by those whose task it is to do so; and every horse of the said company shall be thus branded with the same mark; and no horse belonging to a man-at-arms shall be accepted or listed unless it be valued at thirty pounds *tournois*, or more; nor for the varlet, unless at twenty pounds *tournois* or more. And the leaders of the companies shall be further commanded that each must be ready, together with his men, to be reviewed whenever he shall be required to appear; and that afterwards, as soon as it may be done, an armed muster shall be taken by the leader or lord of his own company, at which each shall be called by name and family name, and close attention shall be paid to see whether he is riding the horse which was listed, and whether he is properly armed, as he ought to be. And those who shall take the muster shall oblige the men-at-arms and those wearing a coat of mail to swear that the horses and the equipment which they have for the muster are really their own, and that they own them in such a way that they may, and will, serve us properly, and without fraud. And we wish and order that the said musters be frequently taken, with the men either armed or unarmed, at least twice a month, and that they be ordered to attend a muster without notice and in an unnamed place, so that they may borrow neither horses nor equipment from another. And if numbers or armour be not fully maintained, then let money be withheld from their wages as a fine which shall be decreed, according to the default, by him who shall take the muster or cause it to be taken, if those who are to suffer the fine cannot present a proper and reasonable excuse; and the said fine, with the details, shall be enrolled on the lists sent to our Treasurer for War, so that a deduction may be made, at the appropriate place and time, from the pay of the defaulter.

(3) We further wish and order that the said men-at-arms shall be made to swear that they shall not leave their captain's company, nor place themselves under the command of another, without the permission and leave of the Constable, Marshal or Master of the Crossbowmen, or of whoever has the task of granting such permission; and in this case those who leave in such a manner shall have their names erased from the list on which their companies' names have been recorded.[6] And we also wish and order that those who lead the companies shall swear that they shall maintain the number of men-at-arms and men equipped with a coat of mail thus [properly] armed and maintained as they will have been at their muster, as best they may, without deceit; and that if they know of any of their company who shall be doing otherwise, they shall present him before the Marshal or other, as appointed. And the same oath shall be sworn by the bannerets who serve under the leaders of companies, as well as by knights, esquires and those equipped with coats of mail who shall serve under the bannerets; and we wish the said bannerets to know the names, family names and persons of the men-at-arms and others who shall be in their companies.

(4) We also wish and order that the said muster and oath-taking be undergone by those equipped with coats of mail and by the men-at-arms. And if any men-at-arms should arrive in small groups, having no master or leader, we wish and order that steps be taken by our Constable, Marshal, Master of the Crossbowmen or other responsible persons that a suitable knight, of whom they approve, be chosen, to whom shall be assigned a company of twenty-five or thirty men, and that those of this company be expressly ordered, on our behalf, to obey and follow the said knight, as they would any leader, into the country and into the towns; and that each shall be reviewed, both armed and unarmed, with the said knight, in the manner outlined above; and that the knight take all possible steps that no fault be found with his company. And we wish that a knight who shall have such a company shall have a forked pennon, bearing his arms, and shall have wages similar to those of a banneret. . . .

(7) And we further order that if any horse listed on a muster roll be wounded, killed or lost, let him to whom it belongs inform and tell the Constable, Marshal, Master of the Crossbowmen or other responsible person, without delay, so that a replacement may quickly be provided him, in order that he may serve us and not have occasion to accept our wages without serving us or being able to do so.

(8) . . . And we wish that all footsoldiers be grouped in companies and detachments of twenty-five or thirty persons, and that each captain be given double wages, and that they be mustered before the appropriate persons, or before those who shall be detailed to [take the

[6] See III.7.B on this point.

musters]. And each captain may have a forked pennon bearing whatever arms or cognizance he may choose. And all the crossbowmen and all those armed with shields, each armed as he should be, shall be reviewed where they should be, and the names and family names of the captain and of all the companions serving under him shall be recorded; and each shall appear before the person taking the muster, and shall draw his crossbow and shoot several times; and he who is taking the review shall look closely to see that the crossbowmen on foot and those armed with shields shall have all their arms, each according to what he is; and if any part of their armour is lacking, they shall be punished and fined, a sum being taken from their wages according to their default, the which default, together with the fine imposed, to be notified to the Clerk of the Crossbowmen, in the above-said manner. And musters are to be taken at least twice a month.

II.1.B   Charles V summons the people of the bailiwick of Rouen to arms against the English. This document illustrates the use made of the *arrière-ban*, or the general call to arms, to help defend the the kingdom in time of necessity [1369]. (French text in Froissart, *Chroniques*, XVIII, 505–6.)

Charles, by the grace of God king of France, to the bailiff of Rouen or his deputy, greeting.

We have heard that our enemies, who are in the parts around Calais and elsewhere in the kingdom, are intent upon a raiding expedition to bring as much trouble and destruction as they are able to our kingdom and to our good and loyal subjects. For this reason we, who wish to act so as to oppose their evil plans and intentions, order you with all our authority, by these presents, that you cause it to be published and proclaimed, in all the accustomed places in your bailiwick, that all the citizens and others of the good towns and those [living] in the countryside in the said bailiwick shall, at the risk of failing to do our will, be duly armed and mounted, and that those who cannot reasonably procure mounts shall [at least] be adequately armed, each according to his rank and ability, so as to resist our said enemies, and do and carry out what you think best for the proper defence of our kingdom. Those who refuse are all to be compelled to act by whatever means and methods may be necessary. And to accomplish this we give you due authority, and we order all our subjects to obey you in this matter.

Given at Sainte-Katherine-above-Rouen, on the 17th day of September, 1369.

II.1.C   Part of an ordinance, issued by Charles V in 1374, concerning military developments in France. The early clauses are chiefly concerned with measures to be taken to stop desertions from the royal army. In the text printed below, emphasis is more upon the need for proper military units which may be effectively controlled by officers acting on behalf of the king. (French text in *Ordonnances des Roys de France de la Troisième Race*, ed. D. F. Secousse, V, 660–1.)

. . .

(13) Item, the men-at-arms whom we shall in future employ at our wages shall be grouped into companies, each of one hundred men-at-arms; and each company shall have a captain; and when there are less than the above number of one hundred men-at-arms, they shall have no captain, but shall join another company when they wish to receive their wages.

(14) Item, the said captains of one hundred men-at-arms, together with their men, shall be ordered by us to be under the command of lieutenants, leaders of war and other officers, at our pleasure and command.

(15) Item, in future none shall be a captain of men-at-arms in our service, for the defence, good and safekeeping of his locality, without our letters and authority, or those of our lieutenant, leaders of war, or of other princes and lords of our kingdom, under penalty of forfeiting horses and equipment, and all movable possessions and lands.

(16) Item, none shall be recognised other than those captains appointed with a hundred men-at-arms, as stated above; each of these shall receive one hundred francs per month; as for our lieutenants and leaders of war who will have charge over greater numbers of men-at-arms, it will be our pleasure to give them due recognition by our command.

(17) Item, as soon as the musters shall have been taken and the men-at-arms shall have received their wages, their captains shall lead them directly, and as soon as they may, to the frontiers to which they are assigned, without allowing them to delay in the countryside; and there they shall maintain them in the places most suitable and advantageous from a military point of view, under the command and ordinance of the lieutenant and leader of our war for that region.

(18) Item, our lieutenants, Constable, Marshals, Master of the Crossbowmen, other captains of men-at-arms, those who hold office at present and those who will do so in future, shall, before their letters of appointment as captains are given to them, swear on the holy Gospels of God, on their honour, faith and loyalty, that they shall keep the ordinances set out above, and everything contained in them, and will hold and accomplish them in every detail, and will cause them to be held, observed and accomplished loyally and honestly, without doing or allowing anything to be done to the contrary. And it is our wish that the above ordinances be published in Paris, on the frontiers and in other important places within the kingdom, as may seem right to our council and officers concerned with the war.

II.1.D Philippe de Mézières, one of Charles VI's councillors, uses a
fictional discussion in an allegory to advise his king to effect
changes in the French army. In place of an army raised *ad hoc*,
he advocates a greater measure of professionalism which, he
claims, will defeat even a numerically superior enemy [1389].
(French text from Philippe de Mézières, *Le Songe du Vieil
Pèlerin*, ed. G. W. Coopland, II, 382–4.)

'What more shall I say?' said Queen [Truth]. 'In both the Old
Testament and in the New, and in the time of the Old Pilgrim,[7] thousands of examples could be cited. To assemble an army and then
gamble on a loss of eighty per cent, as one might in trade, is not something which can be done without remorse. One must go to war with
thought and deliberation. That is to say, my son,' said the Queen, 'if
you are involved in war, your frontiers must first of all be guarded with
great care, and better pay must be given than it has been the custom
to grant in times past. Secondly, you must know the men-at-arms
and foot-soldiers in your kingdom, and how many you should have
to serve your royal person and the common good of the kingdom
when you summon your army. These men-at-arms must be properly
disciplined, as will appear more clearly from something which is written below. Let them remain at home, ever ready and equipped with
all that is necessary, awaiting to come at your royal majesty's earliest
summons.'

'It is my advice, my son, that you make little use of that royal right
which is called the *arrière-ban*, which is the cause of many disadvantages
which it would take too long to list here. It is as well that you should
remember, my son, that a good number of first-rate soldiers fighting
with your gallant and royal majesty will, when allied to wise counsel
and with the help of my Father, bring you greater victory than would a
large crowd of your subjects, some of whom will have come voluntarily,
others through the *arrière-ban*, but all of whom will lack discipline, like
men coming to a fair. And you should also recall, my son, that it is an
easy thing, as Judas Maccabees said, for my Father to give victory to the
bravery and discipline of a relatively small number of men-at-arms,
rather than to the crowd whose only advantage lies in its size, and to
which a sense of false glory and presumptuousness all too easily comes.[8]
How extraordinary [that this should be], since it is only too common for
a rabble of such people to be badly organised.'

'In our opinion, my son,' said the Queen, 'when the aforementioned
number of first-rate soldiers, sometimes less, sometimes more, are all
alert and waiting in their homes for the order to rally to you and
accompany you into battle, you should be careful, my son, not to

[7] The author of the work.
[8] See I.5.B.

remain in the company of ladies in your palaces, nor to lead a life of pleasure once war has been declared. But rather, with a small and select company, and at small expense, you should yourself go with care to visit and comfort your good towns and your loyal subjects, not staying for long in any one place, and taking care not to stray far from your enemies' frontiers. And then, my son, when the opportunity arises and you shall have been fully advised, through your loyal captains and secret spies,[9] concerning the state of your enemies and whether it is expedient that you should personally summon your army and go into battle, then shall you secretly summon your chosen men-at-arms a number of times, while publicly appearing to set off elsewhere. Thus by good and secret advice, and by constantly seeking the help of the divine goodness of the Holy Spirit, and of the Virgin Mother, you will shortly find yourself in the presence of your enemies who will all be caught completely unawares by your great foresight, discreet planning and great military sense. And then, my son, above all, as was said earlier, if they offer to make a good peace, take care not to refuse it out of a sense of pride, or avarice or desire for vengeance, if you wish to emulate my Father in this way.'

II.1.E   A chronicler's dramatic, and at times somewhat overpainted, picture of the important French military reforms of 1445. The emphasis is upon the rôle of the king in achieving these results: he initiates and controls the deliberations in the royal council; he pays the soldiers; he publishes the ordinances, and takes steps to ensure that they are maintained. (French text in *Chronique de Mathieu d'Escouchy*, ed. G. du Fresne de Beaucourt, I, 51–60.)

In the year one thousand four hundred and forty-five, during the king of France's stay at the said place of Châlons [-sur-Marne], he summoned all the members of his council on a number of occasions, both into his presence and elsewhere, to seek advice, opinions and decisions concerning certain important matters which greatly concerned the government and rule of his kingdom, matters which he and certain members of his private council had long ago considered and had taken certain steps to resolve and bring to a conclusion. The most important of these were the war and [the conduct of] his soldiers, [for] he desired with his whole heart that a proper solution and manner of proceeding should be found, by which the soldiers who belonged to him should be paid and maintained in adequate numbers, and then placed and assigned to the towns and castles of his said kingdom, wherever it seemed right; and that all other pillagers, robbers and men of evil intention, of whom there were a great number who did nothing save destroy, rob, and pillage his vassals and subjects, should be chased away and expelled; and that they

[9] See IV.3.I and IV.4.A.

should be informed and ordered that, within a short time, each of them, under pain of death, should return and go back to that part of the country from which he came, and should begin to work the land and practise his trade, each according to his position. The said plan had many times been proposed in the king's presence, as we have said, on occasions when a number of the great princes of the blood, other noblemen, members of his council and captains of the greatest authority had been with him; they, each in turn, when asked what they thought, gave their advice and opinion, and what seemed to them ought to be done for the best.

The majority was agreed that, if they could come to a decision, it would be a most honourable, profitable and useful thing for the king and his kingdom, and for all its other lords. But many had two doubts on the matter. The first was that if the aforementioned soldiers, or at least those of mean or small estate who were very numerous in several of the companies, were to hear the news of what was being planned, they might get together, under certain captains of little authority, in such great numbers and power that only with considerable difficulty would the king, his princes and well-wishers be able to defeat them and expel them from the said kingdom. For, as some within the royal council said, the like had been seen many times in the past, in the days of king Charles the Rich,[10] ancestor of the present king, when the great companies had ruled France for long periods, as is found in the histories written concerning that period.

The second doubt which some expressed was that the king was much weakened and reduced in his finances and revenues by reason of the wars which he had long fought against his enemies. Further, his lands, towns and subjects, in different parts of his kingdom, were in great ruin and poverty, so that it was simply not possible to derive large sums of money from them to pay the soldiers mentioned above, so that this could only be done by utterly ruining the said lands and subjects. And there were those who presented many other different reasons of doubtful validity.

The king listened to all these statements and conflicting opinions which each made in turn, with great willingness, for he was very glad to hear them. Sometimes he answered them himself, suggesting reasons for putting aside doubts which had been declared, for he had long had this business very much to heart. There were often in the council with him his son, the Dauphin,[11] the king of Sicily, [12] the duke of Calabria, his son, my lord Charles of Anjou,[13] the earl of Richmond, constable

[10] Charles VI of France.
[11] He was to become king, as Louis XI, in 1461.
[12] René, nominally king of Sicily. See VI.1.c.
[13] Charles, brother of René.

of France,[14] the counts of Clermont, Foix, Saint-Pol, Tancarville and Dunois,[15] and with them a good number of other councillors, both ecclesiastical and lay. And, to bring about results, some of these lords were ordered on the king's behalf to discuss matters secretly with certain of the principal leaders who had charge of soldiers and who were largely these lords' men, in order to have their opinion on the above-mentioned points, and also that they might urge and persuade their companions to agree to do the will of the king and of his great council.

These captains brought a fairly favourable response to the said lords. They had good reason for so doing, for it had been promised to them that they would be among the best and first to be provided for. Those whose task it was, therefore, later reported to the royal council, which was meeting almost continually at Sarry, a castle which belonged to the bishop of Châlons and which was a long league's distance from Châlons, where the king was staying. Once again this matter, which was of such great importance, was put to the council and, as before, it was debated at some length in order to see how it could be settled to the honour of the king and his kingdom. Finally, after long and mature deliberation, all agreed with the king that they would help him and give him assistance to put this policy into execution and to sustain him as best they could.

And then it was proclaimed, both by the king and the aforementioned members of the council, that there would be fifteen captains, each having under his command one hundred lances; and each lance was to consist, for [purposes of] its payment, of six persons, three of them archers, the fourth being armed with a dagger, together with a man-at-arms and a page,[16] the which man-at-arms, accompanied as is stated, would receive wages, for each month (?) thirty francs in good money. The captains were to be allocated to the good towns, by provinces and dioceses, in the different parts of the kingdom; thus each captain would get to know his place [of command], and where he and his men had to be. At the same time it was also proclaimed what they were to receive and obtain in wages, both from the good towns and from the surrounding country. There were to be certain persons, appointed in the baili-wicks, seneschalcies and provostships, who would collect and distribute the sums of money mentioned above, giving account to the said captains at the appropriate time and place, as far as their responsibilities extended. These captains were chosen and appointed by the king and the lorsd of the council. They were summoned into the king's presence, and were

---

[14] Artur, earl of Richmond.

[15] John, bastard of Orleans.

[16] Other, more reliable sources, suggest a different combination of men. (See *Chronique de Mathieu d'Escouchy*, ed. Beaucourt, I, p. 55, n. 2; V. de Viriville, 'Notices et extraits de chartes et de manuscrits appartenant au British Museum de Londres', *Bibliothèque de l'École des Chartes*, 2nd series, 3 (1846), pp. 124–5.)

told and ordered that they must keep and maintain the said ordinances
to the letter, or risk incurring the displeasure of the king and the said
lords; neither were they to cause, nor allow to be caused, any violence
or harm to merchants, men of the land or others, of whatever condition
they were, if they did not wish these same troubles to be inflicted upon
them [in turn]; further, they were only to engage people on whom they
could rely and for whom they could be responsible.

This done, they were informed in writing of the places to which they
had been appointed, and what their duties were to be. And soon after
these captains had been told the number of men they must have, and
they had made their choice, as best they could, from all the companies,
of the most capable and the best equipped, up to their particular
number, it was ordained, as stated above, that the remainder who had
not been engaged should return in haste, and without delay, to their
home regions, without pillaging or robbing defenceless people; otherwise, if they failed to do this, measures would be taken and justice
would be meted out as if to the most shameless of people. And the
better to put this into effect, certain letters were sent from the king into
several bailiwicks to the officers serving there. When the existence of
these ordinances and injunctions came to be known, the men at once
went off to many and diverse places and dispersed, without staying
together, so that within fifteen days there was no news of them in all the
king's dominion.

As for the fifteen captains mentioned above, when they had been
appointed and allocated, in the manner stated, to command their men
throughout the provinces, dioceses, bailiwicks, seneschalcies and
provostships of the kingdom, they began to rule, govern and maintain
order in the good towns with great discretion and care, without causing,
or allowing their men to cause, any act of violence or harshness to the
good people and inhabitants thereof, or to merchants or ploughmen of
the country round about. And if, by chance, any of them acted otherwise, and complaint was made to these captains, they immediately
caused [the guilty] to be punished without mercy, causing restitution to
be made to those who had suffered the damage.

And although the number of soldiers paid in this way rose to some
9 or 10,000 horses, there were not many of them in the towns: at Troyes,
Châlons, Rheims, Laon or other similar towns, there were no more than
twenty-four or thirty of them, according to the size and strength of the
towns. For this reason, the soldiers were not numerous enough to
assume control or ascendancy over the said good people and inhabitants. And in this way royal officers and justices had control over them,
looking out for any trouble, and seeing whether the captains did their
duty properly.

There were others still, appointed by the king, who organised musters fairly frequently to check their equipment, so that they maintained themselves, as they should, without selling or losing their horses or equipment; and when one [man] was missing, by death or other cause, another was appointed in his place. For there were many who, at their own expense, consistently followed the captains in the hope of being appointed when an opportunity arose; and they sought out every means of achieving this. And if it happened that the king became involved in any operation, in whatever part of the kingdom it might be, he at once sent some of his messengers to the above-mentioned captains, or to certain ones among them, and immediately, without delay, they would come to him wherever he would have them come. And in this way he found himself quickly provided with a good number of well-equipped soldiers, by the co-operation of his princes, chivalry and nobility.[17]

II.1.F   Charles VII, by an ordinance of 1448, establishes the famous *francs-archers* (so called from their exemption from certain taxes) who, it was intended, were to form the nucleus of a permanent, national army in France. (French text in *Ordonnances des Rois de France de la Troisième Race*, ed. L. G. de Bréquigny, Paris, 1790, XIV, 1–3.)

Charles, by the grace of God king of France, to the provost of Paris or to his deputy, and to those elected to supervise the levy of taxes for war in the said district, greeting. Having managed to put an end to the very disorganised life and pillaging which has long been the lot of our subjects, and having put order into the maintenance of our soldiers, we have [now] taken steps to ensure the safety and defence of our kingdom and lordships, in case it should happen that, by means of the truce which now exists between ourselves and our nephew of England,[18] we may not achieve the good of peace. For it is right and proper that we should establish and ordain in our kingdom a certain number of men for its defence, men of whom we can make use in our service in time of war without our having to employ others than our own subjects for this purpose. Thus, after long and mature deliberation with several princes and lords of our blood, we have wished and ordained, and wish and ordain by these presents, for the good of, and at the least charge to, our subjects, that in each parish of our kingdom there shall be one archer who will always keep himself ready and sufficiently equipped [for war], with a sallet,[19] dagger, sword, bow, sheath [of arrows], jerkin[20] and a short coat of mail. These men are to be called *francs-archers*, and will be

[17] Compare this part of the text with the views of Philippe de Mézières (II.1.D).
[18] Charles VII was the uncle of Henry VI of England. A truce between the two had been negotiated at Tours in 1444.
[19] A form of helmet.
[20] A close-fitting jacket.

selected and chosen by you in the said provostship and district, for the aforesaid declared purpose, from among the better endowed and more prosperous as may be found in each parish, granting no favour or special consideration to money or to special requests which could be made to you. And they will be obliged to prepare themselves with their above-mentioned equipment on all feast days and holidays, so that they may become more skilled and accustomed to the said way of life, and be ready to serve us as and when we order them to do so. And we shall have them paid four francs per man every month which they serve us. And in order that they shall be better able and more anxious to keep themselves prepared in the above-mentioned state and condition, we have ordered, and now order by these presents, that each and every one shall be free, quit and exempt not only from all direct and other taxes which may be imposed on our behalf on the kingdom, [but also] from the duty of maintaining our soldiery, from [all] guard duty, and all imposts whatever, except from *aides* which we may order to be levied for the war, and also from the salt tax. By these presents we forbid our commissioners and all those ordered to impose and assess the direct tax and others on our behalf, that they should assess them; and we [further forbid] all lords, captains and castellans that they oblige them hence-forth to do guard duty. And for their greater benefit we wish and order that you should issue them with your letters of franchise concerning these matters, such as seems good should be done, the which [letters] being regarded as if obtained from us.

And in order that they shall be more attracted to serve us and to maintain themselves in the manner described above, we wish and order that each and every one of the said archers shall take an oath in your hands to serve us faithfully and loyally, [fully] equipped, against all and everybody, by carrying out all proper functions in all our wars and affairs whenever summoned by us, and that they shall serve none, either in war or bearing the said equipment, without our orders, at risk of losing their franchises. Further, we wish and order that the said *francs-archers* should have their names and family names recorded by you, as well as the parishes in which they may live, and that these be registered in the office of those collecting the taxes, so that we may summon them promptly whenever we need to do so. And we order and command, by these presents, that you put this, our ordinance and will, into proper execution in the said provostship and district, according to the instruc-tions given to you. And [you shall] oblige all whom it may concern to keep and maintain it by all the usual manner and means employed in affairs concerning us, in spite of any obstruction or opposition which there may be; for we wish that no concession be made in the execution of each and every one of these, and for this we have granted, and [now] grant you, full power, commission and authority to act. We also order and command all our justices, officers and subjects that they obey and follow you, and each of you, diligently in this matter, and that they give you every aid, advice and assistance which need may make you ask for. And we wish that full credence be accorded to a copy of this, as if it were the original.

Given at Montil-lès-Tours, on the 28th day of April in the year of grace 1448, and of our reign the twenty-sixth.

Thus signed: By the King in his Council.

J. Delaloere [Secretary][21]

II.2 THE ENGLISH ARMY

England's chief military need was the provision of an effective army to fight extended campaigns of aggression in France and elsewhere. The challenge was met by the development and adaptation of the social system of indenture, or retainer, already in existence before the war began, in order to meet military requirements. The idea that military service was a duty owed chiefly for defence for a period of up to forty days a year was put aside. In its place there came into existence an army which consisted in large measure of men who had volunteered for service, and who were not averse, in return for pay and other material considerations, to serving abroad. It was the development of this system which made the prolonged English campaigns in France possible and which, it is hardly an exaggeration to say, changed the nature of warfare during this period.

II.2.A Many were retained to serve a lord not only in time of war, but in peace time, too. This indenture, dated September 1397, records the terms according to which Nicholas de Atherton contracted to serve in the retinue of John of Gaunt, duke of Lancaster, in both peace and war, and Gaunt's undertaking to pay him regularly for his services. (Anglo–Norman text in 'Indentures of Retinue with John of Gaunt, duke of Lancaster, enrolled in Chancery, 1367–1399', ed. N. B. Lewis, *Camden Miscellany XXII*, Royal Historical Society, London, 1964, pp. 109–10.)

This indenture, made between the most high and powerful prince, John, duke of Guyenne and Lancaster, on the one hand, and his esquire, Nicholas de Atherton, on the other, witnesses that the said Nicholas is retained and bound towards the said duke, to serve him both in time of peace and in war, for the period of his life, and to work with the said duke in whatever parts it may please him, adequately and properly mounted and equipped for war as is fitting for his rank.

[21] On some effects of these military developments, see V.4.B.

In time of peace the said Nicholas shall be paid by and receive his board from the said duke whenever he may come in response to letters sent to him on behalf of the duke, or at his command, in the same way as other esquires of his rank and condition.

And the said Nicholas shall receive from the said duke as his fee, both in time of peace and in war, ten marks a year for the period of his life, from the issues of lands and lordships belonging to the said duke in his duchy of Lancaster, through the hands of his present receiver, or of his successor, at the time of Easter and of St Michael,[22] in equal portions.

In addition to this, the aforesaid Nicholas shall, in time of war, take from the said duke wages of war or wages and board equal to those taken from the duke by esquires of his rank for the [duration of the] expedition, and he shall be paid the said wages by the hands of the said duke's war treasurer who shall at the time hold office.

With regard to prisoners and other profits of war taken or won by the aforesaid Nicholas or any of his men in the service of the said duke, [and with regard to] the beginning of his year's war service, and the transportation of himself, his men, horses and equipment, the duke will do to him as he will to the other esquires of the same rank and condition.

In witness of which the aforesaid parties have affixed their seals to these indentures which they have exchanged.

Given at London, [on] the last day of September, in the twenty-first year of the reign of our most redoubted sovereign, king Richard, the second since the Conquest [1397].

II.2.B   This indenture for service in war illustrates not only how the king of England contracted with a captain to raise a force for him, but also underlines the basic duties and privileges of those who served the king on active service abroad [1424]. (French text in *Letters and Papers*, ed. J. Stevenson, II, i, 44–50.)

This indenture, made between the most high, very excellent and most powerful prince, [John], duke of Bedford, regent of the kingdom of France, on the one hand, and Sir John Fastolf,[23] councillor, grand master of the household, lieutenant of [the county of] Maine and of the marches thereabouts for my lord the regent, and governor of Alençon, on the other, witnesses that the said grand master is retained by my lord the regent as captain of eighty mounted men-at-arms, he himself being numbered among them, and of two hundred and fifty archers, for one whole year, beginning at the feast of St Michael last past, and finishing on the same said feast in the year to come, which will be the year 1425. [And they shall] be employed in the conquest of the said land and county of Maine, and of the border country thereabouts, held by the

---

[22] 29 September.
[23] See III.7.C.

enemies and adversaries of our sovereign lord and of the said lord the
regent, and anywhere else in the kingdom of France where it shall be the
will of the said lord regent to ordain.

For which [services] he will have and receive wages as follows: for a
knight banneret, captain of men-at-arms, four shillings sterling a day
in English money; for a knight bachelor, likewise a captain, two shillings sterling; for a mounted man-at-arms, twelve pence sterling a day,
with the accustomed rewards; and for each archer, six pence a day of the
said currency,[24] the English noble being valued at six shillings and eight
pence sterling, or French money at the current rate. And these wages
shall be paid as from the day of the first musters, which the said grand
master shall hold of the said men-at-arms and archers before the commissioners of the king, our said lord, or of the said regent. And after
these musters, payment shall be made to him in advance, from the
revenues of both France and Normandy, by order of my lords the
treasurers and general governors of the said finances, and by the hand
of the clerk of the treasurer of the war-receipts of our sovereign lord the
king in Paris, or by the receiver-general of the said revenues in Normandy, or by one of them, for [the period of] six whole weeks and, at the
end of the first quarter, for the remaining six whole weeks, and thence-
forward quarter by quarter, in advance, according to the musters and
reviews which he shall be obliged to hold before the commissioners and
officers of the king, our sovereign lord, and of the said lord regent, from
quarter to quarter, and as often as he shall be required to do so before
the said commissioners.

And the said lord regent shall have both a third part of the profits of
war of the said grand master, and a third of the thirds which the men of
his retinue shall be obliged to give him from their profits of war,
whether prisoners, booty or anything else taken, and also all other
customary rights. Of the said thirds and rights thus owing to the said
lord regent, the said grand master shall be obliged to certify every
quarter to the said treasurers, general governors and clerk, and to others
as may be required,[25] when he requests his wages, and to account for
them in the Chamber of Accounts through the farmer of the said grand
master or the executor or executors of his testament. And the said grand
master shall have any prisoners who may be taken during the said
period by him or by those in his retinue: with the exception of any
kings or princes, whoever they may be, or sons of kings, and especially
Charles who calls himself Dauphin of Viennois,[26] other important
captains and persons of the blood royal, captains and lieutenants holding
powers from the said kings and princes; and excepting, too, those who

---

[24] These wages are paralleled in III.1.A.
[25] On the division of spoils, see III.2.
[26] He was, in fact, king Charles VII. See IV.2.B and Ch.IV n.7.

killed and murdered the late John, once duke of Burgundy, or who consented to or were accomplices in the crime,[27] and those who consented to and participated in the treason done to the duke of Brittany by Olivier de Blois and his accomplices,[28] each and all of whom shall belong to the said lord regent, and he shall pay a reasonable reward to him or those whose prisoners they shall be.

In return for these things the said grand master has undertaken, and undertakes, to serve the king, our sovereign lord, and the said lord regent, either in person or by means of others appointed by him, for whom he shall be answerable, and to use the said men-at-arms and archers in the conquest of the said land and county of Maine, and of the border country thereabouts, or anywhere else in the said kingdom of France, in the best manner and means known to him, or [in any way] which the said lord regent shall command him. And he shall keep, and cause to be kept and maintained, as best he may, the people and subjects obedient to the king, our said lord, [free] from all force, violence, pillages, robberies, seizure of provisions, horses and cattle, and all other exactions whatever.

In witness whereof, on that part of the present indenture which is to remain with the said grand master, the lord regent has caused his seal to be placed.[29]

Given in Paris, on the 27th day of November, in the year of grace 1424.

Thus signed: By the lord regent of the kingdom of France, duke of
    Bedford.

R. Veret [Secretary]

II.3 MUSTER AND REVIEW

The importance for the crown to be able to maintain an effective control over its forces, largely by the use of economic sanctions, is reflected in the system of the muster and review of soldiers which came to be a characteristic of military life for the soldier in the royal service.

II.3.A   Orders are given for a review of troops preparing for a siege in France in June 1424. This was the only adequate method available to commanders of ensuring that their subordinates kept

---

[27] John, duke of Burgundy, was murdered at Montereau in September, 1419, by men in the service of the Dauphin, Charles; his son, Philip, duke of Burgundy, was an English ally.

[28] Olivier de Blois, employed as his chamberlain by John V, duke of Brittany, had betrayed his master into the hands of the French king, Charles VII.

[29] An indenture took the form of a contract whose terms were set out in duplicate, each party affixing its seal to one half which was then handed over to, and preserved by, the other.

their retinues sufficiently numerous and constantly ready for war. (French text in *Letters and Papers*, ed. J. Stevenson, II, i, 29–31.)

John, duke of Bedford, regent of the kingdom of France, to our very dear and much beloved cousin, John of Luxembourg, lord of Beaurevoir, greeting and love.

We order and command, by these presents, on behalf of our lord the king and ourselves, that you carry out and conduct, or cause your commissioners and deputies to carry out and conduct, month by month, for as long as they are with you in the service of the lord king and of ourselves, the musters, inspections and reviews of the men-at-arms and archers from the country of England who are under the command of our beloved and faithful councillor and chamberlain, Sir Thomas Rempston, knight, appointed with you to the siege of Guise and other places round about, [with the intention of] bringing these into the obedience of our lord the king. You are to receive and pass at these musters sufficient men-at-arms and archers, properly mounted, equipped and arrayed, as may be appropriate, while rejecting those who are not [found] adequate. The names of those who are received and passed at the musters must be listed and certified, or caused to be certified, under your seal or that of your deputy, in order to provide for the payment of our said chamberlain, his men-at-arms and archers, as is customary, and to serve, along with these presents or copies thereof, as a discharge for the person who shall make the payment, as is fitting and reasonable. We command that you and your commissioners and deputies in this matter shall obey and carry out this order diligently.

Given at Paris, under our seal, on the 6th day of June, in the year 1424.

II.3.B   Muster roll of the men-at-arms and archers forming the garrison of Rouen castle for the English government in France on 16 August 1432. (French text in *Rouen au temps de Jeanne d'Arc et pendant l'occupation anglaise (1419–1449)*, ed. P. Le Cacheux, pp. 243–4.)

These are the names of the men-at-arms and archers who form the garrison in the castle of Rouen for its safe-keeping, passed in review by us, John Salvain,[30] knight, bailiff of Rouen, and John Stanlaw, esquire, treasurer of Normandy, on the 16th day of August, in the year 1432.

---

[30] The original spelling has been preserved in the case of names. Also note how a man's name might be spelt in more than one way in the same document.

Jehan Lampet, *lance on horseback*

Lances on foot

Nicolas Basset
Jehan Southewik
Thomas Lampray
Jehan Galles
Thomas ffynk
Jehan Ofmore
Jehan Waltham

Jehan Alain
Thomas Thorneton
Rogier of Barton
Jehan Roux
William Cokffild, at Laigny
Thomas Graunt
Jehan Hardowyk

T[otal] xiii lances on foot

Archers

Jehan Pute
Guy Colleville
Robert Gardiner
Watier Clerc
Jehan Alverlay
Thomas Sprolle
Thomas Aturisbury
William Slye
Jehan Rine
Jehan Telby
Robert Courseil
Hennequin Dumont
Henry Jacquesson
Richard Bossewell
Jehan Brunnell
Davy Watkin
Jehan Raisin
Jehan Briger
Jehan Lobley
Henry Key
Jehan Sclyfford
William Selby
William Stedman

Jehan Dynham
William fforham
Robert Hablay
Rogier Maint
Jehan Warram
Thomas Gifford ⎫
Thomas Esgard ⎬ at Laigny
Estienne Drop
Jehan Modi
Jehan Cauffin
Jehan Poullain
Jehan Dodde
Robert Corbart, sick
William Rambold
Jehan ffischer
William Vant
Thibault, cannoner
Henry, clerk
Thomas Gervaiz
Jehan Guedeney
Jehan Burne
Jehan Beaumont
Robert Hablé, absent

T[otal] xliii archers

[Signed]: J. Salvayn. J. Stanlawe.

II.4 NON-MILITARY PERSONNEL AND TRANSPORT

Medieval armies numbered others than fighting soldiers, men whose task it was to convey a force from place to place, or to help with what were normally non-military skills in the army's attempts to defeat the enemy.

II.4.A Froissart describes the departure of Edward III's army from Calais into French territory in the early autumn of 1359. In addition to the splendour of the fighting army, he emphasises the importance of transport, provisioning and, finally, of the existence of a form of pioneer corps in the English army at this period. (French text in Froissart, *Chroniques*, VI, 222–3.)

Once the king of England had arrived in Calais with the Prince of Wales, his eldest son, and three other of his children, my lord Lionel, earl of Ulster, my lord John, earl of Richmond, and my lord Edmund, the youngest of the four, and all the lords who were accompanying them and their men, he caused their horses, equipment and all their provisions to be unloaded; they then remained in Calais for four days. Then the king had the order given that all should put themselves in a state of readiness to leave, for he wished to ride after his dear cousin, the duke of Lancaster. Thus the said king left the town of Calais with his great array, and set out across the country with the greatest and best equipped train that had ever been seen to leave England. It was said that he had more than six thousand carts there, each well loaded, which had all come over from England. He had drawn up his columns, which looked so splendid and richly bedecked, one and all, that it was a delight and a pleasure to behold them. [The king] made his Constable, the earl of March, whom he loved greatly, ride in the van, accompanied by five hundred men in plate armour and by one thousand archers, [all] going before his own column. After these rode the king's column, in which were three thousand men in plate armour and five thousand archers; and he and all his men rode in close formation after the Constable. Following upon the king's column came the great carts, which extended over a distance of a good two leagues; for there were more than six thousand of them, all harnessed, carrying all the necessities for the army, and such things which it had not previously been usual to take with men-at-arms, such as handmills, stoves for cooking, and many other necessary requirements. And behind came the [third] column, a strong one, led by the Prince of Wales and his brothers, in which there were two thousand five hundred men in plate armour, nobly drawn up and richly apparelled; and all these men-at-arms and archers were in close ranks, [ready] to fight if there should be need. Riding in this way they did not leave behind them a single servant who could have attended them; nor could they properly advance more than three leagues a day. While drawn up in this way, they were met by the duke of Lancaster, and the foreign lords, as is recounted above, between Calais and the abbey of Licques, on a fine plain. And there were in the king of England's host up to five hundred varlets, with spades and axes, who went before the carts and cleared the paths and ways, and cut down the thorn bushes and the thickets, so that the carts might pass more easily.

II.4.B   Order is made to pay carpenters, masons and men of other crafts
         who are to assist the French force involved in the siege of
         Cherbourg in November 1378. (French text in British Museum,
         Additional Charter 34.)

Audouin Chamieron, doctor of laws, bailiff of the Cotentin, and Jean
des Ylles, bailiff there for our lord the king for the lands which [once]
belonged to the king of Navarre,[31] and at present acting on behalf of the
king's general commissioners for the siege of Cherbourg, to Fouquet
Tribout, receiver-general of the taxes for war imposed upon the dioceses
of Avranches and Coutances for the sum given for the payment of
engines, workmen and other equipment raised from the said region and
taken to the siege of Cherbourg, greeting.

We have today seen the muster rolls of carpenters, masons, quarriers
thatchers, pioneers and waggoners from the viscounty of Avranches
whom Jean Legey, viscount of Avranches, has brought to serve at the
siege of Cherbourg, [these being] over and above the number already
detailed for the management of the engines. In which muster there are
twenty carpenters, twenty masons and quarriers, twenty-six thatchers[32]
and eight waggoners. We now order that, from the receipt of moneys
obtained by you, you shall give them payment for the next ten days,
including today; namely, for each of the carpenters, 3 shillings per day,
which for the ten days for them all will amount to 30 pounds; to each
mason and quarrier, 3 shillings which, for the ten days, will amount to
30 pounds; to each thatcher, 2 shillings and 6 pence per day which, for
the ten days for them all, will be 32 pounds 10 shillings; to each wag-
goner, 10 shillings per day which, for the ten days for them all, will total
40 pounds *tournois,* in accordance with [the rate] at which they are
evaluated in the said muster roll, to which this present order is annexed ...
the total being 132 pounds 10 shillings, to be taken from your receipt.

Given at Carentan, under our seals, on the 12th day of November,
1378.

II.4.C   A surgeon petitions Henry V that he may accompany him on his
         expedition to France, and that he may engage others of his
         profession to assist him [1415]. (French text in *Foedera,* ed.
         T. Rymer, IV, ii, 123.)

To our most excellent and most sovereign lord the king.

Your humble, loyal and faithful servant, Thomas Morstede, surgeon,
beseeches you that, of your benign grace, it may please you to grant
letters under your private seal to your chancellor of England, to cause
to be delivered to your said suppliant letters of commission, under your

[31] Charles the Bad.
[32] The thatchers were probably employed to protect the siege engines.

great seal, by virtue of which he may have permission to engage, both from within and from outside franchises, twelve persons of his profession, at his own choice, to go in his company and to be of service to you, most sovereign lord, on your expedition.

Again, may it please you, of your benign grace, to cause indentures to be drawn up, under your privy seal, between yourself, most sovereign lord, and the afore-mentioned Thomas, by virtue of which the said Thomas shall be obliged to serve you, most excellent lord, on the said expedition, as a man-at-arms, taking the same wages and rewards as are taken by others of his rank, with fifteen men in his retinue, of whom three shall be archers and the others men of his profession, each of them receiving the same wages as are taken by the other archers going on the said expedition; and that the said indenture be of the same form as is drawn up for your esquires.

H[umphrey of Gloucester], Chamberlain of England.

The king has granted the petition in its entirety.

II.5 WEAPONS

The provision and supply of weapons was a vital aspect of military organisation which could not be ignored. These documents indicate the sources from which certain weapons were obtained, and how they were made available for use.

II.5.A Edward III orders the sheriff of Oxfordshire and Berkshire, and other sheriffs, to purchase specified numbers of bows, bow strings and arrows for the use of his army in France [1346]. (French text in *Foedera*, ed. T. Rymer, II, iv, 203.)

The king to the sheriff of Oxford and Berkshire, greeting.

Since, for the sake of our expedition of war to France, we have immediate need of a great quantity of bows and arrows, we now firmly order and command you, under penalty of forfeiting all that is forfeitable to us, that, upon seeing these present letters, you shall immediately cause to be bought and provided for us, out of the issues of your jurisdiction, 200 bows and 400 sheaths of arrows, from whatever places may seem best to you in your counties, both from within and outside franchises. And you shall cause the said bows and arrows to be brought and stored within our Tower of London, these to be ready and prepared by the Sunday before the feast of the Assumption of the blessed Virgin Mary next to come, at the latest,[33] [when they shall] be handed over to our beloved clerk, Robert de Mildenhale, according to the agreement made for this purpose between you and him. And when we have knowledge of the expenses which you will have incurred for the purchase,

[33] I.e., the Sunday before 15 August.

provision and conveyance of the said bows and arrows, we shall have the said sum to be owed recorded in your account in our Exchequer.

Given by the Keeper of England, at Windsor, on the 1st day of August [1346].

By the king himself.

Similar letters were directed to those named below concerning the provision of [the numbers of] bows and arrows mentioned from the counties listed, these to be sent to the said Tower by the date stated, namely the same date, as follows:

Sheriff of Gloucester	300 bows and	500 sheaths of arrows
Sheriff of Worcester	100 bows and	200 sheaths of arrows
Sheriff of Cambridge and Huntingdon	150 bows and	250 sheaths of arrows
Sheriff of Norfolk and Suffolk	200 bows and	400 sheaths of arrows
Sheriff of Essex and Hertford	160 bows and	400 sheaths of arrows
	500 bow strings	
Sheriff of Middlesex	100 bows and	300 sheaths of arrows
Sheriff of Kent	100 bows and	300 sheaths of arrows
Sheriff of Surrey and Sussex	100 bows and	500 sheaths of arrows
Sheriff of Southampton	100 bows and	300 sheaths of arrows
Sheriffs of London	300 bows and	1000 sheaths of arrows

On the said Sunday

Sheriff of Warwick	120 bows and	200 sheaths of arrows
Sheriff of Northampton	100 bows and	200 sheaths of arrows
Sheriff of Rutland	50 bows and	100 sheaths of arrows
Sheriff of Somerset and Dorset	200 bows and	500 sheaths of arrows

On the said feast of the Assumption

II.5.B   An indenture, dated 29 September 1475, made between John Sturgeon and William Roos confirming that Sturgeon has delivered the artillery of Edward IV to Roos in France. (Text in Public Record Office, London, E101/55/7; also printed in J. Calmette and G. Périnelle, *Louis XI et l'Angleterre*, pp. 358–61.)

This indenture, made the xxix day of Septembre in the xv yere of the regne of King Edwarde the fourthe, bitwene John Sturgeon, maister of the Kings Ordenaunce, on that *oon* [one] partie, and William Roos, countroller of the same Ordenaunce, on that other partie, witnesseth that the said John hath delivred bi the Kinges commaundement into the kepinge of the said William, the day and yere aforeseid, bi the hands of Thomas Bowes, divers parcels of the Kinges Ordenaunce and Artillerie, suche as weren brought bi the said John owte of Englond for the Kinges grete *viage* [expedition], that is to sey:

First, a chariot with a grete irenne gonne.

Item, a chariot with the chambre of the said grete irenne gonne, and the chambre of the longe *Fowler* [piece of artillery] called the Edward.

Item, a chariot with the grete *brasin* [brass] gonne.

Item, a chariot with the chambre of the same brasin gonne and i *potgonne* [short piece of artillery] of irenne.

Item, a chariot with a grete *bumbarde* [piece of artillery] of irenne.

Item, a chariot with a grete *bastard* [a species of cannon] gonne and her chambre, called the Messenger.

Item, a chariot with a *bumbardelle* [a small bombard] called the Edward.

Item, a chariot with a Fouler and her chambre, called the Fouler of Chestre.

Item, ij chariotts with ij grete potgonnes of bras.

Item, a chariot with a Fouler and her chambre called Megge.

Item, a chariot with a Fowler and her ij chambres called the Fowler of the Towre.

Item, a chariot with a Fouler and her chambre, called the lesse Fowler of the Toure.

Item, a *curtowe* [a cannon with a short barrel] of irenne and i carte of iiii wheles.

Item, grete shot of stones for the said grettest irenne gonne, brasin gonne and bumbarde ... ccxv

Item, shot of stone for the said ij brasin potgonnez ... lxxiiij

Item, shot of stone for the said vi other bastard gonnez, Foulers and potgon of irenne ... ccccciiii^{xx}x [490].

} *Summa* [Total] *vii^{c}iii^{xx}xix* [779]

Item, *tampons* [plugs] for the said grete gonnez, potgonnes and Foulers.

Item, pilowes of lede with ringes of irenne for iiij of the said grettest gonnez.

Item, a crane with vj *polies* [pullies] of bras and a tacle of iii polies of bras to shipe and unshipe the said grete gonnes.

Item, a *gynne* [gin, machine for raising weights] with a vice called a worme with a trestill therto.

Item, a gynne of iiii peces called a stradill gynne, to carte and uncart with the said grete gonnes.

Item, ij *trokils* [a form of pulley] with iiii wheles *hopid* [hooped] with iren, iche of theme to cary the said gonnes over.

Item, bowes of ewe ... mcxxxiiij. Item, bowes of wiche ... ccxxv. } *summa : mccclix* [total: 1359]

Item, bowstrings to the same, *ciiii*^{xx}*ii grossez* [182 gross].

Item, sheffes of arrowes of ix ynches, cccl.

Item, sheffes of arrowes of viii ynches, fethir, mdccl.

Summa [Total] *x*^{m}*clx* [10,160]

Item, sheffes of arrowes of vii ynches, fethir, vii^{m}ix^{c}lx.

Item, sheffes of arrowes unhedid, ccxxvii.

Item, chests to the said bowes, arrowes, and bowstrings, ccl.

Item, shovils and spadez, miiii^{xx}xii.

Item, *mattokkes* [a form of pickaxe] and pikasez, cciiii^{xx}xvi.

Item, felling axes, lxvi.

Item, *handbilles* [a cutting instrument], lxxii.

Item, *malles* [heavy hammer] of lede, cccvi.

Item, gonpowdre, x barells.

Item, sulfre in powdre, xii barells.

Item, brymstone grete unbrokin, a hoggeshede and ii barelx.

Item, salpetir syve tred and *sarced* [sieved], redy to *medill* [mix], xxxviii barrels.

Item, *colopowdre* [? charcoal], ii tonnes, a hoggeshede and xxviii barelx.

Item, grete *crowes* [levers] of irenne, xlvij.

Item, smalle crowes of iren, xix.

Item, grete kutting hamers, viij.

Item, grete kutting *pinsons* [pincers], iij paire.

Item, small pinsons, j pair.

Item, grete hokes of irenne with cheynes to pull downe *hurdesse* [pali-sade of hurdles], loopes *sowes*, [a cover to protect men while mining],[34] and drawebriggez, xii.

Item, i cheyne with an loke for a staye of a potgonne.

Item, a grete crosbowe *of brake* [with a winch].

Item, a foure fotid trestill, a *wyndesse* [windlass] for the same bowe.

Item, shot for the same called Roliens, cxiiij.

Item, *carteclowtes* [ironplate to protect the axle-tree] newe for axeltrees of grete gonnez, xxiij.

Item, grete bolts of irenne for the said grete gonnez, iij.

Item, a *buorne* [?] of irenne.

Item, *cressetts* [torch] of irenne to bere fire[35]   iij.

Item, stele   j barelle.

Item, xvi small chests with [all] of them contenyng vij dosins   cxxii dosins.

Item, *pavices* [shields], xviij.

Item, lanternes, iij.

Item, *sawting* [for assault] laddirs, iii dowble and v single.

---

[34] See the sow mentioned in IV.3.G.

[35] The manuscript here and below is damaged and only partly legible.

Item, a bote of *leddir* [leather] of iii peces.
Item, leddir of ii botes, shapened and served redy to frame.
Item, peces of a *fletingbrigge* [floating bridge], xli.
Item, *horsshone* [horseshoes], cc.
Item, horsshonaills after vii^{xx} to the c . . . x^{m}.
Item, vi *penynaills* [? small nails] after vi^{xx} to the c . . . iiii^{m}cc.
Item, hors colers with traces and *harney* [harness] cccxl   ccxl.
Item, colers withoute tracez. . . .
Item, colers with belles for *thilhorses* [? dray horses], lv. . . .
Item, *cartesadiby* [cart saddles], x. . . .
Item, horsse drawyng haltirs, lx. . . .
Item, *cropers* [crupper, strap] of ledder, cheyned with iren for *charue horsez* [cart horses] xii.
Item, *dorsers* [baskets] to the same, xix.

In witnesse wherof to that oone parte of these indentures remaynyng toward the forseid John Sturgeon, the forseid William hath set his seals; And to that other parte of the same indentures remaynyng the said William, the forsaid Thomas Bowes hath set his seals, the day and yere abovesaid.

II.6 PROVISIONS

No army could be fully effective without adequate and, if possible, regular supplies of provisions. While, all too frequently, armies lived off the land, this could lead to indiscipline and troubles with the civilian population. The three documents which follow show Henry V taking the steps necessary to provide his army with the provisions required in the invasion of France.

II.6.A   Henry V, about to take an army to France, orders that large quantities of bread and beer be prepared for the benefit of the army [1415]. (Latin text in *Foedera*, ed. T. Rymer, IV, ii, 123.)

The king to the sheriff of Southampton, greeting.

Since, as you already well know, we are, with the help of God, soon to set out for foreign parts to regain and assume the inheritance and rights of our Crown which, as is clear to all, have for long been unjustly withheld; and wishing for this purpose to provide in this way for the sustenance of the lords and others in our following who are to set out with us towards these parts; we now firmly order you that, having read the content of these present letters, you shall immediately cause it to be publicly proclaimed on our behalf, in every place within the city of Winchester and the town of Southampton, and in all other centres of trade and hamlets within the said county, as may be expedient and necessary, that each and every one of our liege subjects living there whom it may concern, shall bake and brew, under supervision of

D

yourself, or of your deputy in the said county, until the arrival of ourselves with our following, and that of our other liege subjects, in those parts, from the day of the said proclamation until the feast of St Peter in Chains next to come.[36]

And do not fail to fulfil any part of this order without risking the danger and penalty of our indignation.

Given by the king at Westminster, on the 27th day of May [1415].

By the king himself.

II.6.B   A letter, similar to the above, illustrating how large numbers of animals for slaughter were to be gathered and brought to certain key points for sale to Henry V's army, now assembling before sailing for France [1415]. (Latin text in *Foedera*, ed. T. Rymer, IV, ii, 123.)

The king to the sheriff of Southampton, greeting.

Since, as you already well know, we are, with the help of God, soon to set out for foreign parts to regain and assume the inheritances and rights of our Crown which, as is clear to all, have for long been unjustly withheld; and wishing for this purpose to provide in this way for the sustenance of the lords and others in our following who are to set out with us towards these parts; we now firmly order you that, having read the content of these present letters, you should immediately cause oxen, calves, and cows, to the number of one hundred animals, to be taken by you, or your proper deputies, from wherever they may be found within your county, whether within liberties or outside them (fiefs of the church being excepted), and that you should cause them to be brought with the greatest reasonable speed by their owners or others in their name, to Lymington, Romsey, Alderford and Fareham, in the said county, for the sustenance and provision of the lords and others who are awaiting in the said county, so that they may be sold for the above reason to the said lords and others, in such a way that there may be reasonable agreement [as to the price] between these lords and the said owners or those acting in their names.

In no way fail to do this.

Given by the king, at Winchester, on the 24th day of June [1415].

[Similar letters were sent, on the same day, to the sheriff of Wiltshire, that he should cause the same number of oxen, calves and cows to be brought to Titchfield, in the county of Southampton.]

II.6.C   The need to keep an army, especially one engaged in a siege, well-provided with food and drink is emphasised in this letter from Henry V to the Mayor and Aldermen of London [1418]. (Text in *Memorials of London and London Life in the XIIIth, XIVth and XVth Centuries*, ed. H. T. Riley, pp. 664–5.)

[36] 1 August.

By the Kyng.

Right trusty and welbeloued, we grete you ofte tymes welle. And forasmoche as in the name of Almighty God, and in oure right, with Hys grace we haue leyd the siege afore the Cite of *Roan* [Rouen], which is the most notable place in Fraunce, saue Paris; atte which siege us nedeth gretly refresshing for us and for our hoost; and we haue founde you our trewe lieges and subgitz, of good wille at al tymes to do al thing that might do us *worshippe* [honour] and ese, wherof we can you right hertely thank; and pray you effectuelly that, in al the haste that ye may, ye wille *do* [cause to] ariue as manie smale vessels as ye may goodly, with *vitaille* [provisions], and *namly* [especially] with drinke, for to come to Harfleu[r], and fro thennes as fer as they may, up the riuer of Seyne to Roan-ward with the said vitaille, for the refresshing of us and our said hoost, as oure trust is to you; for the which vessels ther shal be ordeigned suffisant *conduyt* [escort], with Goddes grace; *wetying* [knowing] welle also that ther-inne ye may don us right gret plesaunce and refresshing for al oure hoost aboue sayd, and *yeue* [give] us cause to shewe therfor to you euer the better lordshippe in tyme comynge, wyth the help of Oure *Saueour* [Saviour], the which we praye that He haue you in Hys *sauf-warde* [safe-keeping].

Yeuen under our Signet, in our hoost afore the sayd cite of Roan, the X day of August [1418].

To oure right trusty and welbeloued the Mair, Aldermen, and al the worthi Communers of our Cite of London.

II.7 THE NAVY

The sea was coming to play an increasingly important part in hostilities at this period, not only as a physical barrier between countries at war, but also as a highway to be used to transport men and supplies from one theatre of war to another. All sides came to appreciate its importance in military terms, but the methods used to achieve control of it were normally traditional and usually showed little real determination to attempt to control the sea in any permanent way.[37]

II.7.A Navies were usually raised *ad hoc*, in time of crisis, and were kept in being only for as long as was necessary. Consequently, use had to be made of ships normally employed for commerce and other peacetime purposes. Fairly typical, therefore, was Henry VI's appeal for help in procuring ships to repel French attacks on Calais [?1452]. (Text in *Letters and Papers*, ed. J. Stevenson, II, ii, 477–8.)

[37] See C. F. Richmond, 'The War at Sea', *The Hundred Years War*, ed. K. A. Fowler, pp. 96–121.

By the Kinge.

For asmoche as we, from tyme to tyme, as wel by letters as by credible informacions and dayly reportees, be warned and *acertayned* [informed] that oure adversarie of France is fully *appoyntede* [prepared] and disposede to come in his owne persone in to oure marche of *Calese* [Calais] with al the hast, spede and diligence possible unto hym, to the entente of getyng by meane of seege of oure towne of Calese, and of al other places in the same oure marchis, *trowyng* [trusting] to *mowe* [be able] execute his seid malicious purpose in fewe days; and after that to come, withe al his myght and *puyssaunce* [power] that he shal mowe in any wise *gadre* [to assemble] or make, in to this oure lands, to thentent to dispoyll, distroye, and in jour *hit* [it] and the dwellers of the same, that God ne *wol* [will]. We purposyng, with the grace of oure Lorde, and with the helpe [and] assistence of you and of other oure trewe *sugittes* [subjects], to withstande and *lette* [prevent] oure seide adversaries malicious purpose, without delay or tarying, write unto you exhortyng, and also hertely prayynge and requyryng you, that ye, in furtheryng of oure seide godly purpose, as ye love the *worshipe* [honour] and the welfare of us and of this oure lande, thees oure letters seen, doo al the diligence possible unto you to ordeyne as meny shippes and vessels of *thoo* [those] that bylonge to oure port of A. as ye shal mowe, to come to oure port of Sandewiche without delay or taryyng, so that *that* [they] be there before the last day of *Feverere* [February] next commyng, there to assemble with gret and notable nombre of *carrakes* [carack, a merchant ship,] and also of other shippes of this oure lande, the whiche we have ordeynede to *entende* [attend] upone the passage of oure owene persone in to oure *reame* [realm] of France, as sone as it shal please God that we shal mowe be redy therto, the whiche, as oure Lorde knowethe, is the thyng *erdly* [on earth] that we moost desire; as also to occupie the see in suche wise as we shall mowe have the rule and the gouvernaunce therof, and withstande the malicious purpose of al oure adversaries and enemyes, to the *plesire* [pleasure] of God, and to the worshipe and welfare of us and of this oure lande. And in executione of this oure desire ye faile not, but that ye soo *demeane* [act] you *as* [that] we, withoute delay or taryyng, shal mowe have knowlyche of youre treue *acquytaille* [compliance] therein.

    Yevene [Given] under oure Prive Seel, at Westminster, the xxviij day of   .[38]

        ★ To oure trusty and welbeloved the maire and commynalte of oure towne of Hulle.

        ★ Item, *semblably*, [similarly] to the maire, etc., of Lynne.

        ★ Item, etc., to Newcastelle.

        ★ Item, etc., *Brystowe* [Bristol].

[38] The date is not completed.

Item, to Dertemouthe.
Plymmouthe.
Fowy.
Falmouthe.

II.7.B   For an island kingdom such as England, with dependencies and
interests on the European mainland, it was important to be able
to convey troops abroad free of threat from enemies. Henry VI
demands that English trading vessels sailing for Bordeaux shall
be made available to accompany those ships taking soldiers to
succour Bordeaux, it being hoped that their number would serve
to discourage attacks by the French [1453]. (Text in *Letters and
Papers*, ed. J. Stevenson, II, ii, 489–91.)

By the Kyng.

Trusty and welbeloved. We doubte nat but it is come to youre
knowelache howe we have disposed and ordeigned a notable armee and
puissance [force] to be sent at this tyme unto oure duchie of Guyenne
for the defence and saufgarde thereof ayenst the myghte and malice of
oure adversaries and ennemyes. Nevertheless, for asmoche as we be
credibly accertaygned that oure saide ennemies, and *namely* [especially]
of the parties of *Brytaigne* [Brittany] and Spayne, have ordeygned and
sette to the see a greet numbre of shippes and men of werre, to thentente
to *forbarre* [prevent] and *lette* [hinder] our saide armee of thaire purpose
and goyng into oure saide duchie, by the whiche, if thay so sholde doo
(that God forbede) to greet an hurte and inconvenient mighte and were
like to ensue to the same our duchie and subgittis there, that we ne
wolde. For somoche we write unto you theis lettres, desiryng, praying
and nevertheless charging you that by alle the wayes and meenes possible unto you, ye exerte, stire, moeve and enduce, and also straitely
charge on oure behalf, alle the oweners and maistres of shippes belonging to oure port of Plymmouthe and there being, that this yere *dispose*
[intend] thayme towardes oure citee of Bourdeaux, that thai be redie by
the last day of this monethe to accompany oure saide armee towardes
oure said duchie. And *over* [in addition to] this, that ye do openly to be
proclaimed, in suche places as ye thinke most expedient, that alle
persones that wol dispose thaim to be redy in maner abovesaide with
thaire shippes to accompaigny oure said armee, shalle frely passe
withoute paying of any custume for any *vitaille* [provisions] that thai
shalle carie withe thayme, what ever it be. And that *that wol differre*
[those (who) will defer] thaire going unto [after] the tyme our said
armee [shall] be passed, shalle in noo wyse enjoye that benefice, but
duely pay alle manere custumes according to oure lawes and statutes,
any proclamaicion afore this made to the contrarie notwithstanding.
And we wol that ye faille not in execution of this our commaundement,

as ye desire the worshipe and welfare of us and of alle this oure lande,
and the seuretee and *savacione* [safe-keeping] of oure saide duchie and
subgittes there.

Yeven [Given], etc., at Westminstre, the xvij day of August, the yere,
etc., xxxj [1453].

To the maire and custumers of our towne and port of Plymmouthe.

Item, *semblable* [similarly], to the maire and custumers of oure
towne and port of Dertemouthe.

Item, semblable, to the baillief and custumers of Fowey.

Item, semblable, to the maire and sherrief of the towne of *Bristowe*
[Bristol].

By order of the king, on the advice of his council, there being present
the lords Treasurer, the dean of St Seurin [Bordeaux], Thorpe, etc.[39]

Langport [Secretary]

II.7.c   Report of an indenture, similar in nature to those made for war
         service on land, whereby Sir Baldwin Fulforde agrees to defend
         the sea against the enemies of the English king [1460]. (Text in
         Letters and Papers, ed. J. Stevenson, II, ii, 512–15.)

Henry, by the grace of God king of Englande and of Fraunce and
lorde of Irlande, to the tresorere and chamberlayns of oure Eschequiere,
greeting.

For asmoche as by endenture made the *thridde* [third] day of the
present monethe of *Feverere* [February], betwixt us, on that one partie,
and oure trusty and welbelovede Bawdewyne Fulforde, knyght, on that
other partie, the same Bawdewyne is witholdene towardes us to doo us
service upone the see, at suche places convenable as we shalle assigne
hym, if *wynde and wedire* [wind and weather] wolle serve, for the
resistence of oure enemyes and repressing of thaire malice, with the
nombre of a *m* [1,000] menne, wele and sufficiently *harneysede* [equipped]
and *arraiede* [prepared] for the werre, and competent nombre of shippes
for the same, for and duryng the terme and space of a quarter of a yere,
the said quarter to begynne, as *towardes* [regards] the *vitaillyng* [pro-
visioning], at the begynnyng of the *talowyng* [greasing with tallow] of
the saide shippes, and as towardes the wages, at the weying up of
thancres and makyng saile of the saide shipps. And the saide Bawdewyne shalle take daily wages of ij s[hillings] for hym self, and vj d[pence]
by day for every maistre of the saide shippes, and for everyche of the
remenaunt of the m. men above-saide, ij s[hillings] iij d[pence] *be* [by]
the weke, during the tyme of a quartere of a yere abovesaide.[40] Of the
whiche wages the saide Bawdewyn shalle receyve a m [pounds] at the
makyng of the saide endentures, and the remenaunt at thende of the first

---

[39] The last clause is in Latin.
[40] Contrast the sailors' wages with those paid to soldiers (II.2.B and III.1.A).

vj wekes of the saide quartere. And in caas that the saide Bawdewyne be not content ne paide of the saide remenaunt at thende of the saide vj wekes above rehercede, thanne he be dischargede *anenst* [against] us of any ferther kepyng of the see, in that partie, the said endenture not-withstandyng. Also we shalle make the said shippes to be *competently* [adequately] furnyshede of gonne powdere, bowes, arowes, and *strenges* [strings]. And the saide Bawdewyne, duryng the tyme abovesaide, shalle put hym in his fulle *devoire* [effort] and diligence in and aboute the saide kepyng for the *wele* [good] of us, relief and comforte of our subgittes, frendes, alyes and othere beynge undere oure *saufconduit* [safe conduct] or *saufgarde* [safeguard], and doo alle the hurt, harme and *noissaunce* [mischief] that he shalle *mowe* [be able] unto oure enemyes.

And we shalle have a quartere of al manere of prises and *preies* [takings] as wel prisoners as othere, that duryng the tyme aforesaide shalbe takene by the saide Bawdewyne, or any of his said felishippe, and alle othere shares of olde tyme due unto us by the custume of the see, except suche as ben traitours and rebelles unto us, whiche, if any hap to be take, shalle *oonly* [entirely] and hoolly remayne unto us.[41] And the saide Bawdewyne and his felisshepe, that *soo* [in this way] shalle take theym, shalle have such rewarde for thaim as is ordeynede by us, that is to say, for every lorde, mli. [£1,000], and for everych of the othere, that is to say, sir Johane Wenloke, sir James Pykering, knyghtes, and Thomas Colt, *v.c.* [500] marc.[42] And we shalle ordeyne and *deputee* [appoint] suche persone, or persones, as it shalle please us, to be and goo with the saide Bawdewyne, and receyve for us the saide quartere of alle suche prises, as is above rehercede, and shares, by endenture to be made betwix the saide Bawdewyne and the saide persone or persones assignede; and upone suche endenture had, the saide Bawdewyne, his retenue and owners of the saide shippes, be quyted and dischargede ayenst us and oure heires for evere, of any manere accompte, action, clayme, or demaunde thereof to be made or had in any wise.

And the saide Bawdewyne, nor noone of his felishipe, shalle not attempte nor breke our saufconduyt, suertee, or saufgarde, nor in any manere wise take any goodes or merchaundises of oure liege people, alies or frendes, withoute thaire assent, and as in the saide endenture playnely it is conteynede.

We therfore wolle and charge you that unto the forsaide Bawdewyne ye doo pay for hym, and for every maistre of the saide shippes, and for *everiche* [every one] of the *remenaunt* [remainder] of the saide m. men, the wages in the saide endenture specified; and also doo and parfourme

---

[41] Compare this statement with those contained in II.2.B and III.2.A.

[42] All three were Yorkist supporters; the first two, at least, had been attainted in 1459. On the buying of prisoners, see III.2.A and Keen, *The Laws of War*, pp. 146–8.

in alle thinges in oure behalve after theffect and *contynue* [contents] of
the same endenture.

Yevene [Given] undere oure Pryve Sealle, at oure *palois* [palace] of
Westminstre, the xx day of Feverere, the year of oure regne xxxviij
[1460].

J. Brewester [Secretary]

III

THE ENTICEMENTS OF WAR

THE ATTRACTION OF war cannot be explained solely by the desire of men to help further dynastic quarrels or recover lost territories. In England, the twelfth century had already seen the employment of paid mercenaries, and the thirteenth was to witness the further decline of the army based upon the fulfilment of military duty and obligation. The long wars between England and France, which began in the fourteenth century, finally put an end to this declining practice, so that armies now came into existence for very different reasons, among the most notable being the enticements which could be placed before soldiers to make them serve the king's cause, abroad if need be. Increasingly, therefore, wars came to be fought by men who were, to a greater or lesser extent, committed to the profession of arms and to military values, men to whom war had become a business.[1]

The indenture, or contract, made between the king, his chief captains and those who were to be engaged to serve under them, was the basis of this expanding military system. By studying these, we can see what factors persuaded men to take up war: the undertaking to pay a wage to each soldier for a specified length of time; and an agreement that all ranks, whether noble or not, would be granted a share in what were euphemistically termed the 'advantages' of war, such as booty and profits received from the ransom of prisoners. These spoils of war were an enticement: the manner of drawing up indentures seems strongly to suggest that they were seen as supplementing wages, but few would have denied that these 'advantages' were, in effect, a substitute for pay which, for a variety of reasons, was all-too-frequently not forthcoming. Spoils, whether legalised or not, were an integral part of the wage structure of the late medieval soldier.[2]

The existence of such enticements had its dangers, for they held out a strong appeal to men who were more concerned with winning the material advantages of war than with following the noble profession of arms. The possibility of raising large sums, in a few cases even small fortunes, by financial exploitation of war was ever present. Lack of

---

[1] See M. R. Powicke, *Military Obligation in Medieval England*.

[2] See C. T. Allmand, 'War and Profit in the Late Middle Ages', *History Today*, 15 (1965), pp. 762–9.

discipline in armies could easily lead to such exploitation, which was sometimes encouraged, albeit unofficially. In many cases men joined together to form armed bands of marauders who caused havoc among the poorly defended civilian populations during the fourteenth and fifteenth centuries. They took advantage of the weakness of government, and of a state of almost constant war, to pursue their own selfish ends, frequently in total disregard of the wider context and military needs of the Anglo-French conflict. Critics saw that the answer to this problem lay chiefly in the enforcement of discipline and, secondly, in the ability to pay armies regularly, so as to give soldiers no excuse for taking the law into their own hands. It was to these ends that the authorities were constantly reminded to direct their efforts.

III.1 WAGES

The wage was the soldier's basic pay, the rate being normally specified in the indenture of service. The money was received by the captain, who was responsible for paying his soldiers according to their rank and the number of days which they had served. The muster (see II.3) was the method used to check that soldiers were physically present, and had thereby earned the money which could be theirs.

III.1.A Mandate for the payment of English troops about to proceed into Gascony under the command of John, viscount Lisle. The wages were standard for the period[3] [1453]. (Text in *Letters and Papers*, ed. J. Stevenson, II, ii, 479–80.)

Henry, by the grace of God king of England and of Fraunce and lord of Irland, to the tresourer and chambirlains of oure Eschequer, greting.

For asmuche as oure righte trusty and welbeloved cousin, Johne, viscount Lisle, is *witholde* [retained] by endenture made betwix us and hym to do us service of *werre* [war] for a quarter of a yere in oure duche of Guyenne, for the suerte and *saufgarde* [safekeeping] of the same, undre therle of Shrouesbury, our lieutenant there; and the said Johne shal have with hym contynuelly duryng the same tyme upon the said saufgarde *iiij*^{xx} [4 × 20 = 80] speres, hym selfe accounted, wherof shalbe ij banerettes and iiij knightes horsed, *harneysed* [equipped] and arraied, as it apperteynethe unto thaym, and *viij c.* [800] archiers on fote, wel and convenablie arraied, as it belongithe unto thaim. And the said Johne shal take daylie wages during the said tyme, that is to say, for hym self *vj. s.* [= 6 shillings] by the day, for eithre of the said banerettes iiij.s. by day, for everie of the said knightes ij.s. by day, and for *everiche* [each] of the remanent of the said speres

---

[3] See II.2.B for further evidence of this.

xij.d. [12 pence = 1 shilling] by day, with rewardes accustumed, and for every archier vj.d. by day; of the whiche wages and rewardes the said Johne shal be paied half in hand at the making of the endentures, and that othre half at the see side at the day of making of *monstres* [muster] of hym and of his said retenue, by the handes of the tresourer and chambirlains of oure Eschequer in England for the tyme beyng; and the said quarter shal begynne at the day of the making the monstres of the saide Johne and his said retenue, whiche shal be at the portes of Plymmouthe or Dertmouthe, the xxvj. day of *Feverer* [February] next commyng, before suche persones as it shal like us to depute therto, as in the said endenture it is conteyned *al at large* [in detail]; we *wol* [will] and charge you that unto the said Johne ye do make payment, aswel of the said daylie wages of vj.s for hym self and of iiij.s for eithre of the said banerettes, and for *everich* [each] of the said knyghtes ij.s by day, and for everiche of the remenaunt of the said speres xij.d. a day, with rewardes accustumed, as for everiche of the said archiers vj.d. by day *aftir* [according to] theffect, purport and *continue* [content] of thendentures abovesaid.

Yeven [Given] undre oure Prive Seel, at Westminster, the xxx day of Januarie, the yere of oure regne xxxj [1453].

Langport. [Secretary].

[On the dorse in Latin] Received in cash, by the
hands of Ralph Travars,
chaplain, for this term,
£1,216–10s–7d.

III.2 PILLAGE AND BOOTY

The taking of pillage, together with the booty which it produced, was an important aspect of medieval warfare, finding official recognition, even a measure of encouragement, in both the indenture system and in the laws and conventions by which war was governed. Strictly speaking, such material profits were shared among the ranks, although the manner of so doing varied slightly in different parts of Europe, according to the status of those involved. But the principle remained the same: he who took a risk in war, whether by paying an army or by hazarding his person in battle, stood to gain part of the benefits which an army was expected to derive from war.

III.2.A Part of a discussion concerning the legality of pillaging the enemy: the theoretical nature of the statements which it contains should be emphasised [early fifteenth century]. (Text in Christine de Pisan, *The Book of Fayttes of Armes and of Chyualrye*, ed. A. T. P. Byles, pp. 217–20.)

Chapter XIV

. . .

Now, good mayster, here me a lytel yf thou be so pleased. I aske of *the* [thee], yf whan men of *werre* [war] are taken in to wages, and that of theyre payement be noo *faulte* [default] made, Whethere it behoueth them wyth theyre wages truly payed to take *vytailles* [provisions] vpon the countrey, and to dyspoylle and take dyuerse other thynges as they comonly doo thys day in the realme of Fraunce.

I ansuere the certeynly that nay, and that suche a thynge is noo poynt of the ryght of werre, But it is an evylle extorcyon and a grete vyolence, made wrongfully and wyth grete synne vpon the people. For thus as thy self *haste* [hast] sayde here to fore, that a prynce that wyl make werre ought before hande to *aduyse* [consider] and see where & how hys fynaunce shal be made and taken; and, aboue all thynges, he ought to ordeyne so that hys folke be well payed, wherby they may truly paye that whyche they take, be it vytaylle or other thynges. And then it were a Iuste thynge to punysshe wel theym that wythout money shulde take eny thynge *what someuere* [whatsoever] it were. But by argumentacyon thou myghtest ageyn saye to me, and yf caas were that the ennemyes cam in to the lande sodaynly, wherfore it were nede to make a sodayne deffense, or euere that the prynce might haue *purueyed* [provided] for so grete a fynaunce as muste be had for to paye monethly a grete quantyte of men of werre. But yf a tresore be had, I ansuere the that in al thynge that is of nede, men muste helpe *hem* [them] self as they can best after theyre powere. For *whan* [if] that thys caas were, the prynce shulde be ynoughe excused yf he suffred them to take, that is to wyte, al *onely* [only] vytaylles necessaryly as they passed forthe for sustenaunce of theyre bodyes, onely to the lest hurt vpon the poure labourers that myght be *doo* [done], and not that they shulde doo as the wolues to whom suffyseth not one shepe whan they entre in to the folde, but stranglen and kylle all the hole flok. *Semblably* [similarly], many of oure men of werre doo the same. For there, as a henne or a Lambe myght suffyse them, they take and kylle x or xij of them. And suche waste of goodes they make euen as they were *veray* [truly] wolues rauyshynge wythout conscyence as thoughe ther were noo god, or that they neuer shulde deye. Alas, wel be *thoo* [those] uttyrly blynded that thus doo. For more in *parell* [peril] of dethe they goo than other folke, and lesse than eny other men they take hede therto.

Chapter XV.

What men ought to doo with the *proyes* [spoils] that be goten in werre.[4]

Another manere of questyon I wyl to the make. I aske of the, what

[4] See Keen, *The Laws of War*, Ch. IX.

men ought for to doo wyth the thynges that be wonnen vpon the ennemyes in bat.aylle.

Der loue, to thys questyon byhoueth to be ansuered by dystynctyon
of cases. For, fyrst, after the *cyuyle* [civil] lawe is to be vndrestande of
what astate and condycyon the persone is that hathe conquested a
thynge by faytte of werre. And there is a manere to vndrestand in what
cases & in what werres thees lawes haue place. For yf a werre be made
by *maundement* [command] or callyng of the kynge or prynce that hath
power to ordeyne and sette vp a Iuste werre,[5] som lawes be reserued to
suche a lorde and not to other folke, that is to wyte that all the *getynge*
[spoils] ought to goo atte the wylle of the prince or of the lyeutenaunt or
hed capytayne. For *syth* [since] that the men of werre are atte the wages
of the kynge or prynce, what someuere they take, be it prysoners or
other proye, oughte be to the lorde *after* [according to] the lawes; And
auncyently it was *woned* [accustomed] to be thus doon, *What that*
[although] of grace in tyme present by longue custome in Fraunce and
in other landes is lefte to the men of armes that whyche they conquere
and gete, yf the thynge that they conquere be not of so grete a prys that
it passeth the pryce and Somme of ten thousande frankys, the whiche
thynge, be it a prysoner or other good *moeuable* [movable], is *yolden*
[surrendered] vnto the kynge or prynce, by al thus that he is *holden*
[obliged] to gyue to the sayd man of armes that hath goten hit, what so
euere he be, the sayde pryce of x thousand Francs.[6] And suche a thynge
is a gode custome in a land. But the forsayde lawe affermeth the decree
that sayth playnly that al the proye ought to be after the prynces wylle,
And ought to *departe* [distribute] it iustely amonge them that haue
holpen to gete hyt, euery man after hys meryte. And that thys thynge be
of a trouthe, noo man myght not susteine the contrarie. For the same is
approued by the *ryght writon* [written law] that namely assygneth therto
suche a reason, that is to wytte that if it were soo that the prysonners or
proyes shulde be to the man of werre, all thus and by the same reason
shulde be theyrs the castelles and townes that they take, the whyche
thynge were neyther good nor Iuste that they wyth the money of the
kynge or prynce, and had at hys expenses, shulde gete for theyre owne
behoue [advantage] eny grounde. For that whiche they doo is doon as of
the kynges owne werk-men that he sette awerke for hym and in his
name; therefore ought not the proye to be theyrs wyth theyre wages,
but onely thys that the prynce wyl gyue them of a specyall grace, the
whiche grace, to saye trouthe wel and largely, hit behoueth them as to
them that setten in aduenture so dere a *catell* [treasure] as is the blode,
the *lymes* [limbs] and the lyffe. And the more that a prynce is hygher in
the degre of noblesse, so moche more he ought to rewarde theym that

---

[5] See I.1.A.
[6] On this point, see II.7.C and Keen, *The Laws of War*, pp. 146–8.

wel haue deserued it. And of the proyes wonnen in erthe, the noble and worthy auncyent kept nothyng therof for theyre owne self, but onely hyt suffysed them to haue the name and the *worshyp* [glory] of the dede doon by theyre men, whyche had the proffyt therof. And by suche a waye they *gate* [won] the hertes and loue of theyre men of werre, that they brought atte a gode ende theyre grete and merueyllouse entrepryse.

III.2.B　The importance and manner of the division of spoils is emphasised by the reference to the subject in Henry V's ordinances of war [1419]. (Text in *The Essential Portions of Nicholas Upton's De Studio Militari, before 1446*, ed. F. P. Barnard, pp. 45–6.)

Of the thyrde partes paid in warres

All maner of captaynes, knyghtes, squyers, men of Armes, Archers, what so euer they be, shallbe bounde to paye the iij^{de} parte of All theyr gaynes in warre faithfully, And wyth owte fraude, to theyr imediate captayne or maister, in payne of lesing the hooll principall somme so goten, And Aresting of theyr body vntill they haue made theyr fyne wyth theyr saide captayne or master. Also we woll that All maner of men, Ryding or taryeng wyth us in oure hoste or vnder our baner, thoughe they Receue no wages of vs or our Realme, As physiciens, surgens, barbors, marchauntes, And suche lyke, we charge that they paye of All theyr goodes dewly And lawfully begoten by war, to vs or our cheffe captayne, the iij^{de} parte therof.

III.2.C　Evidence of the strict measures, based upon the ordinance contained in the last document, which could be applied within a garrison to ensure that the profits of war were properly recorded and duly distributed [1443–4]. (French text in *Chronique du Mont-Saint-Michel (1343–1468)*, ed. S. Luce, II, 165–7.)

Here follow the absences and profits of war of the men-at-arms and archers of the garrison of Tombelaine, who are in the retinue of the high and powerful lord, my lord the duke and earl of Somerset, captain of the said place, certified by me, Jehan le Mestre, clerk and deputy of Thomas d'Aultry, controller of the said garrison, all as I found and got it from the register made for this purpose for the quarter of the year beginning on the 29th day of December 1443 and finishing on the 29th day of March [1444].

First, the absences and new arrivals:

James Hobson and Ralph Clerc, archers, left on the 6th day of January, and returned on the 9th day of the said month: each 3 days.

... [A further list of names, with their periods of absences, follows.]

The profits of war

John Flourison, archer to Richard Harper, a mounted lance, took a horse, sold for 6 golden *salus*.

The said Flourison, archer to the said Richard Harper, man-at-arms took a prisoner ransomed for 12 golden *salus*.

Roger Mill, archer to Makin of Longworth, won a sword, sold for 37 shillings and 6 pence *tournois*.[7]

I Jean le Mestre, above mentioned, certify to all whom it may concern that there were no other absences or profits of war recorded during the said quarter, by any of the soldiers belonging to the garrison of the said place of Tombelaine, concerning which I have any information. Witnessed with my sign manual on the [   ][8] day of the month of March, the controller of the said Tombelaine, Thomas d'Aultry, having been delayed at Chateaugontier by the enemies and adversaries of our lord the king.   J. le Mestre.

I, Thomas d'Autré, the controller above mentioned, certify these facts to be true, as they are contained in the above record. Signed with my seal.   D'Autré.[9]

. . . [The total of absences, and the sum to be deducted from the wages payable to the garrison, is drawn up]

Total of the said profits of war made by the archers in the service of the lances:

18 *salus*, being worth 27 pounds 37 shillings (sic) and 6 pence *tournois* in money. Of these, 28 pounds 17 shillings and 6 pence *tournois*, a third belongs to the lances, totalling 9 pounds 12 shillings and 6 pence *tournois*; of which third, a third belongs to the captain, namely 64 shillings and 2 pence *tournois*; and of this third, a further third belongs to the king, equal to 21 shillings and 5 pence *tournois*.

III.3 PRISONERS AND RANSOMS

One of the chief aims of war was the capture and ransom of the enemy, both soldier and civilian, an activity which presented every soldier with an immediate prospect of a prize of war. Both the many lengthy and costly court cases concerning prisoners and their ransoms, and the unwillingness of the English to kill their prisoners when ordered to do so by Henry V during the battle of Agincourt, are a clear indication of the importance attached to the financial advantage to be derived from this aspect of war.[10]

III.3.A Part of a discussion in which Christine de Pisan exposes a justification for the proper practice of ransoming prisoners [early fifteenth century]. (Text in Christine de Pisan, *The Book*

[7] Money of Tours.
[8] The manuscript is blank here.
[9] See Chapter II, note 30.
[10] See Keen, *The Laws of War*, Ch.X.

of Fayttes of Armes and of Chyualrye, ed. A. T. P. Byles, pp. 223–4.)

Chapter XVII
. . .
Wel I undrestande the, maister. Now telle me, that *syth* [since] that we crysten men atte thys day haue lefte the auncyent lawes to putte in *thraldom* [bondage] or to slee the prysoners, I aske of the yf Iustly men may demaunde of a prysoner a *fynaunce* [ransom] of gold or of siluer or of som other moeuable goodis after this that men vsen comonly in faytte of werre. For yf I remembre me well, thou hast sayde here byfore that to a prysoner is *myldefulnes* [consideration] due of ryght vnto hym; and me semeth that sith it is due to hym *after* [according to] ryght, men doo hym wronge thenne to make hym paye reanson where as men doo to hym noo *misericorde* [mercy].

I telle the yet and ansuere vpon a newe, that veryly is myldefulness due vnto hym in two maners; that is to wyte, that the lawe ought to be respited to hym and the lyf saued, and more harde, I telle the, that the *mayster* [captor] is *holden of ryght* [obliged by law] and bounde to helpe his prysoner *aienst* [against] another that wolde *offense* [hurt] hym. Item, with this is myldefulnes due to hym in suche a manere that yf it were possyble that a man of armes had al that he is worthe vpon hym atte that *owre* [hour] that he is taken, *altogider* [everything] may be to the mayster that taketh hym without that he shewe hym fauour and doo to hym myserycorde. But of *ryght wryton* [written law] he ought to be myldefull vnto hym, so that in takyng of his prysoner reanson whyche is permytted in ryght of armes, by especyall of one natyon ayenst another whan they doo werre togyder, as englysshe men and Frenshe men and other in lyke wyse, ought to be taken *heede* [care] that the reanson be not so cruell that the man be not vndoo therby, and his wiffe & children distroied and brought to pouerte. Other wise it is tirannye ayenst conscience & aienst al ryght of armes. For it apparteyneth not that a gentylman shulde begge hys brede after the payement made for hys reanson, but ought to be lefte hym wherof he may lyue, kepyng his astate. And wel ought to be praysed the vsage of ytalye, in which werres, whan a man of armes is taken, he comonly *leseth* [loses] but onely his horses & *harneys* [equipment]; So nedeth hym not to selle his *lyflode* [livelihood] nor to desheryte hym self for to paye his reanson. Thus mayst thou see in what manere is reanson *couenable* [reasonable], Iuste and good after the ryght of armes whiche is permytted. But for to putte a man in an *euyll* [evil] pryson and constrayne by tormentynges to paye more *then* [than] hys power may bere it, is an *homynable* [abominable] horreur and the dede of a cruel crysten tyraunt *wers* [worse] than a Iew. And *wote* [know] thou for certeyn that that whiche he hath bi suche wayes of hys prysoner, it is ryght euyll goten, and he is bounde to yelde it *ayen* [again], or ellis it is hys dampnacyon. Soo kepe hym self there *fro* [from] euery man.

III.3.B A captor might, for various reasons, experience difficulties in obtaining payment of a ransom due to him. As the following petition, sent by the Commons in Parliament to Henry IV, suggests, he ran a decided risk if he allowed his prisoner to get into the hands of others, even into those of the king [1406]. (Anglo–Norman text in *Rotuli Parliamentorum*, III, 597.)

Item, the Commons supplicate on behalf of John Skelton, knight, that since our much redoubted lord the king, by his honourable letters, ordered the said John to come before him, bringing with him Mordok of Fife, a Scot, his prisoner, the said John, at his coming, gave up the said Mordok to the keeping of the bishop of Winchester, then chancellor of England, the earl of Somerset, the earl of Westmorland and Master Thomas Erpingham. This was done on condition, given with their assurance, that they would compensate the said John for his said prisoner, or would otherwise make free restitution of him to the foresaid John, by a certain day already passed. But in fact no agreement has actually yet been made, nor has the prisoner been restored, to the great loss of the said John. In addition to this, the said Mordok is a guarantor and hostage to the said John Skelton for the lord of Graham, a Scot, to the value of 350 marks. May it please our much redoubted lord the king that the said John have restitution of his prisoner, or else that he receive his value in compensation, considering the long litigation incurred and the expenses which the said John has incurred and is still incurring, provided that the Commons of the kingdom be in no way called upon to pay for the fulfilment of this petition and request.

The king and his council will consider this request favourably if it is presented to them.

III.4 APPATIS

Appatis, a form of protection money, was of two kinds. It was sometimes raised, especially in frontier areas, with official approval, and in such cases was a levy paid to a local garrison for the military protection which it could provide. All too frequently, however, it was a sum paid under duress by the population of a town or district to keep a group of marauding soldiers at a safe distance. In both respects it may be seen as an advantage of war won by the soldiery, sometimes for doing little or nothing.

III.4.A Statement of the *appatis* paid by the city of Rheims to the
company of Guillaume de Flavy, which had threatened Rheims
with its unwelcome attention [1437]. (French text in P. Champion,
Guillaume de Flavy, capitaine de Compiègne, p. 205.)

To the venerable and discreet person, Master Jean Remond, provost
of the [cathedral] church of Rheims, for and on behalf of Guillaume de
Flavy, captain of Nesles, for the payment of the sum of 300 pounds
tournois, which it has been agreed shall be allotted and paid by the
inhabitants of the said town of Rheims to the said Guillaume de Flavy,
so as to be spared the pillaging and robbery which his men from Nesles
might have carried out upon this city and the surrounding countryside
during the months of July, August and September, 1437; the sum of
160 pounds; and to Jean Gibour, citizen of Rheims, the sum of 16
pounds *parisis*,[11] for his wine and generosity in having lent the said sum
of 160 pounds *parisis*, so that the said Guillaume de Flavy could be paid,
for no other way could be found of raising the above-mentioned sum, as
appears more fully in an order of my lord the captain of Rheims, dated
the 18th day of January, in the year 1437. The which two sums, totalling
176 pounds *parisis*, have been paid to the said lord provost of the
[cathedral] church and to Jean Gibour, by virtue of the said order, and
by their own quit-claim written on the back of the said order.
             Paid...................... 176 pounds *parisis*.

III.5 LAND

Land, won on behalf of a king or prince, belonged to him; no soldier
had a right to it. Not infrequently, however, such as in Normandy after
Henry V's conquest, it was given to men who had served successfully in
war. It brought its own rewards, such as revenues and, perhaps, titles;
but, since land ownership was frequently associated with expensive
military responsibilities such as defence, it might not be so lucrative as
certain other forms of reward already described.[12]

III.5.A The text of the following grant of land, made in August 1450,
illustrates clearly how some Norman lordships changed hands
several times as rewards during the course of the Hundred Years'
War. (French text in Archives Nationales, Paris, Collection
Lenoir, vol. 75, pp. 81–2.)

Charles, by the grace of God king of France. We make it known to
all, both present and to come, that during the reign of our ancestor king
John [II], the late Godfroy d'Harcourt, in his lifetime knight and lord of

---

[11] Money of Paris.
[12] See C. T. Allmand, 'The Lancastrian Land Settlement in Normandy,
1417–50', *Economic History Review*, 21 (1968), pp. 461–79.

the viscounty of Saint-Sauveur-le-Vicomte, the lordship of Auvers, and of the barony of Néhou, declared and showed himself to be an enemy of the French crown, going to live with the English, our ancient foe, making open war upon our above-mentioned ancestor, and committing against him acts of felony, rebellion and open treason.[13] He continued committing these for so long that he went from life to death while living in the English obedience, so that the said viscounty of Saint-Sauveur-le-Vicomte, the lordship of Auvers and the barony of Néhou, with their appurtenances and rights, were declared confiscated and were taken over by our ancestor. He, exercising his right and moved by certain reasons and considerations, gave the said lands and lordships to the late John Chandos, an English knight, who enjoyed his rights for a certain while.[14] And since then these lands and lordships have been given by our predecessors to certain of their servants, to the late Bureau de la Rivière, knight, and then, later on, to Charles, lord of Ivry, the which persons, as a result of these gifts, successively enjoyed the said lands and lordships, Charles d'Ivry, indeed, holding them from the year 1394 until 1415, when he went from life to death at the battle of Agincourt. And so the said lands and lordships, having been occupied for about thirty years by our said enemies, have once again come into our possession as a result of the reconquest which we have made of our duchy of Normandy. And since we may now dispose of them, considering the facts stated above and the good disposition which we have towards our beloved and loyal chamberlain, André, lord of Villequier, on account of the many good and honourable services which his predecessors have done to our predecessors, and which the said lord has himself done to us since his youth, he having been continually in our service and close to our person, which we hope he will continue to do in the future, we, moved by these reasons and others, have granted, given, ceded, and now grant, give and cede, by these presents, by our special favour, the said viscounty of Saint-Sauveur, the lordship of Auvers and the barony of Néhou to our said chamberlain, for him and his heirs, procreated in legal marriage, to hold and enjoy henceforth and for ever. Given, etc., August, 1450.

III.6 THE CONSEQUENCES OF ENTICEMENT

The lure of riches all too easily gained, together with the frequent failure to pay armies adequately, and thus maintain firm discipline, led soldiers to group themselves into freelance bands, usually under an acknowledged leader, bands which brought terror to the hearts of

[13] For Harcourt, see IV.3.A.

[14] Chandos was given these lands by Edward III rather than by the French king.

the civilian population. Their methods indicate clearly what kind
of men they were, what they sought, and why people lived in fear of
them.

III.6.A An account of the typical activities of the companies, as these
        bands were known, in fourteenth-century France. The chron-
        icler's evident disapproval of their activities should be noted.
        (French text in Froissart, *Chroniques*, V, 227–9.)

Although the truces which had been arranged between the kings of
France and England were properly observed between the persons of
the kings themselves, and between people, too, where their power,
authority and writ were recognised, none the less many adventurers, who
were really brigands and thieves, became active, especially in the far
corners of France where the local knights were not up to fighting, or
were not ready to take up arms against them. There they captured their
towns and castles, and gathered around themselves a considerable
number of similar sorts of people, bearing arms, men of the German
nation and others who, under the guise of war, perpetrated their wicked
deeds and enterprises; none opposed them and it was said by some that
they were openly tolerated and endured by the royal officers, knights
and esquires in the areas in which they were active, and that these
shared the loot and the booty with them. I say to you that such activities
and feats of arms, found all over France, made her into a training ground
for all such iniquities and evils, and that these groups multiplied rapidly
because of the easy time and facility which they enjoyed from the start,
as you will have observed in the history of past events.

There was one particular brigand (I think that he came from Germany) who held dominion in Limousin and Languedoc; they called
him Bacon. He had other brigands under him, and they looked up to
him as their leader and chief because he was the most wicked and the
most daring of them all; (he paid them well, too, regularly every month).
He was too cunning and subtle to rob and capture towns and castles by
escalation; on such occasions, he and his companions would ride twenty
or thirty leagues through the night along little-known paths, and would
arrive at the place which they had in mind at very first light; they would
then climb the walls at the point at which they had set their sights and,
once in the town, they set fire to five or six houses. The townspeople
were much alarmed and, leaving everything, fled; whereupon the
brigands broke open chests and jewel-cases, and took whatever part of
the contents tickled their fancy. Furthermore, they would also take the
richest citizens as prisoners, in addition to the very towns which they
had captured, and would then ransom them to the people of the district,
and even to the very townsfolk whom they had expelled. In this way
much wealth was gained according to what they could raise. On one

occasion this brigand, Bacon, wickedly amassed much money by capturing the town of Donzenac, in the county of Limoges, then by pillaging it and, finally, by selling it back, when he eventually came to leave, for the sum of 10,000 *écus*. Then the said Bacon and his men took the town and castle of Comborne, together with the count of the said place, his wife and children, and ransomed them for the sum of 24,000 *écus*; in the meanwhile, he retained and used the castle for warlike purposes for as long as the said count continued to take up arms for the countess of Montfort, since the said Bacon was himself a supporter of the wife of my lord Charles of Blois.[15] Then he finally sold the castle to the king of France, for which sale he received the sum of 24,000 *écus*, raised from the country all around: and the count of Comborne then made his peace with the king of France. Then the king decided to take this Bacon into his service, and he became the king's inspector of arms and served both king Philip [VI] and king John [II] well, and was always well provided with roan-coloured chargers, and palfreys, together with plenty of silver and gold. And he lived the good life for as long as he lived.

Similarly, at about that time, there was in Brittany another soldier of the German nation; he was called Crokart, and had been a varlet in the service of the lord of Erkele, in Holland. But he became so successful in the Breton wars, chiefly by capturing towns and castles and then selling them back, as well as by ransoming men of substance, that when he had done enough of this sort of thing and had finished with war and all such evil acts, he was worth 60,000 ancient *écus*. The said Crokart was one of those who fought on the English side at the Fight of the Thirty,[16] fighting so well on that side and achieving such fame that king John of France told him that if he wished to leave the English side and become French, he would make him a knight and give him a wife together with 1,000 *écus* a year. But he refused this offer. Then Crokart went back to Holland, where he flaunted his newly-won wealth; but seeing that the lords whom he had once known were not impressed, he returned to Brittany just as the duke of Lancaster, Henry of Derby, was besieging the city of Rennes. The duke welcomed him and retained him in his household with twelve horses. Then, as I shall tell you, fate overtook the said Crokart. One day he was riding a fine horse which had cost 300 *écus*; he had only very recently purchased it and wanted to try it out to see whether there was anything that needed doing. He had had shoes put on the horse, but this had been badly done, so that when he came to jump a ditch, the horse fell and caused his master's neck to be broken. So ended Crokart.

[15] The houses of Montfort and Blois were on opposite sides in the war of the Breton succession, in which the kings of England and France were deeply involved.

[16] Fought in March, 1351. Froissart's account is given in IV.3.j.

III.6.B In the fifteenth century, the companies of professional soldiers
came to be known as *Écorcheurs*, or Flayers. The text of this
deposition suggests that, even when escorting the Dauphin of
France, they had but scant respect for other people's persons or
property [1444]. (French text in A. Tuetey, *Les Écorcheurs sous
Charles VII*, II, 309–31 [extracts only].)

Inquest carried out by us, Huguenin Belverne, notary at Luxeuil,
Gautier Courbenay of Faucogney, deputy to the provost of the said place
and notary to my lord the duke of Burgundy, Nicolas Huguot, Gautier
Henrion and Jean de Molin, deputies for my lord of Burgundy's
representative in the lands of Faucogney and Luxeuil, ordered to this
task by the very reverend and worshipful lords who are members of the
ducal council at Dijon, carrying out the orders contained in certain
instructions sent by them to us concerning the depredations wrought
in the lands of Faucogney and Luxeuil by Frenchmen, as well as by men
from Lorraine and Bar, and by others, too, since peace was established
between the king [Charles VII] and my lord [Philip] duke of Burgundy at Arras, the which inquests were begun on the 4th day of
November, in the year 1444, in the manner which follows:
    First,
    Regnault Bellebos of Amblans, living at Luxeuil in a district called Le
Chasne, states on oath that during the month of July last past, when my
lord the Dauphin passed through the lands of Luxeuil and Faucogney,
on his way to Germany where he is at present, he took in five of my
lord the Dauphin's men, who were quartered in groups on the outskirts
of Luxeuil. He does not know the names of the captains, because it was
not safe to come too close to them since they beat and ransomed all
whom they could lay their hands on, the which men at arms from the
aforementioned five lodgers caused him great harm, both by burning,
looting and breaking some of the contents of his house, and by spoiling
his oats, hay, fodder and other goods, to the value of six francs.
    . . . Jean Garnier, living at Le Chasne, near Luxeuil, sworn on oath
as above, states that the people of my lord the Dauphin, at the time
mentioned above, caused damage to his thatch, which they broke up,
and to his windows, as well as by removing from his home six silver
vessels and several other possessions which they broke up and burned,
all this costing more than twenty francs, not to mention the almost
unlimited amount of stores which they needed.
    . . . Jehanette, widow of the late Jean Frisse, living at Luxeuil, sworn
on oath as above, states that at the said time the soldiers of my lord the
Dauphin broke down three doors, took the metal hinges of the windows
of her house, damaged the roof of her house in four places, and then
broke into cupboards and several other small wooden containers, the
damage caused by such activities totalling some two francs. In addition,

they wrecked and spoiled three cart-loads of hay, which could have been worth one franc.

. . . Jean Lambert . . . aged about sixty years, sworn on oath as above, states upon God's holy Gospels that, at the time described above, when the Dauphin was himself quartered in the town of Luxeuil, certain companions in his troop took the son of him who gives this evidence, a young man of about 32 years, called Girard Lambert, from the home of him who presents this evidence, and after they had severely beaten him because he refused to pay a large ransom which they were demanding, led him away at once to their quarters in the outskirts of Luxeuil; and because they could not have the ransom on that very day, they tied his hands behind his back and took him to the top of the tower of the entrance gate of the said suburb of Luxeuil, and from the top of the said tower they caused him to fall to the ground, thus causing him to die instantly.

. . . Mathiot Roussell . . ., aged about eighty years old, sworn on oath as above, solemnly declares by his oath that in the year 1439, when the French were returning from Germany where they had been, they caused him the following damage: they took a mare and her foal, costing four and a half francs; they seized and took away four quarters of rye, worth at the time three golden florins; two quarters of oats worth fourteen *gros*; also four lengths of cloth and one sheet worth four pence, and several other of his possessions worth six pence. He further states that in the month of August last passed, the men serving my lord the Dauphin caused damage as follows: they captured him and took him away as a prisoner to the town of Lioffans, where they beat him very severely and put him in prison, and demanded from him a ransom of 100 florins; but happily, with God's help, he was able to escape, and thus avoided paying the said ransom. He also claims that they caused him to lose 140 sheaves of rye, valued at three francs and, over and above this, hay and fodder, which could well be worth one franc, the damages costing him the sum of thirteen francs and nine *gros*.

III.7 ENTICEMENT; INDISCIPLINE AND ITS SOLUTIONS

Men reacted to the existence and to the outrages of the companies in very different ways. Some, as we have seen, bought their freedom, but such a method was essentially self-defeating. A king might use threats to move the companies from a particular territory. But neither method dealt fundamentally with the continuing problem, for neither faced squarely the reasons which had brought the companies into being. It was not everyone who saw that only by the strict use of discipline, through the courts, and by the ability to pay properly and regularly, could the problem be satisfactorily solved.

III.7.A Faced with the need of dealing with captains who broke the terms
of a treaty which he had made with the French king, Edward III
felt obliged to threaten them with the most stringent penalties
if they failed to stop their unlawful activities [1364]. (French
text in *Lettres de Rois, Reines et autres Personnages des Cours de
France et d'Angleterre*, ed. J. J. Champollion-Figeac, II, 170–2.)

The King to Eustace Dabelichecourt, Robert Scot, Hugh Calveley,[17]
knights, and to all other persons of the English nation and from our
other lordships, being outside Brittany and within the kingdom of
France.

You must be well aware that, by means of treaties which we have
promised, sworn and agreed, just as our children, the prelates and others
of our kingdom have also done, with our well-beloved and dear brother,
the king of France, with his kingdom, his lands, territories and subjects,
that we will not permit any of our own subjects, nor any others, to go to
or enter the kingdom of France, or any other lands belonging to our said
brother, there to make war or to cause damage or trouble in any way,
whether they be paid by us or any other person, for any manner or
reason whatever; and that we shall prevent and hinder them from doing
this, so that if any of our subjects act to the contrary, or cause trouble or
harm to our said brother, to the kingdom of France or to any of his
subjects, either by land or by sea, we shall punish them, or cause them
to be punished so severely that it will be an example to all others, as
these and other matters are contained in greater detail in the text of the
said treaties.

We have recently heard, on good authority, that, under cover and
colour of the war which the king of Navarre[18] is now waging on his own
authority against our said brother, the king of France, and against his
subjects, both in Normandy and elsewhere, within the realm and outside it, you have entered into the said kingdom with a large following
and number of men at arms, archers and others, and that you are openly
making war there by seizing, robbing and ransoming the people,
burning and destroying buildings, violating and ravishing widows,
virgins and other women, taking, occupying and detaining fortresses,
and by causing other great evils, damage and troubles to our said
brother, to his subjects and to his kingdom, against the terms of peace
contained in the said treaties, to the great shame, scandal and blame of
ourselves and our said estate, and to that of all our sons, prelates and
other great men of our realm; which facts displease us very greatly, so
that we can in no manner ignore them, but must try to remedy them.

For this reason we command you, on your honour and at risk of
forfeiting to us your lives and property, that, having heard the order

[17] See VI.2.B.
[18] Charles the Bad.

[contained] in our present letters, you shall at once cease, abstain and desist from all such troubles caused by this enterprise; and when you have made sufficient reparation and remedy, and have returned to all whom it concerns what you have wrongly taken, you and all your men shall leave the said kingdom of France, without tarrying there any longer or causing any further damage. And we wish you all to understand quite clearly that, if each and every one of you does not fully and properly comply with the command contained in these our orders, as soon as we shall be fully ascertained that you have come to learn of them, we shall punish you so severely that it will be an example to all others, for we shall take unto ourselves and our domain all your goods, possessions, and lands, and will banish and exile you out of our kingdom and all our lordships, and will proceed against each of you as we would against traitors and rebels, as in a case of treason, just as we are obliged by our oath to do.

We therefore command and order all seneschals, captains, castellans, justiciars and officers of our said brother of France, and each of them, that they shall cause to be announced, published and proclaimed, openly and expressly, that which is contained in our present order, in places, meetings and public assemblies within their areas of jurisdiction and authority; that they shall present our said order to each of you if they can come safely into your presence; and that they shall then notify us and our council, by their letters and properly authenticated copies duly sealed, or by any means which can legally and reasonably achieve this, the which should contain the text of these our present letters, the details of the names and surnames of the malefactors, and an indication of when our said order is to be put into effect and practice, so that, from then on, we may proceed with this in sure and certain knowledge, as we are held to do by the terms of the said peace, and must do for the sake of our good faith, the law and reason.

Given by the witness of our great seal, in our palace of Westminster, on the 14th day of November, in the year of grace 1364.

III.7.B The existence of indiscipline, and of its threat to military endeavour, were openly recognised in the text of Henry V's war ordinances [1419] which, when applied by the army's law officers, the Constable and Marshal, constituted a serious attempt to control one of the most pressing problems which faced any medieval commander in the field. (Text in *The Essential Portions of Nicholas Upton's De Studio Militari, before 1446*, ed. F. P. Barnard, pp. 33–4, 35–6.)

Here folowyth the statutes [of war of Henry V]. All thoughe the greate goodnes And graciousnes of the moste hye Artificer haith ordered And dysposed that his subiectes shulde be meke, charitable, And in theyr conversacion honest, yet for All that, onrewly couetousnes, mother of stryffes, enemy of peace, occasion of *grutche* [dispute] And malice, engendryt And bredyth dayly so grete debate Amonge people that, *but yf* [unless] iustice dyd Repreue And subdue theyr wykkyd Assaltes And poures, The vniversall goode order of our cristen *hooste* [army] shulde be clene distroyde, And Also the comon welthe vtterly vndone, whereby we lyue And Regne, And therfore lawes And constitucions be ordeyned *be cause* [in order that] the *noysome* [harmful] Appetit of man maye be kepte vnder the Rewle of lawe, by the wiche mankinde ys dewly *enformed* [taught] to lyue honestly, to hurt no man, And to geue euery man his owne; And for by cause our hooste maye At bothe tymes, that ys to saye bothe in peace And in war, *After* [according to] good order be Rewlyd And gouernyd, And the comon welthe kepte in prosperite; Also, on the other parte, that the constable And marshall of oure hooste maye in theyr causes shewyd Afore theym more discretely Iudge and disscerne; We therfore, by the councell of our lordes, nobles, and gentilmen, haue made certen statutes And constitucions, And causyd theym openly to be proclamyd in our hooste, comaunding that All And euery one of oure capitaines in our saide hoste haue theym in wrytting, that oure publisshing of theym maye be taken for sufficient *monition* [warning], And that euery one of our subiectes in the saide statutes and constituciones pretende no ygnoraunce.

. . .

To what maner of personnes men of warre shall be bounde to obeye. *Whe* [we] ordeyne more ouer that All maner of men beyng wyth in our hooste, what so euer degree, state, condicion, or countrey he be of, that he be lowely obedient to our constable & marshall in All lawefull And honest thinges, vnder payne of forfayting body And goodes. Also we comaunde that All *soudiars* [soldiers], And All suche that reseue wages of vs And oure Realme, be lykewyse obedient vnto theyr immediatt captaynes And maisters; keping such watches And *wardes* [guard-duty] that ys put to theym, or that shall be Reasonably Apointed vnto theym; And that they go nott frome the same watches And wardes in Any maner of wyse wyth owte speciall licence of theyr saide captaynes and maisters, vnder payne of aresting body And goodes, vntill by the discrecion And allowance of the marshall, the saide captaynes or maisters be fully content.[19] Also when *scantnes* [scarcity] *chaunceth* [occurs] of *vitayle* [provisions], or of prouender for horse, yf the captaynes thinke yt necessary to send to Any villaige Aboute for suche vitalles, *whe* [we] comaunde that All maner of saudiars be Redy to Ryde or goo for the same, At the Assignement And ordinaunce of theyr forsaide captaynes or maisters; or ells, yf they be disobedient herein, to be punysshe After the *payne* [penalty] ordend in the statute next Aboue wrytten. More

[19] On this point, see II.1.A (3) p. 47.

ouer As touching chapmen or vitallers that other Ryde wyth the hooste
or Resorte to oure markettes wyth in to bye And sell there, we woll they
be obedient to the constable, the marshall, And clerke of markett, As to
oure owne persone. Also we woll that All maner of bargenes, trespaces,
couenauntes & treatys, done wyth in oure hooste, so that bothe partyes
or the one of theym be Abyding in oure hooste, we woll they be shewed
And finally determined in oure owne courte At the iugement of the
constable And marshall; or, in his Absence, of the marshall, what so
euer persones they be.

. . .

III.7.c William Worcestre, servant of Sir John Fastolf,[20] a leading
English captain in France in the first half of the fifteenth century,
reminds Edward IV of the results, in years past, of extortion by
English armies in France. He advises him to see the wisdom of
giving regular pay to his soldiers, thereby avoiding the disastrous
political and military consequences of exploiting a hostile
civilian population [c. 1475]. (Text in *The Boke of Noblesse*,
ed. J. G. Nichols, pp. 71–2.)

How a prince, be he made regent, governoure, or duke, *chieveteyne*
[commander], lieutenaunt, capetaine, conestable, or marchalle, make
alwaie just paiment to *her soudeours* [their soldiers], for *eschewing*
[failure] of [which] gret inconvenientis might falle.

And overmore, most highe and excellent prince, of youre benigne
grace and providence, if it please youre highenesse to have considera-
cion, in way of justice and keping, to remedie one singuler offence and
damage to youre liege people, the whiche by Goddis law, and by law of
reason and nature, is the contrarie of it righte dampnable, and which
grevous offence, as it is voised *accustumablie* [commonly], *rennythe* [is
practised] and hathe *be* [been] more usid under youre obeisaunce in
Fraunce and Normandie than in othir *straunge* [foreign] regions: and to
every welle advised man it is easy to undrestande that it is a thing that
may welle *bene* [be] amendid and correctid, and to be a gret *mene* [means]
to the *recuvere* [recovery] of youre londes in the saide adverse partie;
that is to say, that shalle be *men of soude* [mercenaries] and of armes, as
well *tho* [those] that shalle be undre youre lieutenauntis as the chiefteins
and capetains, may be duely paide of her wages by the monithe, lyke as
Johan regent of Fraunce[21] payd, or by quarter, *bethout* [without] any
rewarde gyven, bribe, *defalcacion* [misappropriation] or *abreggement*
[underpaying], or undew *assignacion* [promise of payment] not *levable*
[leviable] assigned or made unto them, aswelle in this londe as in

[20] See II.2.B.
[21] John, duke of Bedford, brother of Henry V, was Regent in France for his
nephew, Henry VI, from 1422 until 1435.

Normandie, to deceyve hem, or cause hem [to] be empoverisshed in straunge contreis, as it hathe be accustumed *late* [lately] in the saide contreis. And that suche paymentis be made content bethout delaie or nede of long and grete pursute, upon suche a resonable peyne as the cause shalle require it. And that none of youre officers roialle, nethir *hir debitees* [their deputies] or commissioneris, shalle darre doo the contrarie to take no bribe, rewarde, or defalke the kingis wagis; wherebie youre souldeours shalle not have cause to oppresse and charge youre *obeissauntis* [subjects] and youre peple, in taking their *vitaile* [provisions] bethout paieng therfor, whiche gret part of theym, in defaut of due payment, hathe ben accustumed [to do], by x. or xij. yere *day contynued, or* [daily continuously before] the said londes were lost, uncorrectid *ne* [nor] punisshed, as turned to the gret undoing of youre saide obeisauntes, and one othir of gret causis that they have turned their hertis frome us, breking theire allegeaunce by manere of cohercion for suche rapyn, oppressions and extorcions.

IV

THE PRACTICE OF WAR

THE POSSIBILITY OF war was an ever-present factor in late-medieval life. For the old nobility, its chivalric aspects were of great importance, finding expression both on the battlefield, and in the jousts and tournaments which were so popular at this period. To some, indeed, the tournament was almost an alternative to active war, since it could certainly be as dangerous; to others, the joust provided opportunities both for achieving fame and practising the skills associated with the handling of weapons. Likewise, men of meaner rank were expected to practise the use of arms, and keep themselves in readiness for war.

Once war had been officially declared by legitimate authority, and the formalities had been properly observed, the realities then took over. If the Hundred Years' War is famous for its great battles, it is hardly notable for the number of such battles. Military leaders, one is tempted to say, tended to shun major encounters. Instead, war was characterised by a multiplicity of smaller encounters, which did not involve large armies, and by the activities of semi-independent bands of men, most of them led by soldiers of daring and experience, who attacked targets, both human and material, in a war of attrition. In many respects this was how the war was conducted. The typical activities of these bands (or guerillas, if one may use this modern term), such as attacks on towns and villages which were not always important from the military or strategic standpoint, formed the most common and least pleasant side of war, while chivalric combat, a dying concept by the end of the fifteenth century, added notes of both generosity and unreality to war's unpleasantness.

War at sea, too, was fast becoming an essential part of international conflict. No longer may we look upon sea engagements as a somewhat quaint way of waging war, peripheral in their effects; no war which had to take account of the insularity of Britain, of the long coast-line of France, and of the existence of the skills of the Castilian and Genoese galleymen, could ignore the importance of naval activity. Maritime conflict was now to be an important and integral part of the history of war.

Finally, there was the development of new weapons, associated with the general acceptance of the use of gunpowder and with the new

97

attitudes to warfare, in particular to the problem of defence, which this development encouraged. This was, in many respects, a revolutionary breakthrough in warlike activity; men could be killed more readily, as John Wyclif, for one, complained, and material destruction was now achieved more easily than ever before. The initiative had passed over to the aggressor; it was up to the defender to protect himself, and his, with greater effect.

IV.1 TRAINING FOR WAR

Warfare was an art which required much practice. The need to keep men in training, implied in the duty to rally to the country's defence, was generally recognised, but as two of the following extracts suggest, more than a few were lax in carrying out their obligations which, in England, had been impressed upon his subjects by Edward I in the Statute of Winchester in 1285. Even the failure of the nobility to live up to its noble calling of arms was to be sadly remarked upon by William Worcestre in the middle years of the fifteenth century.

IV.1.A Edward III reminds his officers in the shires of his subjects' duty to practise the use of arms, and especially archery, an activity which has been allowed to lapse. They must now resume this practice, under pain of penalties [1363]. (Latin text in *Foedera*, ed. T. Rymer, III, ii, 79; also translated in *English Historical Documents. IV : 1327–1485*, ed. A. R. Myers, p. 1182.)

The King to the Sheriff of Kent.

As the subjects of our kingdom, both noble and non-noble, have, in times past, commonly practised the art of archery in their games, whereby, with God's help, honour and profit have accrued to the whole of our kingdom and great assistance to us in our military enterprises.

Now, however, this practice having been almost totally abandoned, the people amuse themselves by throwing stones, loggats[1] and quoits, others by playing at hand ball, foot ball and with bats, or at cock fighting or with staves, others still with further vain games which are of doubtful value in training, as a result of which the kingdom, within a short space of time, will likewise become destitute of archers (which God forbid). We, wishing that appropriate measures be taken to prevent this, order you that you should publicly cause it to be proclaimed, in suitable places within your county, both within and outside liberties, that all able-bodied persons within your county should, on feast days, when there is a holiday, practise with bows and arrows, and with crossbows and bolts, in their games, so as to learn and exercise the art of archery. Forbidding all and every one, on our behalf, to play at the throwing of stones,

[1] Heavy poles. This was an old game.

loggats or quoits, at hand ball, foot ball or with bats, at cock fighting or
with staves, or other worthless games of this kind, which can do them no
good, under threat of imprisonment if they should in any way exercise
themselves or take part in these activities.

Witnessed by the King, at Westminster, on the 1st day of June [1363].

By the King himself.

IV.1.B William Worcestre, observing that the English nobility are
abandoning the arts of war for other, less chivalric, activities,
encourages Edward IV to win them back to their traditional
disciplines so that England may once again win victories [c. 1475].
(Text in *The Boke of Noblesse*, ed. J. G. Nichols, pp. 76–8.)

How lordis sonnes and noble men of birthe, for the defense of *her*
[their] londe, shulde excersise hem in armes lernyng.

And also moreover for the grettir defens of youre *roiaumes* [realms]
and saufe garde of youre contreis in tyme of necessite, also to the avauncement and encrece of chevalrie and *worship* [honour] in armes,
comaunde and doo founde, establisshe, and ordeyne that the sonnes of
princes, of lordis, and for the most part of alle *tho* [those] that ben
comen and descendid of noble bloode, as of auncien knightis, esquiers,
and other auncient gentille men, that while they *ben* [be] of *grene* [young]
age ben drawen forthe, norisshed, and excersised in disciplines, doctrine,
and usage of scole of armes, as using *justis* [jousts], to *can renne* [learn to
run] withe speer, handle withe ax, sworde, dagger, and alle othir
defensible wepyn, to wrestling, to skeping, leping, and rennyng, to make
them hardie, *deliver* [adventurous], and wele *brethed* [bred], so as when
ye and youre roiaume in suche tyme of nede to have theire service in
enterprises of dedis of armes, they may of experience be apt and more
enabled to doo you service honourable in what region they become, and
not to be *unkonnyng* [incapable], abashed, ne astonied, forto take
entreprises, to answere or deliver a gentilman that desire in worship to
doo armes in *liestis* [lists] to the *utteraunce* [bitter end], or to certein
pointis, or in a quarelle rightfulle to fight, and in cas of necessite you
and youre roiaume forto *warde* [protect], kepe, and defende frome
youre adversaries in tyme of werre. And this was the custom in the daies
of youre noble auncestries, bothe of kingis of Fraunce as of Englande. In
example wherof, king Edward iij^{de} that exersised his noble son Edwarde
the prince[2] in righte grene age, and all his noble sonnes, in suche
maiestries [skills], whereby they were more apt in haunting of armes.
And the chevalrous knight Henry duke of Lancastre,[3] which is named
a chief auctour and foundour in law of armes, had sent to hym frome
princes and lordis of straunge regions, as out of Spayne, Aragon,

---

[2] Edward, the Black Prince.
[3] Henry of Grosmont, created duke of Lancaster in 1351.

Portingale [Portugal], Naverre, and out of Fraunce, her children, yong knightis, to be *doctrined* [taught], lerned, and broughte up in his noble court in scole of armes and for to see noblesse, curtesie, and worship. Wherthoroughe here honoure spradde and encresid in *renomme* [renown] in all londis they came untoo. And after hym, in youre antecessour daies, other noble princes and lordis of gret birthe accustomed to excersise maistries apropred to defense of armes and gentilnes to them longing. But now of late daies, the grettir pite is, many one that ben descendid of noble bloode and borne to armes, as knightis sonnes, esquiers, and of othir gentille bloode, set hem silfe to singuler practik, *straunge* [different] frome that *fet* [feat], as to lerne the practique of law or custom of lande, or of civile matier, and so wastyn gretlie theire tyme in suche nedelese besinesse, as to occupie courtis *halding* [holding], to kepe and bere out a proude countenaunce at sessions and shiris halding, also there to *embrace* [attempt to influence a court illegally] and rule among youre pore and simple *comyns* [commons] of *bestialle* [stupid] contenaunce that *lust* [desire] to lyve in rest. And who can be a reuler and put hym forthe in suche matieris, he is, as the worlde goithe now, among alle astatis more set of than he that hathe despendid xxx or xl yeris of his daies in gret *jubardies* [danger] in youre antecessourys conquestis and werris. So wolde Jhesus they so wolle welle lerned theym to be as good men of armes, *chieveteins* [commanders], or capetains in the feelde that befallithe for hem where worship and manhode shulde be shewed, moche bettir rathir then as they have lerned and can be a captaine or a ruler at a sessions or a shire day, to endite or *amercie* [punish] youre pore bestialle peple, to theire enpoveryshyng, and to enriche hem silfe or to be magnified the more, but only they shulde maynteyn your justices and your officers usyng the goode custom of youre lawes. And than ye shulde have righte litille nede to have thoughte, anguisshe or besinesse for to conquere and wyn ayen youre rightfulle enheritaunce, or to defende youre roiaume from youre ennemies. And that suche singuler practik shulde not be accustumed and occupied undewly withe suche men that be come of noble birthe, but he be the yonger brother, havyng not whereof to lyve honestly. And if the vaillaunt Romayns had suffred theire sonnes to mysspende theire tyme in suche singuler practik, using oppressing by colours of custom of the law, they had not conquered twyes Cartage ayenst alle the Affricans.

IV.2 DECLARATION OF WAR

As Aquinas had taught, the just war had to be officially declared by and in the name of properly constituted authority. The formal expression of intent was, on occasion, entrusted to royal ambassadors; at other times, heralds were employed on such missions, all being granted immunity for the duration of their mission. The texts illustrate both the manner used by a herald to deliver his master's defiance—all the emphasis is upon the courteous formality of the occasion—and the rather less formal challenge, in which the language is a little more brusque and curt, of the written act of defiance, or *diffidatio*.

IV.2.A The herald of René II, duke of Lorraine (who has assumed his master's name), is received by Charles, duke of Burgundy, to whom he issues a formal challenge to war [1475]. (French text in *Lettres de Rois, Reines et autres Personnages des Cours de France et d'Angleterre*, ed. J. J. Champollion-Figeac, II, 495–6.)

Copy of the commission carried out by a herald of arms, called Lorraine [Herald], acting on behalf of his master, the duke of Lorraine, before the person of my lord Charles, duke of Burgundy and Brabant, etc., then present at the siege of Neuss, on the Rhine.

First, his entrance and respectful greeting, made in the form of a supplication, as follows:

'Most high, most excellent and most illustrious prince, greeting, honour and most humble reverence to your gracious highness from my most high and most powerful sovereign lord, the duke of Lorraine, René, second of that name. I am sent as his most humble and most obedient herald of arms, in order to say and set forth to you what I have been commanded and ordered to do. And because I would neither dare nor wish to presume to interfere by declaring my message without begging you to grant me audience and licence to carry out my orders, I am not willing to proceed further before it should be your wish to accord me permission to do so.'

Reply made by the said duke Charles:

'Herald, you shall say what you have been ordered to say on behalf of your master, and you shall remember what you have said so as to certify that you have said it, as is appropriate to one holding your position.'

The declaration of the commission by the said herald, who wore his hat in the manner of one who speaks as his master's mouthpiece, and bearing his coat of arms:

'You,[4] Charles, duke of Burgundy, on behalf of the most high, most powerful and most dreaded prince, my lord the duke of Lorraine, my most dreaded and sovereign lord, do I now defy with [war of] fire and

[4] Here, and for the remainder of the text, the singular form of the pronoun (*toy*), and not the more formal plural (*vous*), which would be the ordinary form of respectful address, is used by both speakers.

E

blood, [to be waged] against you, your lands, subjects and allies. I have no orders to add anything to this.'

Reply made by the said duke Charles to the said herald, as if he had been speaking to his master:

'Herald, I have listened to and heard the declaration of your commission, by which you have given me cause for joy. And to show and to prove to you that this is truly the case, you will wear my cloak and take this gift, and tell your master that I shall shortly find myself in his lands, and that my greatest fear will be not to find him. And so that you may have no fears about your return, I give orders to the marshal of my army, to Toison d'Or, King of Arms[5] of my Order, that they accompany you in good safety; for I should be grieved if you did not make your report to your master, as is proper to a good and loyal officer of arms.'

The gift which Charles made to the herald of arms.

At the departure of the said officer of arms, the cloak of cloth of gold which the duke had been wearing was handed over and, with it, a goblet of gold-plated silver, in which were five hundred golden florins.[6]

IV.2.B Edward III writes to Philip VI to defy him to surrender the crown of France, and to challenge him to war. In his reply, the French king rejects Edward's claims, and undertakes to expel the English army from France [1340]. (Text in *The Great Chronicle of London*, ed. A. H. Thomas and I. D. Thornley, pp. 35–7).

A Copy of the lettir sent from kyng Edward unto the Frensh kyng.

Edward, by the Grace of God kyng of Fraunce and Engeland and lord of Ireland. To sir phylyp de Valoys.

By long tyme we have yow exortid by messangers and othir manyfold maner of weys to thende that ye shuld Restore unto us and to do to us Reason of owir Rygthfull enherytaunce of the Realme of Fraunce, the whych ye have long tyme occupyed with grete wrong. And for that, that we see well that ye entende to persevir in yowir Injurious witholdyng wythowte to do unto us Reason. For owir Rygth to demaunde we are entryd Into the land of *Flaundrys* [Flanders] as Soverayn lord of the same and passe by the Cuntre. Doyng yow ferther to undirstand that we have takyn, with the helpe of owir lord Jhesu Cryst, the Rygth wyth the

─────────────

[5] The senior herald was often known as a King of Arms. In this case he was the herald of the Burgundian chivalric Order of the Golden Fleece (*Toison d'Or*).

[6] Heralds and envoys were often given financial reward by those to whom they had been sent. For the text of a similar mission, that of the English herald, Garter, King of Arms, to the French court in 1475, see Philippe de Commynes *Mémoires*, ed. J. Calmette, II, 31–2: *Memoirs*, trans. M. Jones, pp. 238–40.

power of the sayd Cunt*** and with owir people theym Alyed, beholdyng
the Rygth which we have In the herytage that ye us witholde wyth grete
wrong. And drawe us toward yow to make a short ende upon owir
Rygthfull demaunde and chalenge, yf ye wyll toward us approche. And
for so moche that so grete powar of men of Armys that come on owir
partyes may not long hold theym *to gydirs* [together] withowte grete
dystruccion of people, which thyng every good Crystyn man *awgth*
[ought] to eschue, And Specially a prince or othir that have the governaunce of people. We therfor moche desire that In *short* [few] days they
may mete, And for to eschue the more mortalyte of the people so that
the quarell apparent atwene us to the dystruccion of our chalenge may
stand in tryall atwene us twoo which thyng we offir unto yow for the
cawsis abovesayd, How be it that we Remember well the noblesse of
yowir persone and your grete wysdam and *advysement* [consideration].
And In caas that ye wyl not thereof, that then in owir chalenge be sette
to afferme the batayll of yowir sylf wyth an hundryth personys of yowir
party of the most *Suffycient* [accomplished], And we In lyke wyth als
many. And yf ye wyll not that oone way nor that othir, that then ye
wyll assyngne a certayn day before the Cyte of Tournay to ffygth wyth
strength agayn strength withyn x days aftyr the sygth of these lettres.
And we wolde that all the world knewe that these thyngis abovesaid In
this our desyre is not for pride nor for grete *presumpcion* [arrogance],
but for that, that owir lord mygth sett the more Rest and pease among
the christen, And for that that the Enemyes of God mygth be Resystyd
and Crystyndum enhaunsyd; And the way that ye wyll chose of these
offyrs abovesayd, wrytyth agayn to us by the *bryngar* [bearer] of these
lettres to hym makyng hasty delyveraunce.

Gyvyn undyr our grete seale at *Elchyn sur le scaut delez Tournay*
[Espléchin near Tournai]. In the yere of grace MCCC and xl, the xxvij
day of *Julet* [July].

The Answer of the French kyng

Phylyp, by the Grace of God kyng of Fraunce, to Edward kyng of
England.

We have seen A lettir sent to phylyp de Valoys brougth to our Court,
In the which lettir were certayn Requestis, And for so Moch as the said
lettir cam not to us the sayd Requestis were not made unto us lyke as it
apperyth by the tenure of the said lettyr We therfor to yow make noon
Answere.[7] Nevirthelesse for that that we undirstand by the said lettir

[7] English kings were reluctant to accord to their opponents the title 'King of
France' as this diminished, and even denied, their own claim to the French
throne. In his letter Edward III calls Philip VI 'Sir Philip de Valoys': in II.2.B,
Charles VII is referred to in an English document as 'Charles who calls himself
Dauphin of Viennois'.

and othirwyse that ye ar *enbataylyd* [come armed] In our Realme of
Fraunce, doyng grete damage to us and ouir said Realme and to the
people, Movid of wyll withowte Reason, not Regardyng that whych A
lyege man owgth to Regard to his lyege and Soverayn lord, ffor ye ar
entryd In to ouir homage yn yowir sylf Aknowlagyng as Reson is to the
kyng of Fraunce and promysyd obeysaunce swych as a lyege man owgth
unto his Soverayn lord, lyke as it apperyth by yowir lettirs patentis
sealid with your grete seale, the whych we have by us, and for that,
shuld yow be obedient unto us. Owir entent ys swych that, when we
shall thynk yt good, to chase yow oute of ouir Realme to ouir honour
and Mageste Royall, and to the profyt of ouir people: And in this
doyng we have feythfull hope in owir lord Jhesu Cryst, from whom all
good to us comyth, ffor by your entirprise, which is of wyll not Resonable, hath been *lett* [prevented] the holy voyage ovir the see, and grete
quantite of cristyn people put to deth, and the servyce of God left, and
holy chirch unworshyppid and *un anournyd* [unadorned] with many
grete Reverencis. And in that, that ye thynk to have the Flemyngis In
yowir Ayde, we thynk us to be assuryd that the good Tounys and the
comons wyll behave theym sylf In such wyse *agayn* [towards] us and
agayn ouir Cousyn, the Erle of Flaunders, that wyll save theyr honour
and *trowth* [loyalty]. And In that, that they have misdoon tyll now, hath
been by evyll counsayll of such people whych Regard not the comon
wele of the people, but of thayr aune proufyt allonly.

Gyvyn In the ffeyld of the priory of Seynt Andrew besyde Ayre,
undyr the seale of ouir secret Sygnet In absence of ouir grete Seale, the
xxx[th] day of Julet, the yere of Grace MCCCxl [1340].

IV.3 WAR ON LAND

War on land took on many different aspects. It was most typically
characterised by the *chevauchée*, the organised raid deep into the enemy's
territory.[8] Great battles were less common, but they were to witness, at
first, the domination of the archer over the cavalry, and then the
increasing effectiveness of artillery, two of the chief military characteristics of the period. Significant, too, were the sieges of, and assaults upon,
walled towns and fortresses. Nor may one ignore the activities of the
small bands of soldiers who achieved results by daring and surprise. If
war, to some, was still predominantly chivalric, it was fast becoming less
so, for many were those who now took part in it with intentions which
discounted chivalry, while the means which they employed to achieve
their ends only served to undermine it further.

IV.3.A War might consist largely of expeditions, or *chevauchées*, under-
          taken not with the express intention of defeating the enemy in

[8] See H. J. Hewitt, *The Black Prince's Expedition*, pp. 46–9.

battle, but rather in the hope of demoralising his subjects and
bringing material advantage to those who took part [1346].
(Text in Froissart, *Chroniques*, IV, 389–92, 395–6.)

When the English king's fleet had arrived safely at la Hougue, and
was anchored or drawn up on the shore, the king leaped from his vessel;
but with his first step on land he fell, and with such force that the blood
gushed from his nose. The knights who were around him said: 'Sire,
return to your ship, and do not land here today, for this is an omen for
you.' The king instantly replied: 'Why? I look upon it as very favourable
for me, a sign that the land desires to have me.'

His people were much pleased with this answer. The king and his
army lay that day, the next night and the following day upon the sands.
In the meantime they disembarked their baggage and horses; and there
was a council held to consider what they should do. The king created
two marshals for his army: one was Sir Godfroy d'Harcourt,[9] the
other the earl of Warwick; and he made the earl of Arundel his constable. He ordered the earl of Huntingdon to remain with his fleet, with
a hundred men at arms, and four hundred archers. He then held
another council to discuss the order of march; the army was divided
into three companies, one of which should advance on the right, following
the sea-coast, and another on the left, while the king, with the princes,
his sons, would remain in the centre. Every night, the marshals' companies were to retire to the king's quarters. The men-at-arms thus
began to march, as it had been resolved. In the meanwhile, those on
board the fleet coasted the shore, capturing and taking away every
vessel, great and small, which they came upon. The archers and foot-
soldiers advanced along by the sea-coast, robbing, pillaging and stealing
everything they found. Both the armies of land and sea advanced in this
way until they came to a strong town and a good harbour called Barfleur, which they soon gained, the inhabitants having surrendered
immediately, for fear of losing their lives; but this did not prevent the
entire town from being pillaged and robbed of gold, silver, jewels and
everything precious that could be found in it. There was so much
wealth, that the servants of the army set no value on gowns trimmed with
fur. They made all the townsmen leave the town, and embarked them
on board the fleet with them, for they did not wish that, after they had
passed on further, the people should assemble together to attack them.

After the town of Barfleur had been pillaged, but not burnt, they
spread themselves over the country near the sea-coast, where they did
much as they pleased, for there was none to oppose them. They went on
until they came to a large and wealthy town, a port called Cherbourg,
which they burnt and pillaged in part; but they could not capture the

[9] See III.5.A.

castle, as it was too strong, and well garrisoned with men at arms. They therefore went on, and came to Montebourg and Valognes, which they pillaged and set fire to. In this way they plundered and burnt a great many towns in that region, and acquired so many riches and possessions that it would have been very difficult to have counted their wealth. Afterwards, they marched to a very large and well enclosed town called Carentan, which had a strong castle, garrisoned by a large number of soldiers. Those lords who were on board the fleet disembarked with their men, and made a vigorous attack upon it. When the townsmen saw this, being afraid of losing their own lives and possessions, they surrendered, saving their lives and those of their wives and children, in spite of the soldiers who were there: and they gladly offered the English all that they had, thinking that they had nothing to lose. The men at arms, on seeing this, retired into the castle, which was very strong; whereupon the English entered the town, but did not think it right to leave the castle in this way; they therefore stayed in the town, and kept up a strong assault against the castle for two successive days, so that those within, not seeing any assistance coming to them, then surrendered, on condition that their lives and fortunes were spared: they marched out, and withdrew to another part of the country. The English did what they pleased in the town and castle, but finding that they could not conveniently hold them, burnt and destroyed both, and then forced the inhabitants to embark on their fleet, and to go with them, as they had done to those of Barfleur, Cherbourg, Montebourg and all the neighbouring towns on the sea-coast which they had captured and plundered.

We will now return to the expedition of the king of England. As soon as he had sent [part of] his army under the command of the earl of Warwick, one of his marshals, and the lord Reginald Cobham, along the sea-coast, as you have heard, he set out from St-Vaast-la-Hougue, where he had arrived, under the guidance of Sir Godfroy d'Harcourt, because he was well acquainted with all the roads and ways of Normandy. Sir Godfroy, as marshal, advanced before the king, with a vanguard of five hundred men in armour and two thousand archers, riding some six or seven leagues' distance before the main army, burning and destroying the country. They found it rich and plentiful, abounding in all things: the barns full of every sort of corn, and the houses with riches, the inhabitants prosperous, having carts, horses, swine, sheep and the finest cattle in the world which are reared in this region. They seized whatever they chose of the good things which they saw, and brought them to the king's army; but the common soldiers did not give any account to those appointed by the king of the gold and silver which they had found, and which they kept for themselves.[10] In this manner

[10] Froissart stresses this, since soldiers had to declare the value of their gains. See III.2.B, C.

did Sir Godfroy proceed daily on the right of the king's company, and each night he returned, with his party, to the place where he knew the king intended to fix his quarters. Sometimes, when he found plenty of forage and booty, it would be two or three days before he returned. The king, therefore, with the army and baggage-train, advanced towards St Lô, in the Cotentin; but before he got there, he set up his camp on the banks of a river, for a period of three days, to await the return of his soldiers whom he had sent along the sea-coast. When they had joined him, and had put all their booty in carts, the earl of Warwick, the earl of Suffolk, the lord Thomas Holland, the lord Reginald Cobham and their company, advanced on the left, burning and destroying the country in the same way as Sir Godfroy d'Harcourt was doing. The king rode between these two, and each night they encamped together.

IV.3.B   This eye-witness account of the battle of Agincourt shows how physical conditions conspired with the skill of the English archers to defeat the numerical superiority of the French [1415]. (French text in Jean de Waurin, *Recueil des Croniques et Anchiennes Istories de la Grant Bretaigne*, [1399–1422], ed. W. Hardy, pp. 210–18.)

The fact of the matter is that the French had drawn up their battle formations between two small woods, one close to Agincourt, the other by Tramecourt. The place itself was narrow, [thus] greatly favouring the English, while acting very much against the French interest; for the said French had spent all the night on horseback in the rain; their pages, grooms and many others, while exercising their horses, had turned up the earth which had become very soft, so that only with some difficulty could the horses pick their hoofs up from the ground. In addition, the French themselves were so burdened with armour that they could hardly bear it nor move forward. For they were armed with coats of steel which were very heavy, right down to the knees or below, in addition to their leg harnesses; and besides this plate armour, the majority also had hooded helmets. Together, this weight of armour and the softness of the sodden earth, as has been said, held them almost immobile, so that it was only with the greatest difficulty that they lifted their weapons; to crown all these mischiefs was the fact that not a few [of the French] were worn out by hunger and lack of sleep. It was wonderful to see all the banners, some of which, it had been decided, were to be displayed.[11] The French agreed among themselves to shorten their lances so that they should be less likely to yield when the time for attacking and closing with the enemy should come; quite a number, too, commanded archers and crossbowmen, but they would not let them use

[11] As a sign of war (Keen, *The Laws of War*, pp. 105–8).

their weapons since the ground was so confined, and there was really only sufficient room for the men-at-arms.

On turning to the English we find that, after the parleying between the two sides, already described, was over, and the delegates had each returned to his own side, the king of England ordered a knight called Sir Thomas Erpingham to arrange his archers in front of the two wings (he and Sir Thomas were to be in charge of the operation), and exhorted all his men to fight well and with vigour in his name against the French, so as to secure and save their very lives. Then the knight, who was riding in front of the formation with only two others, on seeing what the hour was and that all was ready, threw up a stick which he was holding in his hand, shouting "Nestrocq",[12] which was the sign to advance; he then dismounted and came over to join the king, who, likewise, was on foot in the midst of his retinue, his banner being carried before him. The English, seeing this signal, suddenly began to advance, and let out a great cry, at which the French greatly wondered. When the English saw that the French were not coming out to meet them, they moved towards them in very good order, once again giving out a very loud cry, and then stopping to regain their breath. Thereupon the English archers who, as I have said, were on the wings, seeing that they were now within range, began with vigour to shoot arrows upon the French; the majority of these archers had no armour but were only wearing doublets, their hose rolled up to their knees, with hatchets and axes or, in some cases, large swords hanging from their belts; some of them went barefooted and with nothing on their heads, while others wore caps of boiled leather, while yet others still had simply back plates covered with pitch or leather.

The French, seeing the English coming towards them in this way, drew themselves into rank, each man beneath his banner, and wearing his basinet upon his head. The constable, the marshal, the admirals and the other princes strongly admonished their men to fight bravely and valiantly against the English. As they came together, the trumpets and clarions made a great noise on all quarters; but the French soon put their heads down, especially those who were not shielded in any way, such was the effectiveness of the English arrows, which fell so thick and fast that no man dared to uncover himself nor even to look up. They advanced a little, then made some slight retreat; but before the armies could get together again, many of the French were either hurt or wounded by the arrows. When they finally reached the English they were, as reported, so tightly packed together that they could not raise their arms to strike their enemies, except those who were out in front, who struck forcefully with lances which had been shortened so as to be more rigid and in order to come to closer grips with the enemy.

[12] Probably 'Now strike'.

The French, as I shall describe, had made the following plan. The constable and the marshal had chosen a thousand or twelve-hundred men-at-arms, some of whom were to go on the Agincourt side, the remainder through Tramecourt, the intention being that they should split the two wings of English archers. But when they finally approached [the English], those under the leadership of Sir Clugnet de Brabant, who had charge over on the Tramecourt side, now numbered only one hundred and twenty, while Sir Guillaume de Saveuse, a most valiant knight, had charge on the Agincourt side with about three hundred lances. He advanced, with only two others, against the English, followed by all his men and attacked the English archers who were behind their stakes which, however, scarcely stood up since the ground was so soft. Thus the said Sir Guillaume and his two companions came in to attack, but their horses fell upon the stakes, and they themselves were soon killed by the archers, which was a great shame; most of the remainder, out of fear, turned and moved back upon the vanguard, where they caused much disorder and gaps in the ranks, causing them to retreat and lose their footing in the newly-sown ground, for their horses had been so badly wounded by the arrows that they found themselves unable to hold or control them. It was by these, chiefly, that the French vanguard was put into disorder: countless persons began to fall and their horses, feeling the arrows falling upon them, started to bolt behind the enemy, many of the French following their example and turning to flight. Then the English archers, seeing the advance-guard in such disarray, emerged from behind their stakes, threw their bows and arrows aside and, taking up their swords, hatchets, hammers, axes, falcon-beaks[13] and other weapons, rushed into those places where they saw gaps, killing and laying low the French without mercy, not ceasing to kill until the said advance-guard, which had fought but little or not at all, was completely wiped out. They came through, striking to right and to left, to the second squadron which was behind the advance-guard, and here they were joined by the king in person, together with his own retinue. And Antoine de Brabant, who had been sent for by the king of France, was in such a hurry to flee that his men could not keep up with him, for he would not wait for them: he took a banner from one of his trumpeters, made a hole in the middle, and wore it as if it were a tabard,[14] but soon afterwards he was killed by the English. Then began what was both a fight and a great slaughter of Frenchmen, who defended themselves but little since their formation had been broken up, as related above, by their own cavalry, so that the English were able to attack them with greater and greater success, breaking the ranks of the first two squadrons in several places, bringing down men and killing cruelly and mercilessly;

[13] *Becqs de faucquon*: probably scythe-like weapons for cutting.
[14] He was probably hoping to secure for himself the immunity due to a herald.

some got up again with the help of their grooms, who were then able to lead them out of the skirmish for the English were so concerned with killing and taking prisoners that they did not pursue anybody. Then the whole rear-guard, which was still mounted, seeing the confusion in which the other two squadrons found themselves, turned and fled, all except a few of the leaders. It should also be stated that, while all this was going on, the English had captured a certain number of valuable French prisoners.

Then came news to the English king that the French were attacking his people at the rear, and that they had already captured some of his baggage and other stores. This was done under the leadership of one Robinet de Bornoville, who had with him Rifflart de Plamasse, Ysembert d'Azincourt and certain other men-at-arms, as well as about six hundred peasants, who stole the said baggage and several horses from English hands while their guards were busy in the battle. The king, Henry, was much troubled by this loss, but it did not prevent him from pursuing his victory, nor his people from taking many good prisoners who would bring them riches, taking from them nothing but their head armour.

At this moment, when they were the least expecting it, the English experienced a moment of very great danger, for a large detachment from the French rear-guard, among them men from Brittany, Gascony and Poitou, having grouped themselves around some standards and ensigns, returned and, in good order, advanced with determination upon those holding the field. When the king of England saw them coming, he immediately ordered that every man who had a prisoner should kill him, something which they did not willingly do, for they intended to ransom them for great sums. But when the king heard this, he ordered a man and two hundred archers to go into the host to ensure that the prisoners, whoever they were, should be killed. This esquire, without refusing or delaying a moment, went to accomplish his sovereign master's will, which was a most terrible thing, for all those French noblemen were decapitated and inhumanly mutilated there in cold blood, and all this was done on account of this worthless company of riff-raff who compared ill with the nobility who had been taken prisoner, men who, when they saw the English preparing to receive them, just as suddenly turned in flight, so as to save their lives; several of them, in fact, managed to get away on horseback, but there were many killed among those on foot.

When the king of England saw that he was master of the field and had overcome his enemies, he graciously thanked the Giver of Victories; and he had good reason to, for of his men there died but about sixteen hundred of all ranks, among whom was the duke of York, his great uncle, which was a great blow to him.[15] Then the king called together those closest to him, and asked them the name of the castle which was close by; and they told him, 'Agincourt.' To which he replied: 'It is proper that this our victory should always bear the name of Agincourt, for every battle should be named after the fortress nearest to which it has been fought.' When the king of England and his army had stood there, defending their claim to victory, for more than four hours, and neither Frenchmen nor others appeared to challenge them, seeing that it was raining and that evening was drawing in, the king went to his lodgings at Maisoncelles. The English archers went out to turn over the bodies of the dead, beneath whom they found some good prisoners still alive, of whom the duke of Orléans was one. And they took away many loads of equipment from the dead to their lodgings.[16]

IV.3.c An account, not by an eye-witness, of the battle of Castillon, which finally ended the period of English hegemony in Gascony in 1453. The lack of great detail about armaments, together with the emphasis upon artillery, underlines the contrast between this and the previous extract. (Latin text in Thomas Basin, *Histoire des règnes de Charles VII et de Louis XI*, ed. J. Quicherat, I, 263–8.)

The king [Charles VII] arrived in Guyenne with his army, together with many engines and [all] the apparatus of war; without great difficulty he was able to get possession of some of the least defended towns and castles. This done, he began to besiege a town called Castillon, which was necessary to him before he could complete his plan. The lord Talbot was at that time at Bordeaux with many Englishmen, as well as Gascon noblemen and foot-soldiers, knights and men of lesser rank; the French, suspecting that he intended to mobilise them, and that he would not allow the besieged town of Castillon to fall without resistance, fortified their camp as strongly as they could. They dug a deep ditch and added a wall of earth and even great tree trunks around it, placing on this elevation a very large number of machines of war named serpentines and culverins.

There was then in the king of France's service, as superintendent of all these machines and of all the material of war, a certain Jean Bureau,[17] a citizen of Paris, a man of humble origin and of small stature, but of purpose and daring who was particularly skilled and experienced in the use and exercise of weapons of this sort, knowing how to employ them

[15] Edward, duke of York, was a grandson of Edward III, and cousin to Henry IV.
[16] A discussion of the battle, together with a plan, will be found in A. H. Burne, *The Agincourt War*, Ch. V.
[17] See IV.3.H.

effectively, knowledge he had picked up over the years, for he had
served the king of England in a similar capacity. Thanks to this man's
skill, the French camp was so well defended, and the confidence of the
defenders so great, that the castle could not have been taken by the
enemy. The lord Talbot, however, too little aware of the French effort
and confidence, and relying more on the fear which his name had earned
him in many battles, counted more on the ignoble behaviour or the
flight of the enemy than upon his own forces. Failing to appreciate the
strength of the French defences, he very rashly and inadvisedly decided
to attack their camp. Leaving Bordeaux with several thousand knights
and foot soldiers, both English and Gascon, he came rapidly to the
besieged town of Castillon; driven by his desire to fight, he rode
impetuously with his mounted men ahead of his foot-soldiers and his
heavy equipment; and coming upon a group of some four hundred
French archers wandering indisciplinedly beyond their camp defeated
them easily, killing them to the last man.

This good beginning seemed to him auspicious of victory. Not long
afterwards, seeing what looked like a huge cloud of dust rising into the
sky (it was a very hot and dry season) and thinking that it was the
French who, in fear of his mere approach, were abandoning their camp
in flight without daring to oppose him, he urged his troops on even
faster so as to seize booty and pursue fugitives. In this way he arrived at
the French camp, but without his foot-soldiers whom he had left behind.
Too late, he saw that the French had not fled: on the contrary, they were
awaiting the attack with confidence. The dust which he had seen from a
distance had been caused by horses which the French had sent away,
accompanied by grooms, in search of fodder. It was with thoughts of
resistance, not flight, in mind that they had sent the horses away, for
they could have been kept for purposes of flight, had this ever been
their intention.

Having thus arrived with excessive haste with his horsemen before
the French camp, and not waiting for his artillery or men-at-arms who
numbered, it was said, more than ten thousand men, he decided to
attack the castle. One of his captains, or standard-bearers, Thomas
Evringham, a man of rank, hoping to deter him from this imprudent
move by showing him the risks which he and his people were incurring,
very sensibly emphasised the disaster which could befall them if they
attacked the well-fortified French camp too precipitately. He advised
him to await the arrival of his men-at-arms and artillery so that, with
his forces once again united, they could launch a carefully planned
attack or pitch their camp close by, in a place without danger to them,
so that they could starve the French out, and then attack them when
their supplies were low, thereby compelling them to flight. He himself
should have no fears about supplies, since the whole country around

favoured them, and regarded the French as enemies. The French indeed, after only very few days, and having received no supplies, would necessarily experience hunger and discomfort, and would then either have to take to flight or, abandoning the safety of their camp, would attack them. In this way the aforesaid Thomas wisely tried to persuade Talbot to give up his foolhardy plan. But that lord, who was normally impelled to drive the enemy into flight by impetuous daring rather than by a deliberate assault, still thinking that his name alone would cause the enemy to take to flight rather than stand, ordered the said Thomas to bring the standards which he bore up to the ditch built by the French, accusing him of an unaccustomed lack of courage. Both the standard-bearer and the soldiers obeyed their leader at once. They came to the edge of the ditch and at once attacked the camp's defences, striving to force an opening if they could, so as to come to grips with the enemy. On their part, the French remained calm, countering the English with stones, lead and all kinds of other weapons and missiles, and killing a good many of them with shots fired from their serpentines, culverins and arbalests. In this manner the assault was repulsed.

While the fight swung to and fro, many of the English, including Thomas, the standard-bearer, were killed. It also happened, not by chance but rather by design of Divine Providence,[18] that the lord Talbot, leader of the English army, was hit in the lower leg by shot fired from a serpentine or culverin. With Talbot wounded, the attackers repulsed, and many killed by the enemy, the survivors, aghast and stupefied at what had happened, rallied round their leader whom they knew to be wounded. When the French saw this and realised that the English were demoralised, although ignorant of which enemy captain had been wounded, they rushed out from behind their defences and aiming at the place where the wounded English leader stood, they killed him, as well as one of his sons and several lords. . . . Such was the end of my lord of Talbot; with him dead, his army routed, the survivors for the most part fled to the safety of the besieged town of Castillon, seeking a refuge from the drawn swords of the Frenchmen. As for the foot-soldiers who were following up, when they learnt of the disaster and of the death of their leader and the greater part of his knights and nobles, they quickly turned heel for Bordeaux. After two days the besieged, deprived of all hope of rescue, were obliged to hand over the town to the will of the conquerors.[19]

IV.3.D   Sieges were more characteristic of late-medieval warfare than were battles. Much good advice was given as to how these should be carried out, notably by Christine de Pisan who, like others,

[18] See I.5.
[19] This battle is described by Burne, *The Agincourt War*, Ch. XIX.

relied heavily on the works of the early fifth-century writer, Vegetius, now suitably brought up-to-date. (French text in Christine de Pisan, *Le Livre des Fais et Bonnes Meurs du Sage Roy Charles V*, ed. J. F. Michaud and J. J. F. Poujoulat, II, pp. 54–6.)

Battles are of four kinds. The first is when the parties are on open ground, and fight together there; another is when a castle is attacked; the third, when those within the castle defend themselves; and the fourth is when one fights on water, or at sea. With what we have said concerning the assault and capture of towns and fortresses, one way of achieving this is by cutting the water supply, which is what the army must try to achieve; a second way is by starvation, so that the besieging force must take all necessary steps to ensure that nobody gets provisions to those within the castle; steps must be taken, too, to ensure that if any men from the castle are captured, they shall not be killed but only mutilated, so that they will never serve again, but shall be sent back to the castle to help consume the stock of provisions; and the third manner concerns those occasions when those within and those outside fight upon the walls, about which we shall have more to say later.

Sieges of castles and towns should take place in summer, before the harvest is brought in, so that the besieged cannot gather in the harvest; at this time of year, too, ditches are emptier than in winter, so that those within suffer more from lack of water, while those carrying out the siege suffer less in summer than during the cold weather. The besieging army should quarter itself one bowshot's distance from the castle, and dig ditches and build pallisades all around itself, as well as building a kind of fortification for itself, so that the besieged may not capture it by surprise.

The assault should be begun by shooting arrows and bringing up scaling ladders, by mining and digging passages under the ground, and by the use of engines and different cannons which shoot hard, [aided by] structures and other engines which should be brought right up to the wall. The digging of mines must be begun as soon as the tents are pitched, and men must dig under the ground to a depth greater than that of the ditch, thereby creating an access to the walls; the passage must be reinforced with wood and planks, so that it will not collapse; the earth which is extracted must be hidden so that those within the castle shall have no knowledge of what is being done. This mining should continue until the houses within the castle are reached; then, after hay and wood have been placed in the passage, the whole is ignited at night. If the castle is situated upon a rock, or in any other situation which prevents tunnelling, it must be attacked by the use of powerful siege engines or other instruments which can be brought right up to the wall. If projectiles are used at night, pieces of burning material should be attached to the stones shot over, so that, by means of their light, the effectiveness of the shooting can be measured and the weight of the shot to be used estimated.

...

With regard to the attack and capture of fortresses, we learn from the same book [Vegetius] how, with certain wooden engines which are brought right up to the wall, the capture of the place can be achieved. This machine is called a ram; it looks like a house, is built from wood, and is covered with new skins, so that it will not catch fire. At its front there extends a long beam whose end is covered with metal; those who are inside the house manipulate it by using cords and chains, thus making the beam knock the wall and then drawing it back at will, just like a ram who retreats before he wants to attack. And that is why it is called a ram.

There is another kind of engine, which is called a mantlet, made of good, strong planks and exceptionally hard wood, so that the stones projected by the machines cannot harm it. It, too, is covered with fresh skins, so that it will not catch fire. This engine is eight feet wide and sixteen feet long, and is high enough for several men to get into it. It should be led carefully to the wall, whereupon those whom it protects bore into the castle walls. This machine can be of great value on those occasions when it is brought right up to the wall face. When a castle cannot be taken by using either the mantlets or the rams, the height of the walls must be measured, so that castles and towers of wood can be constructed. With these wooden towers, which must be similarly covered with skins and then brought as near as possible to the wall, an attack can be carried out in two ways: either by throwing missiles at those within the fortress; or by lowering drawbridges which reach the walls of the place besieged. Wooden contraptions are made with which such towers can be brought right up to the walls. Those at the top of these wooden towers have to hurl stones at those on the walls; those who are on the middle floor have to lower the drawbridge and then attack the wall; while those at the lowest level must, if they are able, get close to the walls so as to dig mines beneath them.

The attackers should use all these modes of attack at one and the same time; in this way, the maximum alarm will be caused among the defenders of the place.

IV.3.E A fifteenth-century account of the siege and capture of the Norman town of Harfleur by the English under Henry V in September 1415. The emphasis in this narrative is upon the formalities of the siege and the consequent surrender of the town, formalities which, being an essential part of war fought at this time, were common features of such occasions.[20] (Text in *The Great Chronicle of London*, ed. A. H. Thomas and I. D. Thornley, pp. 91–3.)

[20] See Keen, *The Laws of War*, Ch. VIII.

... And thanne sone afterward the kyng [Henry V] with all his *ooste* [army] sayled ovyr the see with a *MM* [2,000] shippes and moo. And the xvj day of August, a litil from Harflete, he landed. And the saturday *next* [following] the Assumpsion of oure lady[21] he leyde siege abowte Harflete. And that siege contynued unto the sonday next before the feste of seynt Mychell,[22] on the which sonday the towne of Harflew was delivered up to the kyng, that is to sey the xxij day of Septembre. But it is to *wete* [(be) know(n)] that the tuysday before, that is to say the xvj day of the same moneth, at xij of the belle withyn nyght, the lordys that were the Captayns and governours of the towne, That is to *wete* [say], the lord *Gaucorte* [Gaucourt], the lorde *Tutvyle* [Estouteville], and moo other lordys, sente oute *herowdes of armys* [heralds of arms] unto the Duke of Clarence,[23] praying hym atte the *Reverence* [honour] of god that he wold, of his high and gracious lordship, graunte hem leve to trete with tho persones that the kyng wold assigne to hem. And the kyng, atte the reverence of god and atte here requeste, assigned the Duke of *Excettre* [Exeter], the lorde Fitz hugh and sir Thomas Erpyng-ham to here what they wold seye and desire. And they desired that the kyng wold not *werre* [war] on hem fro that houre of mydnyght unto the sonday next after the feste of seynt Mychell. And *But* [unless] it were rescued by *bateyll* [battle] by that day be the Frenssh kyng or with the *Dolphyn* [Dauphin], ellis at that day to delyver the towne to the kyng, And they to have here lyves and here goodes. And the kyng sente hem worde yf they wold delyver the towne on the morowe next, after the houre of Mydnyght, withouten ony condicion, he wold accept it; And in none other wyse he bade hem seke no trete. And yit the frensshe lordes prayed oure lordes that they wolde *vouche saaf to be seek* [vouch-safe to beseech] the kyng, atte the reverence of god and of oure lady, that he wolde graunten hem that same tuysday nyght and Wednesday, thursday, Fryday, saturday And the soneday unto an houre after none. And in that meen tyme, the lordes that were Capitaynes of the towne come to the kyng with xxij knyghtes and squyers with hem of the moost *sufficient* [prosperous, important] men within the towne; And they to be sworne upon goddys body, opynly *to fore* [in front of] all the peple. But *yf* [unless] so were that the frenssh kyng or the dolphyn rescued hem by that soneday, by that houre of noone or anone after none, they to delivere the toune to the kyng, and here bodyes and here goodes, to *done* [do] with hem what so evyr hym *lyst* [wished], withoute ony condicion, *with* [except] that the kyng wolde suffre hem to sende to the Frenssh kyng viij persones oute of the towne letyng hem wete in what plyte they stonde. And he graunted hem. And upon the Wednesday by the morowe

[21] The Assumption was celebrated on 15 August.
[22] The Sunday before 29 September.
[23] Thomas, duke of Clarence, brother of Henry V.

thees lordes comen oute of the towne, And xxij knyghtes and squyers
with hem. And thanne come the procession solemply and stately, with
xxiiij Coopes of oo suyte [24 copes of one suit] before goddes body, with
mony worshipfull lordes, knyghtes and squyers, and other much multitude of peple fro the kynges tente, as solempnely done and as stately as
ony man saugh evyr such a thing done before that tyme. But the kyng
was not there presente. And the Frenssh lordes there maad theire othes
upon the holy sacrament. And the othes thus i-done [taken], the frensshe
lordes, with here *felaship* [company], were brought to the kynges tentes,
And there they eten in the kynges halle; But in all this tyme they sawe
not the Kyng. And whanne they hadde eten, they were departed and
delivered to certeyne lordes, forto kepe in hostage tyl the soneday atte
the houre after noone, as it was accorded whan they *resceyved* [took] here
othe. And atte the houre on the soneday after noone, the kyng hadde
a tente *pyght* [pitched] on a hille before the towne. And there he satte in
his astate ryall, and all his lordes aboute hym. And thanne come the
Frenssh lordes, with *iij*^{xx} *and iiij* [sixty-four (3 × 20 and 4)] with hem
of the moost sufficient men that were within the toune, to the kyng; And
to his propre persone yolden up the keyes of the toune, and here bodyes
and goodes, to the kynges grace, without ony condicion. And this was
done the xxij day of Septembre, the yere of oure lord MCCCCxv [1415].

IV.3.F In siege warfare, the traditional methods of attack and defence,
        best expressed in the early years of the fifteenth century by
        Christine de Pisan, who leant heavily upon Vegetius, found
        much favour. (French text in Christine de Pisan, *Le Livre des
        Fais et Bonnes Meurs du Sage Roy Charles V*, ed. J. F. Michaud
        and J. J. F. Poujoulat, II, pp. 57–60.)

We shall now say how those who are in a fortified place should defend
and fortify themselves. First of all, when one wishes to build castles or
towns, one must bear in mind five factors: first, one should note whether
the said edifice is built on rock, or on a mountain, or on some height, or
has water around it, or is by the sea, in which case it is captured only
with great difficulty. When one is building, one should have these
factors in mind.

Secondly, the walls must be built so as to present several angles, so
that those who are defending may cause hurt to their enemies from
several sides.

Thirdly, in the space between the two walls which surround the
castle, earth should be piled like a thick wall, so as to lessen the harmful
effects of stones and engines.

Fourthly, there should be built over the gateways of castles port-
cullises and iron tubes, through which water can be poured (to put out a
fire), or stones or lime dropped in defence of the entrance.

Fifthly, there must be wide ditches, which should be steep and deep.

Towns and castles should be garrisoned, first of all, with good soldiers, able to do their task and numerous enough for the particular place, as circumstances demand. They must have provisions, such as barley, wheat and oats, salted meats and other necessities of human life; and what may not be taken into the castle from nearby towns in time when war is imminent, should be destroyed, so that the enemy may not have advantage from it. Provisions should be distributed by sensible people so that, by orderly rationing, they may be made to last all the longer. The old and the infirm should be distributed among other towns so that they may not uselessly consume the castle's provisions.

If one is afraid that the waters, be they rivers or fountains, which bring water into the castle by conduits, run the risk of being diverted, then tanks must be built to preserve the water, especially if one is near the sea, and the water may be contaminated by the salt. However, Aristotle says in the *Meteorologica* [II, iii] . . . that salt water, if passed through wax, loses its bitterness, and becomes sweet. There should also be vinegar, so that if supplies of wine should fail, vinegar may be mixed with water; this drink gives one renewed strength.

The castle must be provided with quantities of oil, pitch and sulphur, with which to burn the enemies' engines [of war] and with iron and wooden missiles and spears, besides bows, crossbows and all kinds of defensive weapons. There must be also great quantities of hard stone, collected on the walls and in the towers, where there should also be several large containers filled with lime which, when thrown and scattered from the walls upon the approaching enemy, gets into the attackers' eyes, and causes them to be rendered as if blind. . . . And with regard to the protection of fortresses and the methods used to defend them against the enemy, one reads in the same book [Vegetius] that in order to prevent a castle from being taken by mining, or by the hurling of stones or other missiles, the ditches must be dug very deep, so that no mine may pass underneath them. Only if it is built on a strong rock, or is surrounded by a river, is there no problem. Those in the castle must climb to the top of the highest edifice to see whether there is any sign, such as the removal of earth, which may make them suspect that a mine is being dug, and they must listen at the walls for noises of activity; and if they learn of any, they must countermine until they come to the enemies' mine, whereupon they must stop to fight to prevent them mining. At the entrance to their own mine they must have large containers holding water and urine; when they fight, they must feign flight and leave quickly and then, when they emerge, they must empty this water and urine into the mine, whereupon the miners therein will be drowned, a device which has been used many times. . . .

Equally, one may break those contraptions which are outside the wall by the use of a machine which is a catapult on an iron chain; and besides this there should be a forge containing some red-hot iron, which one throws, while it is burning, on to the engines without; and there is no fresh leather which will prevent fire taking hold of the engines.

There is no lack of methods to resist the besiegers. To counter the engine called the ram, one called the wolf has been invented. Those within the castle should have a curved iron with strong, sharp teeth at its ends; they tie it to ropes and, in this way, seize hold of the beam which is called the ram; then, holding it, they pull it up towards themselves, and lash it so high that it can no longer harm the walls of the place. Against wooden towers, the use of burning iron, as already stated, is very profitably employed by defenders. In addition, those within the besieged castle may secretly build a tunnel under the ground, digging in the direction where the enemy will bring their [wooden] tower, so that the ground will collapse under the weight of the construction.

IV.3.G This mid-fourteenth-century account of the siege of Berwick which took place in the early autumn of 1319, demonstrates the ingenuity of the Scottish defenders of that city when resisting the attacks of the English without. The close similarity between the theory expressed in the previous document and the events here described should be noted. (Text in John Barbour's, *The Bruce*, ed. W. W. Skeat, S.T.S., II, pp. 100–5, Book XVII, lines 593–705; E.E.T.S., II, pp. 428–32, Book XVII, lines 589–705.)

And thai that at the sege lay
Or it wes passit the fift day,
Had made thame syndry *apparale* [equipment]
To gang *eftsonis* [again] till *assale* [attack].
Of gret *gestis* [size] ane *sow*[24] thai maid,
That *stalward* [strong] *heling* [covering] *owth* [on the outside] it had,
With armyt men enew thar-in,
And instrumentis als for to myne.
Syndry *scaffatis* [scaffolds] thai maid vith-all
That war *weill* [considerably] hyar than the wall,[25]
And *ordanit* [proposed] als that by the se
The toune suld weill *assalyeit* [attacked] be.
And thai vithin, that saw thame *swa* [sc]
So gret apparale *schap* [prepare] till ma,
Throu Crabbis[26] *consale* [advice], that ves *sle* [cunning],

[24] An engine in which men are placed to approach a wall in safety.
[25] The wall was very low, perhaps only some fifteen feet high.
[26] John Crabb was a Flemish engineer.

Ane *cren* [crane, war engine] thai haf *gert* [cause] dress up *hey* [high]
Rynand [running] on *quhelis* [wheels], that thai mycht bring
It quhar neid war of mast helping.
And *pik* [pitch] and *ter* [tar] als haf thai tane,
And *lynt* [lint] and *hardiss* [hards (of flax)] with brynstane,
And dry treis that weill wald *brin* [burn],
And *mellit syne* [mixed together afterwards] athir othir in;
And gret *flaggatis* [faggots] tharof thai maid,
Gyrdit [tied] with irne-bandis *braid* [broad];
Of thai flaggatis mycht *mesurit* [measured] be
Till a gret tunnys quantite.
Thai fflaggatis *byrnand* [burning] in a *baill* [blazing pile]
With thair *cren* [crane] thoucht thai *till availl* [to lower].
And *gif* [if] the sow come to the wall,
Till lat thame byrnand on hir fall,
And with ane *stark* [strong] cheyne hald thame thar
Quhill [while] all war brint vp that thar war.
Engynys alsua for till cast
Thai *ordanit* [prepared] and maid redy fast,
And set *ilk* [each] man *syne* [then] till his *ward* [place to be guarded].
. . .
And *quhen* [when] thai in-to sic degre
Had maid thame for thair assaling,
On the Rude-evyn,[27] in the *dawing* [dawn],
The Ingliss host blew till assale.
Than mycht men with *ser* [various] apparale
Se that gret host cum sturdely;
The toune *enveremyt* [surrounded] thai in *hy* [haste],
and assalit with sa gud will—
For all thair *mycht* [power] thai set thar-till—
That thai thame pressit fast on the toune.
Bot thai, that *can* [did] thame *abandoune* [give themselves up]
Till *ded* [death], or than till woundis *sare* [sorely],
So weill has thame defendit thare,
That *ledderis* [ladders] to the ground thai flang,
And vith stanys so fast thai *dang* [dealt blows]
Thair *fais* [foes], that *feill* [many] thai left lyand,
Sun ded, sum hurt, and sum *swavnand* [swooning].
Bot thai that held on fut in *hy* [in haste]
Drew tham avay *deliuerly* [quickly],
And *skunnyrrit* [retreated] tharfor *na-kyn* [not at all] thing,
Bot went stoutly till assalyng.
. . .

[27] On the eve of the feast of the Holy Cross, i.e., 13 September.

Than thai without, in gret *aray* [order],
Pressit thair sow toward the wall;
And thai within weill *soyne* [soon] *gert* [caused to be] call
The *engynour* [engineer] that takyne was,
And gret *manauss* [threats] till him *mais* [make],
And swoir that he suld de, bot he
Provit [tried] on the sow sic sutelte,
That he to *fruschyt* [destroy] hir *ilke* [every, each] deill.
And he, that has *persauit* [perceived] weill
That the dede wes weill neir hym till,
Bot gif he mycht fulfill thar will,
Thoucht that he all his mycht vald do;
Bendit [set an engine for casting stones] in gret hy than wes *scho* [she
    i.e. the engine]
And till the sow wes evin set.
In hye he *gert* [caused] draw the *cleket* [trigger, catch],
And *smertly* [quickly] *swappit* [shot] out the stane,
That evyn *out-our* [beyond] the sow is gane,
And behynd hir a litill *we* [space]
It fell, and than thai cryit hey
That war in hir—'furth to the wall.
For *dreid les* [doubtless] it is ouris all.'
The engynour than deliuerly
Gert bend the *gyne* [engine] in full gret hy,
And the stane smertly swappit out.
It flaw out, *quhedirand* [whizzing], with a *rout* [blow],
And fell richt evin befor the sow.
Thair hertis than begouth till *grow* [quake with terror];
Bot yeit than, with thair *mychtis* [strengths] all,
Thai pressit the sow toward the wall,
And hass hir set thar to *iuntly* [exactly].
The gynour than gert bend in hy,
The gyne, and swappit out the stane,
That evin toward the *lift* [sky] is gane,
And with gret *wecht* [weight] syne *duschit* [fell] doune
Richt by the wall, *in a randoune* [with great force],
And hyt the sow in sic maner,
That it, that wes the *mast summer* [the principal beam]
And starkast for till *stynt* [stop] a *strake* [stroke],
In-swndir [asunder] with that dusche he brak.
The men ran out in full gret hy,
And on the wallis thai can cry,
'That thair sow *ferryit wes thair*!' [had furrowed]
Iohne Crab, that had his geir all *yar* [ready],

In his fagattis hass set the fyre,
And *our* [over] the wall syne can thame *wyre* [throw],
And brynt the sow till *brandis* [firebrands] bair.[28]

IV.3.H An account of the difficult passage of a French army, including
much artillery, across the Pyrenees, and of its part in the ensuing
siege of Barcelona in 1462. (French text in Guillaume Leseur,
Histoire de Gaston IV, Comte de Foix, ed. H. Courteault, II,
157–8, 161–2.)

. . .

My lord the count [of Foix] and all the captains went out to meet the
king of Aragon and to do him honour, as was both right and proper
to such a king. The king, too, went out of his way to honour and
welcome my lord the count, and all the captains and soldiers of the
army; he was very pleased and greatly relieved when he saw so fine an
army and so many persons of good class who had come from France
to help him [against Barcelona], and the splendid artillery which had
been brought there. For there were the two brothers, which are two
bombards, not among the largest, but none the less two really excellent
cannon; four large serpentines, made of metal and wonderfully long;
two large stone-throwing cannons of metal, called the two fathers;
two large guns of metal as large as bombards, which threw large fire-
balls; . . . twelve large culverins of metal, and easily one hundred other
pieces of artillery. And the king of Aragon, as well as the Catalans,
wondered greatly how one had managed to bring such large artillery
over the mountains. It was, indeed, a remarkable achievement, for
master Jean Bureau had done this by the sheer weight of men, and by
his use of pioneers and diggers in more than one hundred places where
no beast bearing burden had ever passed; for he had caused a completely new way, along which the said artillery might be conveyed, to
be cut through the rock and the mountains, a way which the Catalans,
since then, have taken to calling 'the French road'. And it is an incredible
thing to see the breaches and passages which the pioneers made for the
artillery; since that day they have always been of the greatest use, and
will continue to be so, for carts may now pass where mules could not
pass without unloading their baskets and their loads.

At San Andres, my lord the count, master Jean Bureau and Gaspard
Bureau, his brother, had the mantels and the covers for the bombards,
as well as the shields on stilts, made up, and all the preparations, which
were required before the siege of Barcelona could begin, were duly
carried out.

. . . After the army had settled down, my lord the count and master

[28] Compare this account of a siege with the theories expressed in documents
IV.3.D and IV.3.F.

Jean Bureau,[29] and Gaspard Bureau, his brother, that very night got the
pioneers and the labourers to dig ditches, trenches and earthworks,
as well as to site and place in position the large artillery, put the covers
over the bombards, and do all such necessary matters. . . . They had an
enormous number of pieces of artillery there, since they had several
founders who, for a long time past, had never stopped the founding of
serpentines, culverins and other pieces of artillery. They also had some
excellent cannons which were so numerous and fired so rapidly above
the army that the reports made by these guns could not be distinguished
one from another; thus could be heard *toup, toup, toup*, as one or two
hundred were fired in less time than it takes to recite an *Ave Maria*.

IV.3.1   Military leaders felt the need for proper information concerning
        the movements, plans, and intentions of the enemy. The use of
        spies, encouraged by Philippe de Mézières in the late fourteenth
        century [see II.1.D], was not uncommon and references to them
        and their activities are sometimes found in chronicles and
        financial accounts [1342–3]. (French text in British Museum,
        Additional Charter 10; also printed in *Chronique de Richard
        Lescot*, ed J. Lemoine, pp. 228–30.)

Expenses and moneys paid out by me, Bertrand Jobelin, on the order
and commandment of my lords of [the Chamber of] Accounts on
certain business concerning our lord the king, mention of which is
made more fully as follows:

First, 29th day of November 1342, at the orders of my lords of the
Accounts, namely my lord Hugues de Pommart, my lord Fauval de
Vaudencourt, Sir Pierre des Essars, and Sir G[uillaume] Balbet,
treasurer of France, there being also present my lords Roger de
Vistrebec and Bernard Franco, I was summoned and ordered to
dispatch messengers to the parts of Brittany as quickly as possible,
to find out and ascertain news concerning the situation of the enemies
of our lord and king and of the king of England's intentions, and to
send frequent news back, by day and night, to my lords of the Accounts,
all at the king's expense, according to their will and order thus made
to me. For this reason, on that very same day, I sent forthwith a
messenger on horseback to the country around Dol in Brittany, to spy
out and make such enquiries, and to report to me the reply of certain
people frequenting the town of Dol, to whom I had written; the said
messenger returned to me at Pontorson, for which expedition [he was
paid] for eleven days, there and back, 4 pounds 10 shillings.

Item, on the 12th day of December, for sending letters from Pontorson to my lords of the Accounts, to make report of the king of
England's coming to Vannes in Brittany, of his plans, of the number of

[29] See above, IV.3.C.

men-at-arms and foot soldiers in his service, and of several allies in Brittany whom he had, who were keeping a watch on the roads, namely my lord Olivier de la Chapelle and my lord G[uillaume] de Cadoudal, knights, who, with a large number of men-at-arms, were observing those who were coming into Brittany on my lord the king's behalf; and that my lord Olivier was at Pillemiq, near Nantes, the other in the forest of Villequartier, near Dol and Pontorson.

Item, to inform my lords how the city of Bordeaux had written to the king of England that he should come to its rescue speedily, otherwise it would surrender the city to the king, our lord.

Item, the said Cadoudal was spying out the land so as to gain entry into the castle of Pontorson and into the Mont-Saint-Michel.

Item, to inform the lords of the Accounts how, on the feast of St. Nicholas in winter,[30] the town of Joué, near Nantes, had been taken, and of many other things, so that they should take such steps as seemed to them proper. For this expedition, paid to J. Lambert who travelled on horse for 17 days, going, returning, awaiting and bringing back the reply of my said lords, at the rate of 10 shillings *parisis*[31] . . . 11 pounds 5 shillings.

Item, for moneys given to two spies who went from Pontorson to Dinan and elsewhere when the town was burned, to ascertain the situation, being away six days . . . 100 shillings.

Item, 24th day of December, for taking letters to my said lords, in which it was reported how the suburbs of Dinan had been burned by the earl of Salisbury, and how it was vital to furnish and defend the castle of Pontorson. Further, how the Cardinals had received letters at Avranches and Pontorson from the king of England, asking that they go to confer with him at Vannes or nearby.[32] For this, paid to a messenger who tarried, went, returned, for twelve days . . . 100 shillings.

Item, for moneys given to two spies, to go to the parts of Brittany, both of them to report on what they found at the castle of Saint-Sauveur-le-Vicomte. For this . . . 4 pounds parisis, worth 100 shillings.
. . .

IV.3.J   Fighting the enemy and the practice of chivalric combat could be reconciled at formal meetings of knights, and others, who offered themselves as champions on behalf of a cause or quarrel. Such an encounter was the Fight of the Thirty, which took place in March 1351. (French text in Froissart, *Chroniques*, V, 289–91.)

At the same time as the siege of Saint-Jean-d'Angély was taking place, there happened in Brittany a most remarkable feat of arms,

[30] 6 December.
[31] Money of Paris.
[32] The cardinals of Praeneste and Tusculum, representing the Pope.

which should certainly not be forgotten, but rather related to bring encouragement of knights bachelors. And so that you may the better appreciate the circumstances, you must know that everywhere in Brittany war was being fought between the supporters of the two ladies,[33] in which war my lord Charles of Blois had been imprisoned. The war was being fought by the supporters of the two parties, some of whom had garrisons in certain castles and fortified towns, some in others. It happened one day that Sir Robert de Beaumanoir, a most valiant knight descended from the best families in Brittany, who was captain of the castle at Josselin, having in his following a large company of men-at-arms of his own lineage as well as other soldiers, came before the town and castle of Plöermel, which was under the captaincy of a German known as Brandeburg, who was assisted by many German, English, Breton and other soldiers; they were all supporters of the countess of Montfort. When Sir Robert saw that the garrison was not issuing out, he went up to the gate and summoned the said Brandeburg under sureties, asking whether he had not with him two or three companions who would be willing to joust with their swords against two or three of his men for the sake of their ladies. Brandeburg replied that their ladies would not encourage them to be killed in a jousting of only one encounter, since this was a trial of fortune which would only too rapidly end. 'But', he added, 'I tell you what we shall do. If it pleases you, we shall take twenty or thirty of our company from our garrison, and we shall come out into an open space, and there we shall fight for as long as we possibly can. And may God grant the victory to those who survive best.' 'By my troth,' replied Sir Robert de Beaumanoir, 'you are talking the right kind of language. I agree with your proposal. Let us fix upon a date.' It was agreed for the following Wednesday; and they further agreed to keep the peace between themselves until that day. And, with that, Sir Robert and his people departed. They chose 30 companions, knights and esquires, from their garrisons: and Brandeburg also chose 30 other companions, all of the best. On the day appointed, Brandeburg's thirty companions heard Mass, had themselves armed, and departed for the field where the contest was to take place. Once there, they got down from their horses, and firmly ordered all those standing about not to interfere at all, for whatever reason, in the contest: Sir Robert de Beaumanoir's champions did the same. The thirty whom we shall call the English awaited those whom we shall call the French for a long time. When these finally arrived, they alighted from their horses and gave their orders as recounted above; then, coming forward to meet one another, they spoke together for a

[33] Jeanne de Penthièvre, wife of Charles de Blois, and Jeanne de Flandre, wife of Jean de Montfort. The parties were fighting out the succession to the duchy of Brittany. See III.6.A.

while, all sixty of them, before retiring a little distance, some in one direction, the others in the other. Then they ordered their people to get well behind them and, one having given a sign, they rushed forward and fell upon one another, fighting fiercely in a mass, defending valiantly any of their companions in danger.

Soon after they had come together, one of the French was killed, but this in no way stopped the others from fighting. Indeed they all fought so valiantly on both sides that they brought Roland and Oliver back to mind. In truth, I don't know who lasted the better; only that they fought for so long that they lost all their strength and breath and will to fight. It then seemed better that they should stop and rest, which they did on both sides, by common accord, agreeing not to fight until they should be rested, and that those who were ready to fight first should call upon the others to continue. At this stage, there were four French dead and two English. Both sides rested for a long time, and drank wine which was brought to them in bottles; they also tied up such pieces of armour which had come undone, and looked to their wounds which needed attention.

When they had rested sufficiently, the first to get up made a sign to recall the others. The contest, thus begun again, was as fiercely fought as before, and lasted for a long time. They fought most valiantly in this second round, but in the end the English had the worse of it, for, as those who saw it have told me, one of the French, who was on horseback, attacked them and knocked them down shamefully, so that Brandeburg, their leader, and eight of his companions were killed. Then Sir Robert Beaumanoir and his people went back to their garrison. It was thus that this work was accomplished.

IV.4   WAR AT SEA

Naval warfare, by the end of the middle ages, was beginning to assume a role of importance in international conflict. The numbers involved in fighting at sea; the use made of naval forces to carry out lightning raids on coastal districts; the importance of keeping the sea-passages open in certain circumstances; the avowed aim of disrupting the enemy's trade and conveyance of military goods and personnel are all a clear indication that the war at sea was regarded as having an increasing role to play in war, a fact which was recognised by all parties in their search for allies, Castilian or Genoese, who might supply valuable maritime support for those unready to provide it themselves.

IV.4.A   The traditional, strongly-built, high-sided vessel of northern European waters enabled ships, even merchantmen, to be temporarily modified and strengthened so as to make it possible

> to fight what at times seemed like a land war fought at sea, employing tactics such as those suggested in this extract. (French text in Christine de Pisan, *Le Livre des Fais et Bonnes Meurs du Sage Roy Charles V*, ed. J. F. Michaud and J. J. F. Poujoulat, II, pp. 60–1.)

On the subject of fighting at sea, or on rivers, Vegetius speaks, first of all, of how one should build ships and galleys: [he says that] in the months of March and April, when the trees begin to have plenty of sap, one should not cut those from which one wishes to build the ships, but rather that this should be done in August, or in July, when the sap of the trees begins to dry; and from these trees planks should then be cut and left to dry, so that they will not warp.

Those who fight on ships and in galleys should be better armed than those who fight on battlefields, for they are less mobile, and yet must receive great hurt from missiles. They must be well supplied with containers filled with black pitch, resin, sulphur and oil, the whole mixed up and enveloped in tow. These containers must be ignited, and then thrown on to the enemies' ships and galleys, which should then be strongly attacked so that they shall have no time to extinguish the fire.

Item, spies should be used to ascertain when the enemy is lacking in anything.[34]

Item, those who fight must always endeavour to manoeuvre the enemy towards the shore, while keeping themselves on the open sea.

Item, to the ship's mast there should be attached a large beam, protected by iron on both sides; this should be used to attack an enemy ship, a mechanism ensuring that this beam is raised so as to be dropped with great force upon the enemy ship, which is damaged by the impact.

Item, there should be an ample stock of large arrows, which should be shot at sails so as to pierce them, so that they can no longer retain wind, and ships may therefore not escape.

Item, there should be a piece of metal, with a good cutting edge, rounded like a sickle and tied to a long pole, so that with it the yards may be cut; in this condition, the ship will no longer be in a proper condition to fight.

Item, with iron hooks and crampons, the enemy ship should be attached to one's own, so that it may not escape when it is at a disadvantage.

Item, one should have several containers, which must be easily breakable, filled with lime or powder, to be thrown on to enemy ships; when these break, their contents blind the enemy.

Item, one should have pots filled with soft soap, for throwing upon the enemies' ships; when these pots break, the soap makes everyone

[34] For spies, see II.1.D and IV.3.I.

slip so that they can no longer stand on their feet, and fall into the water.

Item, one should be provided with sailors who can swim for long periods under water; these should have well-sharpened instruments with which to hole the [enemies'] ships in several places, so that the water will enter; and on to the side which lists the more, quantities of large stones and sharp iron rods should be thrown, so as to pierce the ship and cause it to sink.

IV.4.B An account of the first important naval battle of the Hundred Years' War, in the course of which Edward III defeated the French fleet off Sluys on 24 June 1340. Note how certain of the recommendations made in the previous document are put into practice, and how the impression is given of a land battle fought at sea. (Latin text in *Chronicon Galfridi Le Baker de Swynebroke*, ed. E. M. Thompson, pp. 68–9; also translated in *English Historical Documents. IV : 1327–1485*, ed. A. R. Myers, pp. 68–9.)

In the year of Our Lord 1340, and in the fourteenth year of his reign as king of England, the lord king [Edward III] observed the feast of Pentecost at Ipswich, in preparation for his crossing into Flanders with a small following. But when he heard that the so-called king of the French was planning to impede his crossing by dispatching a large fleet of ships from Spain, in addition to almost the entire French naval force, our king summoned ships from the Cinque Ports and elsewhere, so that he finally had with him two hundred and sixty ships, both large and small. Then, on the Thursday before the feast of St John the Baptist,[35] with the wind blowing favourably, he set sail contentedly; on the following day, the vigil of St John, he sighted the French fleet in the harbour of Zwyn, arrayed like a line of castles and ready for battle. Anchoring at sea, he spent that day deliberating what ought best be done. On the feast of St John, quite early in the morning, the French fleet, now divided into three squadrons, moved a mile or so nearer the king's fleet which, when the king saw it, caused him to say that they should wait no longer, and that he and his men should arm themselves as quickly as they could. After nine o'clock, having both the wind and the sun behind him, with the tide running in his favour and his fleet likewise divided into three squadrons, he began to attack the enemy as they had hoped he would. A fearful shout arose into the sky above the wooden horses, as Merlin had prophecied. An iron cloud of bolts from crossbows, and arrows from bows, fell upon the enemy, bringing death to thousands; then those who wished, or were daring enough, came to blows at close quarters with spears, pikes and swords; stones, thrown from the ships' castles, also killed many. In brief, this

[35] The feast was observed on 24 June.

was without a doubt an important and terrible naval battle which a coward would not have dared to see even from afar off. The sheer size and height of the Spanish ships rendered useless many of the blows cast by the English; but, finally, the first French squadron was defeated, abandoned by its men, and then captured by the English. The French ships were all chained together, so that they could not be separated from one another; thus only a few English ships were needed to guard one group of those which had been abandoned, the remainder being better able to direct their attention to the second French squadron, attacking it with some difficulty. None the less, this squadron was to be disabled even more easily than was the first, for the French abandoned their ships, large numbers of men jumping, of their own accord, into the sea. The first and second squadrons thus overcome, and with the light giving way to dusk, the English, since it was getting dark and they were very exhausted, decided to leave matters as they were until the morrow. During the night, however, thirty ships of the third squadron fled; one great ship, called the James of Dieppe, wished to tow away a certain ship from Sandwich, which belonged to the priory of Christ Church at Canterbury. But her sailors, assisted by the earl of Huntingdon, defended themselves strongly in a conflict which lasted throughout the night. The next morning, when the Normans had finally been vanquished, they found more than four hundred dead men aboard the captured ship. Then, when dawn came, and it was realised that thirty ships had fled, the lord king sent forty well-equipped ships to chase them, appointing as their commander one John Crabbe, whom the English regarded highly for his seamanship and his knowledge of French harbours. What the outcome of this was is not known. Among the first squadron of captured ships, the victors found certain vessels, the first called the 'Denis', another the 'George', the third the 'Christopher', and the fourth the 'Black Cock' which the French had some time previously stolen secretly from the port of Sluys. The number of fighting ships captured was some two hundred, together with some thirty transports; the number of enemy killed and drowned exceeded twenty-five thousand, while among the English four thousand perished.[36]

IV.4.c An account of the attacks carried out by Spanish galleys upon the English shore about 1400. It illustrates both the effective use made of such vessels in war, and the difficulties experienced by those living in the coastal regions which were specially susceptible to this form of lightning attack. (Spanish text in Gutierre Diez de Games, *El Victorial. Crónica de don Pero Niño, conde de Buelna*, ed. J. de M. Carriazo, pp. 193–5; also translated in *The Unconquered Knight*, ed. Joan Evans, pp. 115–17.)

That country where the galleys arrived is called the land of Cornwall;

[36] One must not accept such figures uncritically.

and as soon as they had obtained information about it, the galleys went inland on the tide as it rose up an estuary. The current at the mouth of that estuary was so strong and carried the galleys along with such force that it was impossible to use the oars or to steer or navigate until they had got past the current. The current lasted about as long as a shot from a cross-bow; then they were able to use their oars. And there, inside, was a harbour, well guarded and protected from all the winds, and a wealthy place called Looe,[37] with a population of about 300 citizens; it had no city-wall, but it was sited on the side of a hill and all its streets went down to the sea.

The galleys arrived there. This place was very rich because all its inhabitants were merchants and fishermen.

The captain ordered all his men to arm; then they put the gang-planks in position and everyone disembarked with the captain. He drew up his men in good order, placing a line of heavy shields in front and the cross-bowmen behind them. The captain and Messire Charles conferred together and drew up their troops in agreement. There was a tough fight there, but at last the English were driven back and many of them killed and captured. Then the captain ordered the banners and the men-at-arms to stay outside the town, ready to fight, so that they should not be taken unawares if more Englishmen came up; and he commanded the oarsmen and the cross-bowmen to go in and loot the town, some fighting and others plundering.

When everything had been looted, he ordered the town to be set on fire and it all burned down; the whole business was thus completed within three hours. Then they blew the trumpets, everyone re-embarked and the galleys set out to sea, taking two sailing-ships which were in the harbour. The tide now began to fall, but the galleys went out on the ebb and towed the sailing-ships past the current.

As they were leaving, many Englishmen had arrived. The mouth of the harbour was very narrow now, and on one side of it there was a very high cliff which overhung the galleys. From this and from the other shore, they hurled many stones and arrows on to the galleys; and if the Englishmen who were now coming up had arrived earlier, it would have been very dangerous to disembark, although the cross-bowmen had spent all their time firing.

That night the captain put sailors and supplies on the sailing-ships and ordered them to go to the port of Harfleur in France.

Then Pero Niño and Messire Charles agreed to go sailing along the coast of England; and they came to a great beach called Dartmouth, where they saw a handsome troop of men-at-arms and archers, who were coming from many directions to defend the shore.

[37] There is some doubt as to which place the chronicler meant, but Looe seems likely. Dr. Evans, in her translation, gives St. Ives.

V

WAR AND THE
CIVILIAN POPULATION

WAR, IN THE late middle ages, was coming to involve more and more people. Not merely the soldiers and sailors who fought for a wage or in the hope of material reward, but the non-combatant, or civilian, population was affected as well. This fact was well recognised by contemporaries, some commenting upon the moral dilemmas raised by the participation of the non-combatant in war, others going further by insisting that active steps should be taken by the leaders of society—and not simply by its military leaders—to avoid the shedding of innocent christian blood.

But the non-combatant also had a positive role to play in war. It was, in good measure, his money that was being spent in the furtherance of ambitious dynastic schemes and in the defence of the realm. He might consequently feel that he had a right to a say in the manner of its spending, and he sometimes tried to assert that right. His moral support, too, was considered valuable and was actively sought. Consequently he was kept informed of how war was progressing, for victories made cheerful news, and the non-combatant could be brought in to partake actively in celebrations. Equally, too, he was the target of enemy propaganda, and in this sense war was seen to be becoming a battle for men's hearts and minds, especially in those areas where political loyalties were volatile. All in all, therefore, the non-combatant was the object of considerable attention by society's leaders—and with good reason, for it was he who, in one way or another, bore much of the brunt of war—and especially of its hardships. Whether this was deliberate or accidental is a debatable point. The fact nevertheless remains that all sides devoted much attention to the enemy non-combatant population. Thus the French and their allies ravaged the coastal areas of southern England during certain periods of the fourteenth century, thereby causing much resentment against the English government which failed to defend its subjects adequately; while in both the fourteenth and fifteenth centuries English armies were in France, doing much material harm to the property, persons and morale of their enemies. Naturally the French, upon whose soil most of the war was fought, suffered the most; it seemed easier, more profitable and less dangerous to bring the enemy to his knees by means of pressure brought to bear upon his non-combatant population than to seek him out and defeat him in a battle, thereby risking defeat. Once again, it seems as if every effort was made to influence the outcome of war by attacking the majority of the population, but the majority that did not actively fight. It is a measure of the non-combatant's importance in a society at war that such an attitude could be adopted and such a policy pursued. And it was on account of the unwelcome attentions of the soldiery that the moralists, the lawyers, and the leaders of society sought means of ensuring the non-combatants' protection and safety.

V.1 ATTITUDES TO THE NON-COMBATANT

The general attitude to the non-combatant was one of fellow-feeling, if not of compassion. His predicament in war was understood and discussed by the theorists; the chroniclers not infrequently had occasion to mention and comment upon his plight; and the law-makers tried to ensure that armies did not abuse their power to the detriment of those who were in no position to defend themselves.

V.1.A   Froissart, in his description of the notorious sack of Limoges by the Black Prince's army in 1370, reveals a humanitarian spirit which extended to those who had committed a technical treason against their lord. (French text in Froissart, *Chroniques*, VIII, 41.)

On the next day, as the Prince had ordered it, a large section of the wall was blown up, filling in the ditch at the place where it fell in. The English saw this happen with pleasure, for they were all prepared, armed and drawn up in their ranks, ready to enter the town when the moment should come. The foot-soldiers were able to enter this way with ease: on entering, they ran to the gate, cut the supporting bars, and knocked it down, together with the barriers. And all this was done so suddenly that the townspeople were not expecting it. Then the Prince, the duke of Lancaster, the earl of Cambridge, the earl of Pembroke, Sir Guiscard d'Angle and all the others, together with their men, rushed in, the pillagers on foot, all prepared to do harm and ransack the town, and to kill men, women, and children; for this is what they had been ordered to do. This was a most terrible thing: men, women and children threw themselves on their knees before the Prince crying 'Mercy, gentle sires, have mercy.' But he was so enraged by hatred that he heard none of them; thus none, neither man or woman, was heeded, and all were put to the sword, as and wherever they were found or come upon, men and women who were in no way guilty. I do not

understand how they could have no pity upon the poor people who
were not cut out to commit treason; but these were the ones who paid
the penalty, and paid it more dearly than did the leaders who had
committed this crime. At Limoges, at that time, there was no heart so
hard, who had faith in God, who did not weep bitterly at the terrible
mischief thus perpetrated, for more than three thousand persons,
men, women and children, were killed and executed on that day. May
God receive their souls, for they were certainly martyrs.

V.1.B   Christine de Pisan discusses the position of the 'poure laborers'
         living in a country in which war is being waged. She shows an
         understanding of their position, but an awareness, too, of the
         wider problems involved by the non-combatant's participation
         in war. (Text in Christine de Pisan, *The Book of Fayttes of
         Armes and of Chyualrye*, ed. A. T. P. Byles, pp. 224–5.)

Chapter XVIII

*Whether it is of ryght that men may take vpon the ennemyes londe
the poure laborers.*

I aske *the* [thee] whan a kynge or a prynce hathe werre ayenst another,
though that it be Iuste, whether he may by ryght *ouer renne* [overrun]
the contrey of his enemye takynge al manere of folke prysoners, that
is to *wite* [say], them of the comyn poure peple as ben laborers, shepardes
and suche folke; & it shulde seme that nay. For what reason ought they
to bere the *penaunce* [penalty] of that that they medle not hem self,
where as they can not the crafte of armes, nor it is not theyre office,
nor they be not called for to *iuge* [judge] of werres; & also werres
comen not [are not caused] by suche poure folke, but they be full sory
for it, as they that full *fayne* [gladly] wolde alwayes lyue in gode peas
nor they aske no more. So ought they thenne, as me semeth, to be
free therof, lyke that of ryght ben prestes, *relygyeuse* [religious (persons)]
& all folke of the chyrche, by cause that theyre astate is not to *entremette*
[meddle] hem self of warre. And wyth thys what worship may thys be
nor what pryce of armes for to slee & renne vpon them that *neuere*
[never] bare *harneys* [equipment], nor coude not help hym self wyth
all, and that haue noon other offyce, but poure Innocentes to goo to
ploughe and laboure the lande and to kepe the bestes. To thys I
ansuere the *supposyng* [supposition] in thys manere. We putte *caas*
[case] that the people of Englande wolde make no manere of helpe to
theyre kynge for to *greue* [hurt] the kynge of Fraunce, and that the
Frenshe men went vpon them; wythout faylle, by ryght and reason
and after the lawe, they ought not to hurte nor *misdoo* [harm] *nother*
[neither] in body nor in goodes of the people nor of them that they
shulde knowe that had not meddled them self in nothynge to helpe,

F

nother by theyre goodes nor by theyre counseyll, theyre kynge. But and yf it be so that the subgectes of the same kynge, or of som other in *semblable a caas*, [similar situation] be it ryche or poure laborers or other, gyue ayde, comfort and fauoure for to *maynten* [pursue] the werre, the Frenshmen, after the right of armes, may ouer renne theire lande and take al that they fynde, that is to wyte, prysoners of all astates and al thynges, and be not bounde for to yelde them *ayen* [again.]. For I telle the that suche right is determyned ryght of werre, Iuged by bothe kynges or prynces counseyll, theyre men of werre may gete the one vpon the other. And yf som tyme the poure and symple, thoughe they arme not hem self, doo *abye* [abide by] the bargeyne and be sore hurt therby, it can not be other wyse. For the euyll herbes can not be had out from emonge the goode by cause they be so nyghe eche other wythout that the gode herbes *haue a felyng* [be cut down] thereof. But to beholde ryght well it is true that the valyaunt and gentylmen of armes ought to *kepe* [restrain] hem self as moche as they can that they dystroye not the goode, symple folke, nor to *suffre* [allow] that theyre folke shal Inhumaynly hurt them; For they ben crysten and not *sarrasyns* [Saracens]. And yf I haue sayde that *myserycorde* [mercy] is due vnto the one, Knowe thou that not lesse it is due to the other. Soo ought they to hurt them that ledeth the werre, and spare the symple and peasyble of all theyre *puyssaunce* [power].

V.2 PAYING FOR WAR

Participation in war, as Christine de Pisan noted, could be achieved in other ways than by active fighting. One such vital means was the financial contribution made by the nation through taxation and grants, partly as subsidies voted in assemblies, partly as loans made, more or less willingly, by individuals and communities.

V.2.A   The Dauphin Charles, responsible for the government of France during the captivity of his father, John II, in England, orders the raising of money through local representative bodies in order to finance the war against the English. The duty of the community to help pay for national defence is thereby clearly emphasised [1358]. (French text in A. Coville, *Les États de Normandie*, pp. 367–9.)

Charles, eldest son of the king of France, regent of the kingdom, duke of Normandy and Dauphin of Viennois, to our beloved and faithful Gilles de Maudestour, clerk, and Philippe de Troismons, knight, councillors to both my lord [the king] and to ourselves, greetings.

It is well known that certain evil traitors planned and plotted to sow discord between my lord and us, on the one hand, and the people of the kingdom of France, on the other, so that they might achieve their evil intention and satisfaction of betraying my lord, ourselves, the said people and the said kingdom, the which they planned to have occupied, devastated and destroyed by the English and other enemies, whom they had caused to be brought right up to Paris in large numbers.[1] And this would certainly have happened had not the grace of God come to the assistance of us, the whole kingdom, all our people and especially the good people of Paris who, by divine inspiration, recognised the evil plots and intentions of the said traitors, one of whom was immediately executed, to be followed to death by several others who openly confessed to have known about the said treason.

And because there are still large numbers of the said enemies in several parts of the kingdom, enemies who ravage and lay waste to the country daily (a fact which is most displeasing to us) we now plan, with the help of God and of our good subjects, to go personally against the said enemies with as many men-at-arms and foot soldiers as we may find, so as to bring peace and tranquillity to the kingdom in our time.

In order to achieve this it will be necessary to spend far greater sums of money than we can afford without the help of the good people of the said kingdom. For this reason, our beloved provost of the merchant community, together with the municipal officers and people of our good town of Paris, recognising the great need which faces both themselves and the district around Paris, have graciously granted us a general levy of 8 pence in the pound on all merchandise and commodities; [in addition to this], the salt tax, called the *gabelle*, for up to one year; a tax on wine at certain times, as formerly; 2 shillings in the pound on all income from immovables, all to be used and spent on the above-mentioned needs, and not otherwise, and also for the ransoming of my lord, [the king]; from every seventy households in each of our good towns, one man-at-arms, and from the country folk, one such man-at-arms for every hundred homes, this man to be paid $\frac{1}{2}$d in gold every day.

We now order and command each one of you in the bailiwicks of Rouen, Gisors, Caux, Caen and Cotentin[2] and the parts about, that you should personally act and summon before you at certain specified places, and on certain specified days, the prelates, churchmen, barons, nobles, and the people of the good towns and lordships directly or indirectly subject to my lord the king and to us, and that you should, on our behalf, lay before them the need to act in the manner outlined above, as well as the great benefits and advantages which will accrue to them all, collectively and individually, if this be done. You should also,

---

[1] A reference to the treasonable activities of Étienne Marcel and others in the early summer of 1358.

[2] All these bailiwicks are in Normandy.

in our name, encourage them as far as you can, according to the instructions given to you, that they co-operate loyally with our plan, so that,
continuing to show the great loyalty and obedience which they have
always shown to us and to the kingdom, they may grant us a subsidy
at least as great as the other, the sum to be employed to the same,
above-mentioned ends, the defence and safety of the realm, of themselves and all our other subjects, as well as to the ransoming of our lord
the king, as is written and described above, without any of it being used
for other purposes.

    We order you to issue letters to this effect as often as may be necessary,
letters which will be confirmed by ours; and for the collection of the
said tax we order that you appoint receivers and collectors and any
other officials whom you may think it necessary to appoint, paying them
the wages which you shall consider appropriate; but always do this as
cheaply as you possibly can. And in such places where you may not
carry out our orders personally, we accord each of you our special
permission to name one or more suitable deputies to complete the task
for you.

    Given at Paris, the 13th day of August, in the year of grace 1358.

V.2.B   A revealing account of the methods used to raise money for
         purposes of war by loan in the town of Coventry in 1424. (Text,
         in English except where otherwise stated, in *The Coventry Leet
         Book*, ed. M. D. Harris, I, 74–8.)

A Royal Loan

    Memorandum, that in the tyme of Tho. Wildegrise, then beyng
maiour of the Cite of Couentre, £100 was lant vnto kyng Henry the
vj^t by a lettre of the privye seale direct vnto the maiour and the
cominalte of the said Cite, of the wich lettre the tenour folowith in
thes woordes:[3]

Trusty and well-beloved. For the continuation of the present war
in our kingdom of France, and in order, with the help of God, to bring
the same war to a rapid end and conclusion, as is very much desired,
it will become necessary for us to receive a loan and the provision of
a subsidy and a large sum of money, as will be more fully explained to
you on behalf of ourselves and our council by the reverend father in
God, the bishop of Worcester, and our well-beloved and trusty cousin,
the earl of Warwick,[4] whom, on the advice of our said council, we have
jointly assigned, by our letters of commission issued under our privy
seal, in the absence of the great seal, to communicate and treat with you
concerning the loan of a great sum which you should lend us in this

---

[3] The text of the letter which follows is in French.
[4] Both men were doubtless chosen for their local influence.

great necessity; and to promise to you, in and for our name, sufficient surety for the repayment of such a sum as you may wish to lend us in the circumstances. We therefore sincerely pray you that, for the fulfilment of this task which, with the help of our Creator, will turn out for the good of ourselves, of you and of all Christendom, you should raise the largest loan which you are able, so as to help us to achieve this by means of a loan of notable value, such as will be specified and designated to you by the above-mentioned bishop and earl, adding to these firm faith and belief in the report which they will make to you about this matter on behalf of ourselves and our council.

Given under our privy seal, at Westminster, on the 29th day of March [1424].

And for-asmoche as the said Erle of Warrewyk, the wich was assigned Jointely with the said bischop of Worcestur for to treet of this notable summe aboue namyd, myght not personally com vnto the said Cite for to treate as the lettur of the privy ceale aboue-namyd openly specifiethe, the said Erle vnto the said maiour & burges of the said Cite in Confirmacion of this said mattur his lettre vndur his signet sendythe, of the wich the tenour folowith in thes wordes:— Dere and wel- belouyd, we grett you well *ofte-sythis* [oft-time]. And for-as-moche as now late ther is comyn a commyssion vndur the kynges greate seale, our soueryan lorde, direct vnto the ryght reuerent fathur in God, the bischop of Worcestur, and to vs to comune with you & with other of the moost notabull & sufficiant Burgesses of the Cite of Couentre, that ye wold vpon sufficyant & *couenable* [proper] suertie make *cheuaunce* [loan] of a certen summe of gold vnto our souerayne lord in the supportacion of the highe and notable *astatez* [estates] of his Realme of Ingland and of Fraunce, & of the wellfare & good spede of my lord of Bedford, his vncle, the wich and all Englysche-men that *byn ther* [are there] stonde in grett Jeopardie, but *prouysyon* [help] and remedy be ordenyd from *hennez* [hence] with all possible deliberacion & hast. And for dyuers matters, the wich that touchen our estate & *herettaunce* [inheritance] we may not com personally to you for the said cause at this tyme, but haue buesied us here at *Brystow* [Bristol] with the maiour and Burgessez of that town by the commaundment of the kyng, our said souerayne lorde, in the same & lyke case; the wich town hathe ryght Notabully and kyndly acquyt them, soo that the same reuerent fathur in God comyth vnto you in his propre person in the name of the kyng, our said souerayng lord, be vertue of the commaundment direct vnto vs bothe for the said cheuysaunce; prayng you als hertly as We can, that all this mattur a-fore considred, wich schal-be moore effectually & expressly notified vnto you by the reuerent fader in God than we can do wryte to you at this tyme, Ye woll goodly enclyne you & consent vppon his certificacion for to do make by your good, kynd & wyse discression a *conable* [suitable] prouysion and Cheuaunce of *good* [money] vnto our said souerayng lorde, now in his tendur age[5] & his grettyst nede, and as ye haue full kyndly and notably doon to his wurthy auncestres tofore thies tyme, to his ease and your good *worship* [honour] als effectually and kyndly as we wer with you in propre persone for our loue and for the highe trust we haue in you. Dere & Wel-belouyd, the Trinite haue you allway in his kepyng. Wryton in our manor of Wotton vndur *Egge* [Edge], the xiiij day of Aprill.

Shirley [Secretary].

[The mayor and his council order that £100 shall be collected throughout the wards in the following manner.]

Collectors in Gosforde [Street][6]

Joh. Stafforde, Bened. Marchall, Rad. Alott, Sim. Baker, *deister* [dyer], Joh. Melton, deister.

Total £11 12s.

Jurdenwell

Joh. Recheford, Joh. Prentes, Will. Deyster, Rob. Defforde, Joh. Cooton.

Total £10 4s.

Michparke [Street]

Joh. Lee, smythe, Rob. Danyell, Rob. Pynnok, Joh. Yate.

Total £10.

Erle [Street]

Will. Swane, Joh. Frankelen, Nich. Palmer, Tho. Harres, Joh. Euerdon, Will Frysbye.

Total £11 7s 4d; received £11 0s 8d; still outstanding for Nicholas Metley, 6s 8d.

Bailly [Lane]

Joh. Rounton, Joh. Benett, Ad. Dyer, Joh. Sircoke, Will Brook.

Total £7: received £7.

Brodeyate [Broadgate]

Ric. Bushebury, Rog. Cookes, Rob. Praty, Rob. Saxston, Tho. Lyones.

Total £4 13s 4d; received £4 13s 4d.

Smythford [Street]

Ric. Hickeleng, Joh. Egeston, Joh. Blakman, Wal. Ashebye.

Total £8.

[5] Henry VI was only two years old at this time.
[6] This part of the text is in Latin.

Spoon [Street]

Will. Pratte, Hugo Rigeley, Joh. Deister, *whittawer* [saddler], Joh. Broun, Joh. Essex.

Total £11 7s 4d.

Croschepyng

Joh. Lichfeld, mercer, Rob. Lyrpoole, Joh. Style, deister, Ric. Botoner.

Total £14 10s.

Byschop [Street]

Joh. Lichfeld, bocher, Will. Wymondeswold, Joh. Mongomery, Hen. Knott, Joh. Walgraue.

Total £11 6s.

Grand Total £100.

See further on the following leaf how the above-mentioned sum of £100 was lent, by what persons, and in what manner.

Remember that all these listed below contributed to the £100 lent to the king in the way and manner in which they are listed, as well as on the preceding leaf, where the collectors are listed.

[Gosford Street Ward]

	£	s	d		£	s	d
Tho. Wildegryse	1	6	8	Rob. Tylor		1	8
Laur. Cooke	1	6	8	Joh. Baker		3	4
Will. Crose		15	0	Will. Bagott		3	4
Joh. Wellford		6	8	Rog. Deister		2	0
Joh. Style		6	8	Joh. Knyght		1	8
Nich. Heywood		2	4	Ric. Nicole		5	0
Joh. Wylde		2	0	Will. Cookes		2	6
Juliana Twyng		2	0	Isabella Elford		3	4
Joh. Newby		2	0	Joh. Solyhull		1	6
Tho. Smyth		2	0	Hugh Spencer		1	8
Joh. Sheldon		3	0	Marg. Hall		2	0
Joh. Breton		6	8	Ad. Baxster		6	8
Tho. Mason		3	4	And. Evesham		6	8
Joh. Stretton		6	8	Ric. Beller		1	6
Tho. Stoone		2	0	Hen. Skyll		2	4
Joh. Evysham		5	0	Joh. Luff		2	6
Wyll. Abram		2	0	Joh. Creke		3	4
Ric. Kyng		5	0	Will. Inge		1	8
Hen. Abram		2	0	Ric. Skott		1	8

	£	s	d			£	s	d
Rad. Alett		6	8		Walt. Bonde		1	4
Bened. Marchall		6	8		Will. Colas		1	0
Simon Deister		6	8		Will. Horner			10
Joh. Stafford		3	4		Total	£11.	12s.	
Joh. Melton		3	4					
Ric. Walker		1	8		The above-written sum was			
Joh. David		1	6		paid to the collectors of the			
Tho. Draughton		1	8		said ward.			

[Similar details are given for all the wards of the town]

V.2.c The needs of peace-making, as well as of waging war, forced
rulers to seek money from their subjects. But not all loans to the
crown were raised with the ease which seems to have attended
them at Coventry and Bristol. The evidence of Beverley suggests
strong opposition to such loans being demanded from rather
less prosperous populations [1435]. (Text in Beverley Chartulary,
fos. 22v–23r; also printed in *Report on the Manuscripts of the
Corporation of Beverley*, Historical Manuscripts Commission,
pp. 22–5.)

By the kyng

Trusty and wellebeloved. For as moche as we, now *late* [very]
instanntly [recently], *required* [requested] as wel bi solempne ambassiates
as by lettres of oure holy fader the pope, the general counceil,[7] oure
brother themperoure,[8] our vncle of Burgoigne,[9] and many other, to
entende unto the meenes of pees to be treted bytwix us and oure
adversarie in oure reaume of Fraunce, be condescended to sende oure
solempne *ambassiate* [embassy] of the lordes of oure blode and other in
gret noumbre to mete with thambaxatours of oure said adversarie at
Arras, the firste day of *Juyllet* [July] next comyng; for which cause of
necessite we *most* [must] sende also at the same tyme in to oure saide
reaume of Fraunce a grete armee to holde the feld, the which thing,
as ye in youre discrecions can wele considre, may in no wyse be doon
namely so sone withoute grete aide of *chevance* [loans] of oure trewe
frendes and subgittes; to the which aide at this tyme we have founde
oure *beal* [fair] vncle the cardinal[10] and the remenant of oure counseil
and other[s] aboute oure persone, as wele spirituel and temporel, as
wel *willid* [intentioned] as oure hert can desire, not withstandyng that
many of hem at oure praiere shal goo vnto the same convencion in their

---

[7] The Council of Basle had begun to sit some four years earlier.

[8] The emperor, Sigismund (d. 1437).

[9] Philip, duke of Burgundy (d. 1467).

[10] Henry, Cardinal Beaufort, bishop of Winchester, was Henry VI's uncle.

persones. We desire and pray you that, consideryng the grete good whiche we truste to oure lord shal ensue of thees thinges befor rehersed, ye wolde at this tyme *lene* [lend] vnto us the somme of *CC marc*, [200 marks (=£133.13.4)] for the whiche oure tresourer of England shal make vnto you, be auctorite of Parlement, suche seuretee for youre repaiement as he maketh vnto oure said *beal* [fair] vncle, the cardinal, and the remenant of oure counceill, and other that leene *semblale* [similar] sommes, and gretter, vnto us in this necessitee; the whiche somme we pray you to be delivered vnto oure said tresourer at London at the *oytaves* [week after] of the Trinitee next comyng at the *ferthest* [latest][11], as ye desire the *worship* [honour] and wele of us, and the conservacion of bothe oure reaumes. Geven under oure prive seal, at Westmynstre, the xxviij day of May [1435].

[After the receipt of this request, a protest is sent to the Provost of Beverley on 2nd July]

Unto oure right honourable and worshipful Sir and
Master, the Provost of Beverlay.

Right honourable and worshipful sir and mastre, we *comaunde* [commend] us *til* [to] you.

Like you to *wite* [know] oure liege lord the kyng has directid til us a privy seal of CC marke deliverid til us on Corpus Christi evyn last past,[12] of the *whilk* [which] privy seal the berer of this lettre has a copy to schewe you if it like you. Wheruppon and it like your masterschip to understand that we in the best wise has sembled in oure Gildehalle the most notable persones and other comeners of the town of Beverlay *rehersyng* [showing] til them the privay seal beforseid. Upon whilk thei *yede* [came] to gedir and gaf answer that for divers causis notable thei myght *chevys* [lend] no good vnto oure seid kyng at this tyme. *O* [one] cause was that mennys frehald which in the town of Beverlay thre partes was in decay, and other tenementis that was inhabit with tenantz was so febil that they myght noght weel pay. Another cause was seid that marchandis sometyme usid within the town of Beverlay is so gretly enfeblid, what *be* [by] losse of the see and what with takyng of enemys on the see, that profit of me[r]chandis is no thyng as it was won to be. Another cause, thai have ben so charged with taxis yeerly that has been payd, and yet is for to pay, that withouten over grevous hynderyng til the communite, like chevance may not be made. Another is as it is wele *kennyd* [known] that enmys of divers nacions has been on the coste of Holdernesse, and there has takyn divers schypis, men and theire goodes. Also has renyn up at Withernsea and other places in

---

[11] By 18 June, at the latest.
[12] On 16 June.

Holdernesse,[13] there takyng *scheep* [ships] and men with them; which coast of Holdernesse us moste help and releve [in] tyme of necessite with al oure power in withstandyng the malys of the enemys aboveseid. Also another is certefied til us, that the Scottis wil have oppyn werre whilk til us wil be a gret grevous charge, and warantz come fro Wardeyns of the Marche[14] to reyse the peple as it has be done befortyme. . . .

[At this point the manuscript is damaged and incomplete; it is, however,
    possible to see that the tone of complaint is maintained to the end.
The Provost replies with the following letter]

To the worschipful and entierly welebeloved Frendes, the xij governeurs of the town of Beverlay.

Worschipful sirs and full entierely welbeloved frendes and neghbures, I grete you wel oftentymes of right perfit and hertly affectione, lettynge you wite I have late receyved youre [letter] directid to me be youre commun servant. As for youre excuse to the kyng, oure soverein lorde, of oon loon or chevance of CC marc desired of youre town be the kyng, for his especiale ambassiate and armee at this tyme into Fraunce for the tretee of pees, of the which labour I praye you have me excused. For truly as I stande toward the kyng, as ye knowe, and also that other men of like condicion as ye be of *straingeth* [refuse] thaime noght in this cas, but makis chevance undre suertee suffissante, considerynge the grete and notable cause of the desire therof. And I *couth* [could] noght resonably excuse yow *without* [unless] ye putte you somewhat like othir, and undre like suerte, the whiche is ordenede as stronge as the lordes of the counseil, the which ar chief *lenners* [lenders] at this tyme, can devise. And therfor withouten ye be disposed to do like other of youre degre, desire me noght to entrete in that matere, as weel for your worschyp as for myn. For trewly I wote wele it wolde noght be acceptede of your partie, and I myght be held [responsible] ther with, the whiche I trust ye wolde noght in no wise. Wherfor I counseill you ye [act as] other men of your degrees to do, sumwhate to the kynges plesur, and sendith it hedir be [your] man in haste; and I wil help it to brynge it to as litell somme as I may, with al my hert, [as] wote God. The whiche have you evyr in his holy kepyng. Wreten in haste at London, the viij day of July [1435].

By Robert Rolleston, wardrober and provost.

V.3 INVOLVEMENT IN WAR

Much trouble was taken by the leaders of society to ensure the involvement of the non-combatant in a war, even in circumstances in which

---

[13] Holderness, Yorks, East Riding.
[14] I.e., the Scottish march, or border.

his active participation was not possible. As the evidence shows, this was done in a number of ways which tend to the conclusion that every effort was being made at this period to add a dimension to war by appeals to popular opinion, both at home and abroad.

V.3.A   In the midst of civil strife, while Charles VI leads an army against the duke of Berry, the citizens of Paris demonstrate their belief in the efficacy of prayer and penance as a means of bringing peace to their country [1412]. (French text in *Journal d'un Bourgeois de Paris, 1405–1449*, ed. A. Tuetey, pp. 20–1; also translated in *A Parisian Journal, 1405–1449*, trans. J. Shirley, pp. 62–4.)

And as soon as the Parisians knew that the king was in the lands belonging to his enemies, by common consent they called for processions which were the most devout to have been seen in living memory. Thus it happened that on the penultimate day of the month of May, in the said year [1412], it being a Monday, a procession consisting of those of the Palace at Paris,[15] the mendicant orders and others, all of them bare-footed and carrying several famous reliquaries and the Holy Cross of the Palace, and of men from the Parlement,[16] of both high and low rank, was formed, men walking two abreast, some 30,000 persons following, all of them bare-footed.

On the Tuesday, last day of May, in the said year, some of the parishes of Paris organised processions by their parishioners around their parishes; all the clergy wore their copes and surplices, and each carried a candle and a reliquary in his hand, and went bare-footed; there were carried the reliquaries of St Blanchard and St Magloire, preceded by at least two hundred young children, all bare-footed, each with a candle or taper in his hand; and all the parishioners who could afford it also had a candle in their hands, both the men and the women, all being bare-footed.

On the following Wednesday, first day of June, in the said year, the procession was organised just as it had been on the Tuesday.

The following Thursday was the feast of Corpus Christi, and the procession was formed in the customary manner.

On the following Friday, third day of June, in the said year, was organised the very finest procession to have been seen; for all the parishes and orders of whatever rank went bare-footed, carrying, as related above, reliquaries or candles, in keeping with their devotion, there being more than 40,000 people present, all bare-footed and fasting (not to mention the other mortifications which they may have been practising in secret), bearing more than 4,000 lighted torches. In

[15] A former royal residence.
[16] The supreme court of justice in France.

this manner they carried the sacred relics to Saint-Jean-en-Grève; there, with much emotion, tears and with great devotion, they took the precious Body of Our Lord which the perfidious Jews had boiled,[17] and they gave it up into the hands of four bishops who took it thence to Sainte-Geneviève, accompanied by a large crowd of the common people numbering, some said, more than 52,000 persons. There they sang Mass with much devotion, and then returned the relics to the places whence they had taken them, fasting all the while.

On the following Saturday, fourth day of the said month, in the said year, all the members of the University, under threat of penalty of deprivation, formed themselves in procession, and were joined by the young children from the schools, all bare-footed, each, the biggest and the smallest alike, bearing a lighted candle in his hand; and they went in humility to the Mathurins,[18] and then on to Sainte-Katherine-du-Val-des-Écoliers, carrying a countless number of holy relics. There they sang high Mass, and came away with purified hearts.

On the following Sunday, fifth day of the said month, in the said year, those from Saint-Denis came to Paris, all bare-footed, bearing the bodies of seven holy men, the holy *oriflamme*[19] (the one which had been carried to Flanders), the sacred nail and the holy crown, which was borne by two abbots, accompanied by thirteen processional banners; and there went out to meet them the parish[ioners] of Saint-Eustache, to take their saint's body, which was in one of the reliquaries; and they all went directly to the Palace in Paris. There they very devoutly sang high Mass, and then all departed.

During the following week, very many devotional processions took place daily, one after another, and the villagers of the countryside around Paris assembled with great devotion, all bare-footed, praying to God that by his holy grace peace would be established between the king and the lords of France, for as a result of war, all France had lost both friends and wealth. The open country was barren, except for what one took out there.[20]

V.3.B   Use could be made of the Church and of its ministers to publicise news on behalf of the King. Here Henry VI commands the bishop of Hereford to order prayers and processions for success in the war against France [1443]. (Text in *The Register of Thomas Spofford, Bishop of Hereford (1422–1448)*, ed. A. T. Bannister,

[17] This refers to a tradition that a Jew had once unsuccessfully tried to destroy Christ's body by putting a Host in boiling water.

[18] A famous convent in Paris.

[19] The sacred banner which French kings took with them to war.

[20] A useful plan of Paris may be found in *A Parisian Journal, 1405–1449*. trans. J. Shirley.

pp. 252–4; *Registrum Thome Spofford, Episcopi Herefordensis, A.D. MCCCCXXII–MCCCCXLVIII*, ed. A. T. Bannister, pp. 252–4.)

By the kinge.

Reverend fader in God, right trusti and welbeloved, it is not unknowen unto you how that our adversary of France and his oldest son, that calleth himselfe Dauphin, with all the myght and *puissance* [force] that they can and may assemble, and with all thassistance and help not oonly of thoo that oure said adversary calleth his vassalles and subjects, but also of his allies of other *reaumes* [kingdoms] and contrees, enforcen hem and maken, and be disposed to make, in this season that now is at hande, unto us as *soore* [grievous] and as myghty werre bothe by water and bi lande as they can divise, and namely in our duchies of Normandie and Guienne; and how it be that we, by thadvis of oure conseil, have *do* [done], and dayli do, all diligence possible to us for provision to be made of grete and notable puissance to be sent over to resiste hem in thayr said purpos and to *rebuke* [repulse] hem. Nevertheless for asmoch as we know and consydre wel that the prosperite and welfare of princes and of their reaumes, landes and subjectes, and the getyng and chieving of victories upon thyr ennemyes, resteth not principali in mannes wisdom or strength, nor in multitude of people, but in the hande, disposycion, and grace of God, the which it liketh him to graunte to thoo that sette ther hope and ther trust principali in him, and lowly sue and seke unto him therefore by meens *covenable*, [suitable] that is to say, by sacrifice of humble and devout praiers, bi fastyng and bi chastisyng of them self, bi almes dedis and other blessed werkes; we write unto you exhortyng, requiring, and hertly prayeng yow that ye do all the *devoir* [effort] and diligence possible to yow in this behalve, making all thoo that be called ministers of Goddis chirch, *seculiers* [seculars] *and reguliers* [and regulars (i.e. parish clergy and those members of orders)] withyne your diocise, to go openly and devoutly [in] procession divers daies in the weke al this yere next folwyng, and to pray especially for the prosperite of us and of all oure reaumes, landes and subgects, and especially for the good and gracious spede of all thoo that shal laboure and *aventure* [hazard] their personnes to the withstandyng of the forsaid malicious purpos of our said adversari and of his helpers, *sturing* [urging] hem that, considering the necessitees and the thinges abovesaid, thei encrece therefore and *eke* [also (?both)] their laboures and diligence in prayer not cessing, but all other occupacions and plesieres that be not *behovefull* [beneficial], *forborin* [self-denying] and left *ferforth* [to a great extent] as they shall resonably *mowe be* [be able by] continually emendyng to devout prayers day and nyght, afore noon and after, namely in Goddis hous, where prayers be most exaudible. And over that also that ye exhorte, sture and induce as ferforth as ye shal mowe lay people, man, woman, and child comen to yeres of discrecion, to do as they can and may theyre part to the same *entent* [purpose]. And that in generall ye meve hem all to thentent that her prayers and other good werks abovesaid to be done by hem may somoche be the more acceptable to God that they be *do* [done] in clene lyfe, they be the oftener *shrivin* [absolved]; and over this, to induce hem the more effectually and with the more desire to entende to alle the things above said, we desire that it lyke you to graunte to every personne that shal be present and pray in the said processions, and in like wise to every person that shal say a masse or a nocturne of the *sauter* [psalter] or the vii psalmes or the *letaine*, [litany] or oure ladies sauter, or fast any day or do eny dede of almes or shrive to thentent aforesaid, as often *sithes* [times] as he shal so do, *xl* [40] daies of pardon.[21] And to enable hem the more diligently to continue theyr devocion in alle the thynges abovesaide, us semeth that hit shuld be ful expedient that ye ordeyned, from time to time, good and sturyng *precheris* [preachers] of Goddes word to go abrode in your diocise, that might and wold remembre hem and exhorte hem to the said continuance. And as ye love and tendre the prosperite of us and welfare of us and of all oure reaumes, landes and people, faileth not in fulfillyng of oure desires abovesaid as we trust you. Given under oure signet at oure maner of Eltham, the viii day of Marche [1443].

To the reverend fadre in God, our right trusty and welbeloved the bisshop of Hereford.

V.3.c   Edward III writes to his subjects in England to keep them informed of the successful progress of his campaign in France. The use of naval support should be noted and the text compared to that in IV.3.A. [July 1346]. (French text in Froissart, *Chroniques*, XVIII, 286–7.)

Our lord the king, to the honour of God and of Our Lady, St Mary, and for the comfort of all his faithful and liege subjects in England, announces to them the success and prosperity of his undertakings, granted to him by God, since the time of his coming to la Hougue, near Barfleur, in Normandy.

First, how our lord the king, with his host, moved off from la Hougue on the Tuesday before the feast of St Margaret, and captured the town and castle of Valognes. Moving on, he caused the bridge at [Thouave], broken by his enemies, to be rebuilt; he then passed over it. Then he took the castle of Carentan, and afterwards he marched directly on the town of St Lô, near which, at Pont-Hébert, he found another bridge destroyed in the hope of impeding his advance; but the lord king had it rebuilt at once, and on the following day he took St Lô. Immediately,

---

[21] An indulgence granting remission of spiritual penalties after death.

and without having rested a single day between his departure from la Hougue and his arrival here, he set off in the direction of Caen, where his army rested. Then, soon afterwards, our men began the assault upon the town which was heavily reinforced and defended by about 1,600 men-at-arms, afforced by about 30,000 of the people, also armed; these defended themselves nobly and skilfully, so that the fight was very long and very hard. But, let us thank God for it, the town was finally captured by assault without loss to us, and among the prisoners were the count of Eu, constable of France, the chamberlain of Tancarville, who on the day had been proclaimed marshal of France, and other bannerets and knights, some 140 in number, as well as esquires and rich bourgeois in great number; there were also killed many valiant knights and gentlemen, and a large number of the common people. And the naval squadron which remained with the king burned and destroyed all the sea coast from Barfleur to Colleville near Caen. And also burned were the town of Cherbourg and the ships in the harbour: and more than 100 or more large ships and other enemy vessels were burned by our lord the king and his people.

For all this our lord the king asks his loyal subjects of England to tender devout thanks to God for what he has thus made possible, and that they ask God fervently that he may continue to grant the king his favour. He has ordered his chancellor to write letters, under his great seal, to the prelates and clergy of his kingdom of England that they exhort the people to do the same; and the chancellor and other members of the royal council are to inform the people and citizens of London of what has happened, for their comfort. . . .

V.3.D   The use of propaganda was increasingly employed in attempts to justify war and to rally popular support to a cause, as is here demonstrated by a proclamation issued, in the name of Edward III in 1340, for dissemination in France. (French text in Froissart, *Chroniques*, XVIII, 107–9.)

Edward, by the grace of God king of France and England and lord of Ireland, to all prelates, peers, dukes, counts, barons, nobles and commons of the kingdom of France, of whatever estate they be, these are the true facts.

It is a well-known fact that my lord Charles, of happy memory, formerly king of France, died legally in possession of the kingdom of France, and that we are the son of the sister of the said lord Charles,[22] after whose death the said kingdom of France, as is well-known, came to and devolved upon us by right of succession; further, that Sir Philip

[22] Edward's mother, Isabella, was sister to the last of the Capetian kings, Charles IV, who died in 1328. It was through her that Edward claimed the succession to the throne of France.

Valois, son of the lord Charles's uncle, and thus more distantly related than we, seized the kingdom by force, against God and justice, while we were younger in years, and still holds it wrongfully.

We have now, after good and mature deliberation, and placing our faith in God and the good people, taken up the title to the government of the said kingdom, as is our duty. We are firmly intent upon acting graciously and kindly with those who wish to do their duty towards us; it is not in any way our intention to deny you your rights, for we hope to do justice to all, and to take up again the good laws and customs which existed at the time of our progenitor, St Louis, king of France; nor is it our wish to seek our gain and your prejudice by exchanges and debasement of the coinage, or by exactions, or by raising taxes which were never due; for, thanks be to God, we have sufficient for our state and the maintenance of our honour. We also wish that our subjects, as far as is possible, should be relieved, and that the liberties and privileges of all, and especially of holy Church, be defended and maintained by us with all our power. We wish, further, when dealing with the business of the realm, to have and to follow the good advice of the peers, prelates, nobles and other of our wise and faithful subjects of the said realm, without doing or initiating anything with undue speed and only to satisfy our whim. And we tell you again that our greatest desire is that God, working through us and the good people, should grant peace and love among Christians, and especially among you, so that a christian army may go in haste to the Holy Land to deliver it from the hands of wicked men; this, with God's help, we aspire to do.

And be informed that although we have, on several occasions, offered reasonable ways of peace to the said Sir Philip, he has been unwilling to make any such proposals to us, and has made war against us in our other lands, and is trying to defeat us utterly with his power; thus we are compelled by necessity to defend ourselves and to seek our rights. Yet we are not seeking the deaths, nor the impoverishment of the people, but we wish, rather, that they and their property be preserved.

For which reason we desire and decree, of our grace and kindness, that all people of the said realm, of whatever condition they be, who wish to approach us as our well-beloved and faithful people (as the good people of the land of Flanders have done), having regard to God and our right, thereby recognising us as their lawful king, and who shall do their duty towards us between now and the feast of Easter next to come, be received into our peace and our special protection and defence, and shall fully enjoy their possessions and goods, both movable and immovable, without losing anything or being hurt in any way for their resistance to us in the past; for we wish to save and protect them by all means open to us, as it is reasonable we should do.

And since the above-said things cannot be easily notified to each one of you individually, we are causing them to be proclaimed publicly and to be displayed on the doors of churches and in other public places, so that this may come to the notice of all, to the comfort of our faithful supporters and the terror of those in rebellion against us, so that no man, in future, may plead ignorance of these matters.

Given at Ghent, on the 8th day of February, in the year of our reign of France the first, and of England the fourteenth [1340].

V.3.E The political harm which such propaganda was thought capable of achieving is well recognised in this order of Philip VI that his officers shall take active steps, notably in churches, to counter the effects of the proclamation printed above [1340]. (French text in *Documents inédits sur l'invasion anglaise et les États au temps de Philippe VI et de Jean le Bon*, ed. A. Guesnon, pp. 14–15.)

Pierre le Courant, bailiff of Amiens, to the provost of Beauquesne, or to his lieutenant, greeting.

We have seen the letters of our lord the king which contain the following:

Philip, by the grace of God king of France, to the bailiff of Amiens, or to his lieutenant, greeting.

We know for certain that, through inducement and very wicked and false counsel, the king of England, mortal enemy to ourselves and our kingdom, scornfully using the most wicked deceit and malice, has caused to be written many letters, sealed with his seal, in which are contained falsehoods, lies, treason and things injurious to us, to our kingdom and to our subjects, the which letters he plans to send, or has indeed already sent, to important places in our said kingdom so as to turn the people against us, if he is thus able. And because it is our firm intention that our said people shall never see nor hear the very great fraud, malice, lies and wicked intent of the said king of England, we wish, and therefore order and command you, in order to counter his evil design, that you have it proclaimed and solemnly made known throughout your said bailiwick and jurisdiction, that whoever shall find any persons, of whatever estate or condition they may be, bearing letters from the said king of England or other of our enemies, shall take and arrest them and bring them in custody before you, to have them submit to such sentence and punishment which it shall be appropriate to pass upon persons bearing false and fraudulent letters. And pay special care and attention to all churches and other important places within your said bailiwick and jurisdiction,[23] that no such letters shall be affixed or placed upon them; and if any are found there, they must

[23] This is a clear reference to a passage in the last paragraph of the document printed in V.3.D.

then be removed without delay, and all those who may have placed or
carried or helped in the placing of them there are to be arrested; and
as soon as you shall have these letters, immediately cause them to be
burned. And be so diligent about this as to be pleasing to us, and
inform us of what you will have done and found.

Given in the forest of Vincennes, on the 24th day of February, in
the year of grace 1340.

By virtue of these said letters, we order and command you that you
shall cause their contents to be proclaimed and publicised throughout
all the places of importance within your provostship where such
proclamations and the like are normally made, and that you shall arrest
all those whom you may find bearing such letters, or who may cause
them to be affixed in certain places, bringing them to the prisons of
our lord the king at Beauquesne, so as to see justice done there, without
freeing or giving them up, unless it be by special order from us. Con-
form to and fulfil carefully the points in the said letters, as their form
and contents indicate, so that there shall be no failure in this; for, if
there were to be a failure, we should punish you for it.

Given at Amiens, on the 8th day of March, in the year 1340.

V.3.F   Involvement may also be seen in the triumphal ceremonies which
         accompanied the young Henry VI's return to London from Paris,
         where he had been crowned king of France, a ceremony which
         was the symbolical fulfilment of one of the chief English aims
         in the war [1432]. (Text from 'William Gregory's Chronicle of
         London', in *The Historical Collections of a Citizen of London in
         the Fifteenth Century*, ed. J. Gairdner, pp. 173–5.)

Ande that yere the kyng passyde the see in to Fraunce, and wente
unto Parysse; and he come thedyr the thyrde day of Decembyr. And
the xiij day of the same monythe he was crownyde at Parysse; for there
he was worthely and ryally ressayvyd as they *cowthe* [could] devyse
whythe alle the statys of the towne. And there he hylde hys feste
raylly [splendidly] to alle maner of nacyons that were in that contre,
that yf hyt plesyde hem thedyr for to come. And in Syn Johnys day[24]
in the Crystysmasse weke the kynge remevyd towarde *Roone* [Rouen],
and on the xij evyn he come unto *Calys* [Calais]. Ande the xxix day
of Janyver he londyd at Dovyr. And yn Syn Volantynys day[25] he
come unto London; and he was worthely *fette* [conducted] in to the
cytte whythe the mayre and hys aldyrmen whythe alle the worthy
comyns of the cytte and every crafte in hyr *devys* [livery].

And whenne the kynge come to Londyn *Brygge* [Bridge] there was
made a towre, and there yn stondynge a gyaunte welle arayde and

[24] 27 December (1431).
[25] 14 February (1432).

welle be-sene, whythe a swerde holdynge uppe on hye, sayynge thys reson in Latyn: *His enemies will I clothe with shame* [Ps. 132: 18; Vulg. Ps. 131: 18]. And on every syde of hym stode an antiloppe, that one holdynge the armys of Ingelond and that othyr the armys of Fraunce. Ande at the drawe brygge there was a nothyr ryalle toure, there yn stondynge iij *empryssys* [empresses] ryally arayde, whythe crownys on hyr heddys, the whyche namys folowyn here: fyrste, Nature; the secunde, Grace; the thyrde, Fortune, presentyng hym whythe gyftys of grace. The fyrste gaffe hym *Scyence* [knowledge] an *Cunnynge* [understanding], and the secunde gaffe hym Prosperyte and Ryches. And on the ryght syde of the emperyssys stode vij fayre maydyns clothyde alle in whyte, *i-powderyde* [covered, sprinkled] whythe *sonnys* [suns] of golde, presentynge the kyng whythe vij gyftys of the Holy Goste in the lykenys of vij whyte dovys by *fygure* [appearance] owtwarde, whythe thys resonys: *May the Lord fill you with the spirit of wisdom and understanding, with the spirit of counsel and might, of knowledge and piety, with the spirit of the fear of the Lord* [Isaiah, 11: 2, adapted]. And on the lyfte syde of thes emperysse stode vij othyr fayre maydyns in whyte, powderyde whythe sterrys of golde, presentyng the kyng whythe vij gyftys of *worschyppe* [honour]. The fyrste was a crowne of glorye, the seconde with a *cepter of clennys-s-e* [sceptre of purity], the iij whythe a *swyrde* [sword] of *ryght* [justice] and vyctorye, the iiij whythe a mantelle of prudence, the v whythe a schylde of faythe, the vj an helme of *helme,* [or *helthe* = salvation, prosperity] the vij a gyrdylle of love and of parfyte pes. And thys maydens song an hevynly songe unto the kynge of praysynge and of hys vyctorye and welle comynge home. And whenne he come unto *Cornehylle* [Cornhill], there yn [were] the vij *scyence* [tableaux, scenes], and every scyence schewynge hys propyr comyng wondyrly i-wroughte.

And whenne he come to the *Condyte* [conduit] of Cornhylle there was a tabernacule, and there yn syttynge a kynge whythe a ryalle aparayle. And on the ryght syde sate the lady of Mercy, ande on the lyfte syde sate the lady of *Troughthe* [Truth], and the lady of Clennys-s-e hem inbrasyng with Reson. And by-fore the kyng stode ij jugys of grete worthynys, whythe viij sergauntys of lawe ther presente for the comyn profyte representynge of *dome* [judgment] and of ryghtuysnysse, with thys scryptura:

> 'Honowre of kyngys in every mannys syght
> Of comyn custome lovythe equyte and ryghte.'

And so the kyng rode forthe an esy *passe* [pace] tylle he come unto the Grete Condyte, ande there was made a ryalle syghte lyke unto Paradys, whythe alle maner of *frontys of delys* [appearances of pleasure]. And there were vyrgynnys there, drawyng waterys and wynys of joye, and of plesaunce and comforte, the whyche ranne to every mannys comforte and helthe. Thes maydyns were namyd: Mercy, Grace and Pytte. And in thys Paradys stode ij olde men lyke hevynly folke, the whyche were Ennocke and Ely, *saluynge* [greeting] the kynge whythe wordys of grace and vertu.

And soo rode he forthe unto the Crosse in *Cheppe* [Cheapside]. There stode a ryalle castelle of jasper grene, and there yn ij grene *treys* [trees] stondyng uppe ryght, shewyng the ryght tytyllys of the Kyng of Inglond and of Fraunce, convaying fro Synt Edwarde and Synt Lowys *be* [by] kyngys unto the tyme of Kyng Harry the vj[te], every kynge stondynge whythe hys cote armowre, sum *lyberdys* [leopards] and sum *flouredelysse* [fleur-de-lis];[26] and on that othyr syde was made the Jesse of owre Lorde ascendyng uppewarde from Davyd unto Jesu. And so rode he forthe unto the Lytylle Condyte. And there was a ryalle mageste of the Trynyte, fulle of angelys syngyng hevynly songys, blessynge ande halowynge the kyngys whythe thes resonys in Latyn wrytyn: *He ordered his angels that they should protect you, etc. I shall grant him length of days and show him my salvation* [Ps. 91: 11, 16; Vulg. Ps. 90: 11, 16]. And thenne wente he forthe unto *Poulys*, [(St) Paul's] and there he was ressayvyd whythe many byschoppys and prelatys whythe dene and the *quere*, [choir] and whythe devoute songe, as hyt *longythe* [is proper] to a kynge. Ande so he offerryd there and thankyd God of hys goode speede and of hys welfare. Ans thenne he rode to Westemyster, and there he restyd hym; and on the nexte day folowynge the mayre and the aldyrmen whythe a certayne comeners that were worthy men, and they presentyde the kynge whythe an hampyr of sylvyr and gylte, whythe a *M li* [£1,000]. there yn of *nobellys* [nobles, each worth 6s 8d], &c.[27]

V.4 WAR AND NATIONALISM

War was almost inevitably accompanied by an upsurge in that sentiment which we call nationalism, an increase in men's awareness of the differences between peoples, an emphasis on the divergences in their development and history and on their separate traditions, laws, customs, and present characteristics. This is reflected not only in some of the

---

[26] See B. J. H. Rowe, 'King Henry VI's Claim to France in Picture and Poem,' *The Library: Transactions of the Bibliographical Society*, 4th series, 13 (1933); J. W. McKenna, 'Henry VI of England and the Dual Monarchy: Aspects of Royal Propaganda, 1422–1432', *Journal of the Warburg and Courtauld Institutes*, 28 (1965).

[27] Such royal entries were not uncommon in both England and France at the end of the middle ages. Perhaps the most famous was that made by Henry V into London after his victory at Agincourt in 1415. See *English Historical Documents. IV: 1327–1485*, ed. A. R. Myers, pp. 215–8.

literature of the period, but also in the record of events which passed as history. By means of literature and history men were persuaded to think that they were naturally superior to their rivals and enemies.

V.4.A   In this popular verse, not printed in its entirety here, the English mock their enemies, the Flemings, and their allies, for their failure to capture the town of Calais, and for their fear of the duke of Gloucester,[28] although he had not yet set sail from England on his way to relieve the siege [1436]. (Text in *The Brut*, ed. F. W. D. Brie, II, 583–4; *Historical Poems of the XIV*[th] *and XV*[th] *Centuries*, ed. R. H. Robbins, pp. 85–6.)

. . .

Remembres ye of Brugges, how ye ferst *wan youre shone* [won your shoes/spurs (= achieved fame)],
How ye come forth to scarmyssh vpon an aftirnone
With *pauyses* [shields] & crossebowes, on *Saynt Petirs* [a place outside the walls of Calais] playne,
And how sone the *Calisers* [men of Calais] made you to turne agayne,
And ouerthrewe you sodeynly, or euer that ye *wist* [knew],
And brought you in-to Caleis, tyed fast by the fist.

Remembres ye of *Gaunt* [Ghent] eke, for al youre pride & bost,
Wonnen was youre bulwerk *beside* [in addition to] your gret host,
And slayne all that was therin: & ye, that same night,
Fled ouer *Grauenyng* [Gravelines] watir; *but go that go myght* [only those who could go, went],
And youre lord[29] with you, for dreed and for fere
Of the Duyk of Gloucester; & yette was he not ther.
Wel was hym might go before with *pisone & with paunce* [parts of a set of armour],
And laft behind you, for hast, al youre *ordynaunce* [supplies].

Remembres, ye Picardes, as seege *eke* [also] as ye lay
Of *Guysnes* [Guînes], that strong Castel, how ye fled away
For ryngyng of the larume bell, shamfulli in a *morowe* [morning],
As *ferd* [frightened] as the Flemmynges, with hertes full of sorowe.
Ye lost there your ordynaunce of gunnes that was *cheff* [best]:
To you & to al Pycardis, shame and gret *repreff* [reproach].

[28] Humphrey, duke of Gloucester, Henry VI's uncle, was a personal rival of the duke of Burgundy, whose army was besieging Calais. The English success at Calais was, although not due to Gloucester's intervention, turned to his personal advantage.
[29] A reference to the duke of Burgundy, whom the English accused of having fled from the siege.

Remembres now, ye Flemmynges, vpon youre owne shame;
When ye laide seege to Caleis, ye wer right still to blame;
For more of reputacioun, ben Englisshmen then ye,
And comen of more gentill blode, of olde antiquite;
For Flemmynges come of *Flemmed* [outlaws, exiles] men, ye shall wel
    vndirstand,
For fflemed men & banshid men enhabit first youre land.

Thus proue I that Flemmynges is but a flemed man,
And Flaunders, of Flemmynges, the name first began.
And therfore, ye Flemmynges, that Flemmynges ben named,
To compare with Englisshmen, ye aught to be ashamed!
Ye be nothing elles worth, but gret wordes to *camp* [fight];
Sette ye still, & *bith* [remain] in pees: God gyue you *quadenramp*
    [misfortune]!

Such & many othir rymes were made amonge Englisshmen, aftir the
Flemmynges were thus shamfully fled frome Caleis, & the Picardis from
Guisnes fledd & gon theire way, for drede & fere of the comyng of the
Duyk of Gloucestre, whiche by that tyme was redy at London with his
power & armee to come to the rescows of Caleis, & to shippe at Sandwich, wher-as lay redy in the hauen iij^c [= 300] sailes to abyde his
comyng.

V.4.B   Part of a fifteenth-century tract, drawn up in the form of a
debate between an English and a French herald, presided over
by the mythical figure of Dame Prudence, in which an attempt is
made to demonstrate the superiority of the French over the
English. The emphasis placed upon the military achievements
of the French king should be specially noted [c. 1455]. (French
text in *Le Débat des Hérauts d'Armes de France et d'Angleterre*,
ed. L. Pannier, pp. 22–5.)

Item, let us now speak of the kingdom of France. It is quite true
that in fairly recent times past, in what I would call the present time,
there has been great division in the said kingdom between the lords
of the blood of the said kingdom, and this has led to terrible and long-
lasting war. The saying has it that

> Whose neighbour is friendly
> Will wake up in safety.

When you came to learn of the said war and division, some of you came
to the help of the duke of Orléans, others to help the duke of Burgundy,[30]

---

[30] A reference to English assistance given, in 1411 and 1412, to the supporters
of the dukes of Burgundy and Orléans, at that time contending for control of the
French crown.

burning things up and extending the war in all the ways which you could think of. Then, having seen war and division spread everywhere, you immediately sought to subject the kingdom to your authority, wishing to have yourself regarded as king of France, and causing yourself to be called by that title.

Item, it is true that, as a result of the said division, and also because our king was young of years and still a child, Henry [V], your king of England, achieved great conquests in this kingdom and won many towns and regions, to the extent that during his lifetime, and after his death, your conquests extended as far as the river Loire, and even beyond it. However, this was not done without our fighting great battles with you, nor without considerable resistance on our part.

Item, but let us now see how king Charles, the seventh of that name, who now reigns as king of France, has succeeded in opposing you. For while he was a child and still young, you overran him and waged war against him hard and long, during which time he suffered the greatest ill-fortune and adversity which a king could ever suffer (this would take too long to recall here); but once he had reached the age of his maturity, by his great ability, he found a way of reconciling the lords of his blood and of ending the war which had already lasted too long, and thus he achieved friendship among them.

Item, once this was done, he soon found a way of winning back his own town of Paris and, by siege, his town and castle of Meaux; then he took Pontoise by siege and assault, and was in fact there in person. Indeed, he expelled you from the whole of the Ile de France, as far as the duchy of Normandy.

Item, soon afterwards he assumed the heart of a lion and the courage of a prince, and with a large force and army he entered his duchy of Normandy; and, as much by sieges, battles and surprise attacks as by other means, he expelled you and threw you out of his said duchy of Normandy in one season [1449–50], which is a very short time indeed; nor has he left you a single place in the said region, but has put it all under his obedience, conquering in one year all that you and your king Henry had conquered in thirty three.

Item, following on his good fortune, in the year 1450 he came with a great army into his duchy of Guyenne, where he found several of his towns and castles occupied by you, such as Bordeaux, Bayonne, Bourg, Blaye, Fronsac, Libourne, St Emilion, St Macaire and several others which had remained in your hands after the conquest carried out by Philip, king of France, called Godgiven, who had not been able to complete the conquests during his lifetime, for he died between two campaigns; but our king Charles, a short while ago and within a short space of time, by means of assaults and sieges, conquered the said region and placed it within his obedience.

Item, although, since the said conquest, the town of Bordeaux rebelled against him, and those of the said place gave their oath to the lord Talbot, an Englishman, the king defeated the said Talbot in battle, and then besieged Bordeaux by sea and land in such a way that those of Bordeaux were compelled to place themselves in his grace and mercy.[31] Indeed, he has not left you a single place in Guyenne and has packed you off to England in shame. And believe me, Dame Prudence, that men cannot remember such great and remarkable deeds being done, nor such great conquests being achieved, in so short a space of time, than those carried out by our king, Charles, who reigns at present.

V.5 PROFIT AND LOSS

It was not only the active participant who reaped the advantages or suffered the disadvantages of war. The non-combatant was sometimes in a good position to obtain profit from a war, especially at a time of military success. Likewise, whether he is regarded as the unavoidable or the deliberate victim of war, his losses could be very great, since he was of that section of society which stood to lose the most from a state of war.

V.5.A   Henry VI makes the grant of a house in Paris to his secretary,
         Ralph Parker. This, one of scores of such examples, illustrates
         how the non-combatant might reap the material advantages of a
         war successfully fought in a foreign land [1425]. (French text in
         Paris pendant la domination anglaise (1420–1436), ed. A. Longnon,
         pp. 149–50.)

Henry, by the grace of God king of France and England. We make it known to all, both living and to come, that out of consideration for the good and valuable services which our beloved secretary, master Ralph Parker, has done for us, we, on the advice and by the deliberation of our much loved uncle John, duke of Bedford, regent of our kingdom of France, and by our special favour, have given, granted, ceded and handed over and now give, grant, cede and hand over by these presents, to him and to his legitimate male heirs born to him in direct descent, a house with all its appurtenances whatever, and with the furnishings and equipment within it, all of which formerly belonged to Jean le Blanc, the house being situated in Paris at the Porte Barbette, and attached on one side to the house of the widow of the late Jean Chanteprime, the which house with its appurtenances, furnishings and equipment has come to us as a result of confiscation and forfeiture for the

---

[31] The French captured Bordeaux in 1451, only to lose it to English sympathisers in the following year. They finally regained it in the wake of their success at the battle of Castillon in 1453. See IV.3.C and VI.2.E.

rebellion and disobedience of the said Jean le Blanc. We wish that this house, together with its appurtenances, furnishings and equipment, should now be given to the said master Ralph Parker and to his heirs male, born legitimately in direct descent, so that they may enjoy, use and exploit it from now on fully, peacefully, from generation to generation, perpetually and for always, as their own property and land, paying such taxes, fees and services as may be due and customary; provided, however, that the said house shall not have been granted away to others before today, on which day these letters have been written, by our well beloved ancestors or father, whom God assoil, or by us or by our said uncle.

Thus do we order, by these presents, our good and loyal servants at the Chamber of Accounts, our treasurers and general overseers of our finances . . . and our provost of Paris.

Given at Paris, on the 13th day of the month of February, in the year of grace 1425, and of our reign the third.

Thus signed: By the King, on the advice of my lord the regent of the kingdom of France, duke of Bedford.

J. Picquet
[Secretary]

V.5.B   A pardon is granted by Henry VI to Jean Guérard, for having failed to recognise him as king of France. The document sets out in some detail the misfortunes which might occur to a non-combatant caught up by the events of war [1425]. (French text in *Paris pendant la domination anglaise (1420–1436)*, ed. A. Longnon, pp. 168–71.)

Henry, by the grace of God king of France and England. We make it known to all, both living and to come, that we have received the humble petition of Jean Guérard, a poor man, aged about 34 years, burdened with a wife and small child, in which he maintains that in the year 1419, or thereabouts, a fortnight after the feast of All Saints,[32] the said petitioner, being present and dwelling in our said town of Paris, together with his wife, fearing that a certain Blanot Maunoury, also dwelling in Paris, was threatening to have him arrested and cast into prison (as he had already done on several occasions) and have his goods seized and confiscated because the said Blanot alleged that the said petitioner owed him certain sums of money, the said petitioner fled from our said town of Paris, together with his wife who was at that time pregnant, with the intention of going to Orléans and to Bourges, where he might be able to earn a meagre livelihood and subsistence, since he no longer dared to live in our said town of Paris for fear of Blanot, who was having our said petitioner sought out wherever he

[32] I.e., a fortnight after 1 November.

hoped that he might be found, so that he might have him cast into prison, as stated above.

They travelled as far as Massy, in which place they were relieved of all that they carried, the said petitioner being taken and imprisoned in the castle of Massy, where he was put up to ransom by our enemies and adversaries who were then occupying the said castle, for the sum of twenty gold pence, which he duly paid them. He and his wife then went to Montlhéry, where they remained for a good three months or so, living off their labour and effort; but, not considering themselves to be safe on account of the illegal activities of our soldiers and other subjects there, they moved to Étampes where they rented a house, thinking that they now had the necessary security to earn a living by trade or other means. On the second day after their arrival in Étampes, on market day, the said petitioner was captured in the said town by men from the garrison of Gaudreville, our enemies and adversaries, and was taken away as a prisoner to Gaudreville on the grounds that he was one of our supporters; there he had to pay the twenty gold pence which were demanded of him as a ransom. He then returned to Étampes to his wife, who was just then expecting her child, and they remained there together for the duration of Lent, living off their labour and effort, receiving help from none. At the end of Lent there came to Étampes a certain Pierre Combertin, who suggested to the said petitioner that he should accompany him to Farcheville, and that he would help him as best he could. The said petitioner went there, taking his wife with him, but soon after their arrival the petitioner's wife retired sick to bed, where her illness kept her for about eighteen months, the said petitioner being ill, too, for a period of about seven weeks. He, realising that he had no means of livelihood, nor of looking after his wife who thus lay ill, at the suggestion of the said Combertin, who had brought him to Farcheville, and at the evil suggestion of the enemy, joined the garrison of Farcheville, remaining there for the better part of two years. After that time, the said petitioner and his wife left for Milly in Gâtinais, where they remained until our beloved and loyal cousin, the earl of Salisbury, besieged it on our behalf. On this occasion they lost all their goods, and then went back to Farcheville, where they continued to stay until the Tuesday before the [feast of the] Ascension last past,[33] when the said petitioner who, with others, was out plundering, was captured by the soldiers of Bagneux and Vanves or by other of our supporters; whereupon he was taken to Bagneux, where he remained for one night, and the day following to Fontenay, and then to Sèvres, where he was ransomed, the whole cost of his ransom amounting to some twenty crowns.

He, while at the said places of Farcheville and Milly, and in the

---

[33] I.e., 15 May 1425.

company of members of the garrisons, attacked our subjects and followers, capturing and taking them as prisoners to the said garrisons (which are comprised of our enemies) where he put our subjects to ransom; besides which he has robbed and pillaged wherever there was anything to take, although during all this time, while engaged in these activities, he has not killed anybody, nor assaulted any woman, nor violated any church, nor committed any arson.

The petitioner now sincerely wishes to become our loyal and true subject, and to live in our obedience, and to bring his wife and child there too. However, he would not dare return without being accorded a pardon. . . . We, for pity of him, etc., [The pardon is granted].

Given in Paris in the month of June, in the year of grace 1425, and of our reign the third.

Thus signed: By the Council.

J. de Drosay [Secretary]

V.5.c   Private citizens—more often than not those living on a frontier, or merchants engaged in trade—could seek a form of legalised retribution, known as letters of marque, permitting them to obtain redress from an enemy for wrongs or material losses inflicted upon them. This text shows how this might be done in early fifteenth-century England [1416]. (French text in *Statutes of the Realm*, II, 198–9.)

Item, because our sovereign lord the king has heard and understood, at the grievous complaint of the Commons of his realm in this present Parliament, that . . . our sovereign lord the king's enemies, both in the parts beyond the sea as in the realm of Scotland, have assumed great daring to harm the king's faithful lieges, by slaying some and taking others prisoner, and also by taking their goods and chattels, against the tenor of the truces, both upon the high seas and in the marches of Scotland abovesaid; concerning which the said Commons have humbly besought our said sovereign lord the king to provide some remedy. The king our said lord, always ready, in this case as in others, to take steps to secure the indemnity of his faithful lieges, has declared in this present Parliament that he, the same sovereign lord the king, will grant [letters of] marque in due form to all who feel themselves grieved by any attempts made by his enemies upon any of his faithful lieges against the tenor of any truce made before this time, wherein there is no express mention that all marques and reprisals must cease; and our said lord the king will do likewise to all his liege people who feel themselves grieved against the tenor of any truce which shall in future be made between him and his enemies. And to the greater comfort of his faithful liege people, in order that they may the more readily, and without long delay, have remedy in such a case, our lord the king wills that he or they who feel themselves grieved against the tenor and form of such truces within the realm of England (except on the said Marches of Scotland), or upon the sea, or in the parts beyond the sea, shall complain to the Keeper of the Privy Seal, who holds office at the time, who after hearing and taking note of such complaint, shall make to the complaining party letters of request under the privy seal in due form; and if, after such request is made, the party required does not make, within reasonable time, due restitution or satisfaction to the party grieved, then the Chancellor of England, for the time being, shall cause to be made to such party grieved, if he demand them, letters of marque under the Great Seal in due form. And as for providing a remedy for the king's lieges and subjects who feel, or may feel, themselves grieved in the said realm of Scotland, or in England in the Marches adjoining the said realm of Scotland, against the form of such truce as is said above, our lord the king shall give power by commission to the Wardens of both the East and the West March, and to each separately, to hear the complaints of all his liege people and subjects who may or shall be grieved, and cause letters of request to be made for delivery to the person who has done or shall do such grievance or to the Guardian of the March, or to the Conservator of Truces on the Scottish border, if it can effectively be done, or otherwise to make proclamation in public places upon the Marches that he or they who have done such grievances against the truces shall make due restitution or satisfaction to the party grieved. And if they do not do it within a reasonable time, then, at the demand of every one of the King, our lord's, lieges and subjects who may have been, or who may come to be, grieved in such a case, letters of marque are to be issued in due form under the seals of the said Wardens, or under the seal of the one of them to whom the complaint shall have been made in this case, without any difficulty.

V.5.D   The use of letters of marque, argued Philippe de Mézières, a learned and experienced French soldier and statesman at the end of the fourteenth century, could in fact work actively against the interests of the aggrieved party and his country. Arguing, as his thirteenth point in part of a long allegorical treatise, that trade would assist the regeneration of France after many years of war, he urged the king to oppose methods which frightened or compelled foreign merchants into staying away [c. 1389]. (French text in Philippe de Mézières, *Le Songe du Vieil Pèlerin*, ed. G. W. Coopland, II, 421.)

'Again, my son,' said Queen [Truth], 'for this thirteenth reason you must take very great care that you do not grant to any of your subjects, who may have sustained loss outside your kingdom, any right of reprisal or marque upon any christian kingdom or people, with the effect that your subject, who has suffered a loss as stated above, may cause the honest merchants of the said peoples who come into your kingdom to be apprehended, however just his cause may be. For such a policy will cause these merchants to forsake your kingdom, and you would lose the great benefits of this thirteenth reason.'

'My son,' said the Queen, 'you should realise the great loss which often comes upon a kingdom when the king, foolishly advised, grants to one of his own private subjects letters of marque against another kingdom or another lordship. First, he makes enemies of those who are his friends, and gives pretexts for beginning war; and, secondly, all merchants, merchandise and men, of whatever estate, of the country against which letters of marque shall be granted, are banished from the kingdom and from the lordship of the king who will have granted them. And all this trouble and loss is brought about for the particular profit of a single individual.'

'My son,' said the Queen, 'during the lifetime of the Old Pilgrim,[34] the royal majesty of France, acting through its council of men inexperienced in the pursuit of trade, and acting in all appearances to achieve justice, has granted letters of marque to the subjects of the kingdom [of France], one being directed against the noble and excellent city of Venice, the other against the kingdom of Aragon; these claims, which were the cause of very great loss, could have been settled, and reparation could have been made, for, perhaps, less than two or three thousand francs. Instead, it is notorious among well-informed merchants in the kingdom of France that the said letters of marque caused damage to the kingdom of France totalling probably one hundred times the cost of the compensation which might have been paid.'

V.5.E   As this Commons petition of 1378 demonstrates, war affected trade in another way. In days when no regular navy existed, merchant ships were requisitioned when required for military purposes, not infrequently to the loss of the owners. (Anglo–Norman text in *Rotuli Parliamentorum*, III, 46.)

Item, the Commons pray that as in time past the land of England was well provided with a fleet, both of large ships and of small, by which the said land was, at that time, greatly enriched, and greatly feared, too, by all the surrounding lands; yet, since the beginning of the war between England and France, the said fleet has been very frequently requisitioned for many expeditions to France and elsewhere; as a result of which, the owners of the said fleet have suffered very excessive losses and expenses, both by the loss of ships and boats, and by the depreciation and wastage of masts, chains, anchors, cables and other forms of gear, without obtaining any form of compensation from the king or the

[34] The author of the work.

kingdom, as a result of which many of them have been totally ruined, and the said fleet almost destroyed in all parts of England, to the great loss of the king and the kingdom, to the complete ruination of the owners of the ships, and to the great rejoicing of all the enemies of England.

May it please our lord the king to order remedy in this present Parliament; further, that the owners of the ships shall not be put to such great losses and expenses in time to come as they have had to bear in times past.

The king, by the advice of his council, will take such measures as he may do with advantage.

VI

DIPLOMACY, PEACE
AND THEIR AFTERMATH

BROADLY SPEAKING, DIPLOMACY had two main aims, which may appear paradoxical, and which are only properly resolved in the saying, already quoted, that the best way to peace is through war. Diplomacy was regarded as a weapon of war, and a legitimate one, whether by securing alliances or by demanding concessions which, if refused, could be cited in justification for a decision to make war. It was, at the same time, used as a means of bringing about an end to war and of achieving peace, this being done, on occasions, at the urging of the Church, and by her mediation, sometimes by the mutual consent of the parties concerned.

In either case, since resident or permanent ambassadors were only being introduced at the end of the fifteenth century, diplomacy was carried out *ad hoc* by envoys dispatched, under an elaborate system of safe-conducts, to a foreign court or to a previously arranged meeting place, or convention, the envoys being given detailed and precise instructions concerning the issues on which it was open to them to negotiate. Such gatherings of diplomats, described in a number of important journals, or protocols, kept by the participants, were great and solemn occasions, when envoys and ambassadors, together with their attendants, showed off as best they might the riches and the power of the ruler whom they represented. Sometimes, it may seem to a modern reader, the formalities of these occasions were looked upon by the participants as more important than the end for which they had come together, the achievement of peace.

Peace itself, it it came, could be a very mixed blessing—or so some seemed to think. A treaty might lead to an official ending of hostilities; a resounding victory, like those achieved by the French at Formigny in 1450, or at Castillon three years later, might, in its turn, effectively end a state of war: but at the same time it should be recognised that in societies whose daily existence was so much dominated by war, it was no easy task to settle everything in a moment. Peace there might be, but the after-effects of war had to be faced, and dealt with. There was the problem of the returning soldier, or the soldier with nowhere to go, a sizeable problem if one accepts what many contemporary sources have to tell us about it. There were, too, legal problems, arising largely out of a desire to stabilise the tenure of land and property after a long period of occupation. More positively, there was the question of how to get a country on to its feet again, once the fighting had ended. Such were the problems which faced those responsible for the well-being of societies after long decades of war. There are clear indications that at the end of the Hundred Years' War the diplomats of both sides were becoming increasingly aware that there were consequences of peace which had to be faced. Peace was not synonymous with Elysium.

VI.1 PEACEMAKING

Peace, or at least the cessation of hostilities, was achieved in a number of different ways. Attempts to achieve it were not always successful; sometimes they were but short-lived, while on other occasions they were more long-lasting. The Church was not infrequently involved in diplomacy, acting as a neutral mediator between the parties; on other occasions, the sides negotiated directly with each other through embassies sent for the purpose, while in a few instances rulers themselves became actively involved in negotiations for peace.

VI.1.A In this description the papal envoy makes a desperate, last-minute and unavailing effort to secure a cessation of hostilities between John II and Edward, the Black Prince, before the battle of Poitiers in September 1356. (French text in Froissart, *Chroniques*, V, 397, 414–16.)

At this time there had been sent to France, on behalf of our Holy Father Pope Innocent VI, my lords Talleyrand, Cardinal of Périgord, and Nicholas, Cardinal of Urgel, to negotiate peace and concord between the king of France and his enemies, the principal one being the king of Navarre, whom the king had caused to be imprisoned. And they had discussed the matter several times with the king in the course of the summer, while the siege of Breteuil was taking place; but nothing had come of it all. After the ending of the siege which had led to the capture of Breteuil, the said Cardinal of Périgord had retired to the good city of Tours in Touraine. And there news had come to him that the king of France was hurrying in search of the English; upon which the cardinal, moved and encouraged to bring an end to such a crisis and to reconcile the two lords, if he could do it, by any means, or at least take such steps as would prevent an encounter from taking place, hurriedly left Tours and rode off towards Poitiers, for he understood that the two armies were intent upon going there; and he exerted himself so much that he got there. . . .

As the French were about to advance, for they were seemingly very anxious to find the enemy, the Cardinal of Périgord, who had left the town of Poitiers very early that morning, came up in great haste to the [French] king, and bowing very low before him, in all humility, and with his hands joined as if in prayer, begged him, for the love of Almighty God, that he should delay and hold back for a while, until he had spoken to him. The king of France, who was normally ready to listen to reason, agreed to this saying: 'Willingly, what is it you wish to say?'

'Dear sire,' said the cardinal, 'you have here all the flower of chivalry of your kingdom assembled against what is but a handful of Englishmen when compared with your force. If you should have them in your power and they should submit to your mercy, it would be more honourable and more advantageous to you to do it in this way, than to risk so large and so chivalrous a force as you have here. I therefore pray you, in the name of God and of humility, that I may ride over to the Prince [of Wales] and show him in what danger you hold him.'

This the king agreed should be done, saying: 'My lord, this is pleasing to us, but come back at once.' At these words the cardinal left the king of France and went hurriedly over to the Prince, who was standing with his men in the middle of a vineyard awaiting, seemingly with confidence, the king of France's army. As soon as he came, the cardinal dismounted and presented himself before the Prince, who graciously received him. Thereupon the cardinal, having greeted him, said: 'My good son, you have beheld and pondered upon the might of the king of France. I hope that you will allow me to make an agreement between you, if I can.'

To which the Prince, who was then a young man, replied: 'My lord, saving the honour of myself and of my men, I shall be glad to consider anything reasonable.'

Replying, the cardinal said: 'My good son, you speak well. I shall do what I can for you. For it would be a great shame if the many fine people whom you have on one side and on the other, were to come together to do battle, for too much harm could come of it all.'

At these words the cardinal, without saying anything more, left the Prince and went back to the king of France. Here he began to work out ways of agreement, and to make suggestions, and, in order to get his agreement, he spoke thus to the king:

'You need be in no haste to fight them, for they are yours without the need to strike a blow; they can neither escape from you nor flee. I beg you that for today, and until sunrise tomorrow, you grant them respite and delay.'

The king of France began to reflect about this a bit. But he wouldn't grant this respite at the cardinal's first asking, nor at the second, for a number of members of his council were not in agreement with this, especially my lords Eustace de Ribemont and Jean de Landas, who had the king's ear in such matters. But finally the cardinal, who was working for a good end, begged and urged the king of France so much that he gave in, and granted a respite to last for the duration of the Sunday and until sunrise on the following day.

All this the cardinal reported very quickly to the Prince and to his men, who were not displeased by it, for they were trying all the time to improve their plans and their positions. Then the king of France ordered that a tent of vermilion silk, very rich and finely made, should be erected on the field on the very spot where he had granted the respite, and gave leave for all his men to retire to their lodgings, except for the squadrons led by the constable and the marshals. There, too, were the king's own children, and the great men of his blood, from whom he would take advice in time of need.

Thus, on this Sunday, the cardinal worked through the day, riding to and fro, for he would have wished them to reach an agreement if it had been possible. But he found the French king and his council very unresponsive, since they did not want to make any compromises at all, unless they could have [as prisoners] four out of every five, and the Prince and his men should surrender without fighting, which they would never have done. So there were offers and counter-offers, and many suggestions were put forward. And I was later told by the said Cardinal of Périgord's people who had been present, and could be relied on to know about these things, that the Prince offered to return to the king of France all that he had taken on this expedition, both towns and castles, and to surrender all the prisoners whom he and his army had captured, and to swear not to take up arms again against the kingdom of France for seven whole years to come. But neither the king of France, nor his advisers would agree to any of this, continually insisting on their proposal that the Prince and one hundred of his knights should surrender themselves into the prisons of the French king; otherwise the English would not be allowed to go forward. But this was a peace proposal which neither the Prince of Wales nor his councillors would ever have agreed to.

VI.1.B   Some of the written instructions given by Henry VI to his ambassadors sent to treat with their French counterparts at Arras [1435]. (Text in *Letters and Papers*, ed. J. Stevenson, II, ii, 431–3.)

Instruction *yeven* [given] by the kyng, oure souverain lorde, unto the right worshipful and worshipful fadres in God, John [Kemp], archbisshope of Yorke, William [Alnwick], bisshope of Norwiche, Thomas [Redbourne], bisshope of Seint David, and also to the kynges cosins, Johne erle of Huntyngtone and William erle of Suffolk, and the kynges welbeloved Waulter Hungerford, maistre William Lyndewode, keper of the kynges Prive Seel, Johne Radclife, seneschal of *Guien* [Guyenne], Johne Popham, Robert Shotesbroke, knyghtes, and William Sprever, doctour of lawe, his ambaxadeurs borne in his reaume of Englande, overe thinstruccions yeven unto hem, and also to his other ambaxadeurs borne of his reaume of Fraunce, to be by hem utterred in the mater of pees to be treted bitwix him and his adversarie in Fraunce.

Furst, if the kynges partie adverse wol in no wise be agreed withe thofres made unto hem by the kynges *ambaxe* [embassy] aforeseide, rather than the kyng shulde be demed in eny wise wilful to goo fro the *wele* [good] of pees, or not to be seen put hym in his *devoir* [effort] as *ferforthe* [much] as a good Christen prince oughte, the seide ambaxadeurs shul offre unto the partie adverse al that ys beyonde the *water* [river] of Loire, nothing thereof reserved to the kyng save oonly that he is possessed of in *Gascoigne* [Gascony] and Guiene.

And yf thei wol not be so contented, than the said ambaxatours shal condescende finaly that the kyng shal content hym withe that he is possessed of in Fraunce at this day, and the partie adverse on that other side to holde stille that he now occupiethe *semblably* [similarly], eche of hem as *voisin* [neighbour] to other, withe this that commutacion and entrechange be made of suche places and landes as either party hathe enclaved withinne *thobeissance* [obedience, jurisdiction] of other by suche persones as shal be chosen and appointed therto on either side. And in cas thei falle in eny *variance* [disagreement], than the cardinalx that shal be present in the tretie as persones *indifferent* [neutral],[1] by informacion and advis of suche persones of bothe the parties as han knouleche of the nature and situacion of the places, to reduce the parties to that that reson and equite *wollen* [will], and generaly what particion of lande that by this tretie happe to be made betwix the kyng and his adversarie, be yt by wey of a longe *trewe* [truce] or of a pees final; thenterchaunging of such places enclaved alweyes to be demened and gouvernid by this fourme and ordre abovesaid.

And in eny of thees cases of pees final abovesaid to be concluded with the partie adverse, for as muche as yt [is] thought that mariage is alweyes *oon* [one] [of] the principal thinges that nurisshethe and holdethe *togideres rest* [together tranquillity] and pees betwix princes, poeples and cuntrees that *han* [have] stonde in longe difference, the said ambassatours, as for the *uttermest* [very last] thinge that the kyng wol condescende unto, shal conclude mariage betwix the kyng and suche of thadversaries doughters as shal be thought moste agreable to the kynges plesir, to take hir rather than faille of a goode conclusion of pees for default thereof, withoute lande or moneye.

---

[1] Two cardinals, Nicolò Albergati, representing the Pope, and Hugues de Lusignan, representing the Council of Basle, were to be the neutral presidents of this assembly. See J. G. Dickinson, *The Congress of Arras*, especially Ch. IV.

And yf the partie adverse desire the deliverance of the duc of Orleans[2] oonly by the meene of pees, the said ambaxadeurs shal answere like as ys contened in theire furst instruccion, where is made mencion of his deliverance.

In wittenesse of whiche thing to this present instruccion oure seid souverain lorde the kyng hathe do put to his greet and prive seeles, at Westminster, the last day of *Juylle* [July], the yere of his regne the xiije [1435].

VI.1.c Narrative of the proceedings of the embassy sent by Charles VII to England in July 1445. The essential formality of the proceedings should be remarked. (French text in *Letters and Papers*, ed. J. Stevenson, I, 153–9.)

This is the manner in which my lords the ambassadors of our lord the king were received in England.

In the first place, there arrived at Calais the archbishop of Rheims, my lord of Précigny, master Guillaume Cousinot and master Étienne Chivalier; and there came out to meet them the lieutenant of the town, acting on behalf of the duke of Buckingham, earl of Stafford,[3] half a league out of the town. And on the next day, at ten o'clock, the said lords set out and crossed over the sea.

On the second day following, there came to the said place of Calais my lords the counts of Vendôme and Laval, and the said lieutenant came out to meet them a quarter of a league from the town; and at their entry through the streets, the English and the townsfolk were there, all armed, and our said lords were well and splendidly received and lodged. And they found in the said town the duke of Brittany's ambassadors, namely the bishop of Nantes and the chancellor of Brittany, called the lord of Guémené-Guingan. And they spent two days in the town awaiting a [favourable] wind, and the said lieutenant gave them supper with much honour.

On the following day, as soon as dawn appeared, the said lords left, and came over to England, and rode to a town called Rochester. And there came out to meet them there Sir Thomas Hoo and Sir Robert Roos, very splendidly dressed and riding horses bearing silver harnesses. Then all the ambassadors left Rochester together to travel to London; when they were about a league and a half distant, they arranged themselves to receive the English lords who were coming out to meet them. And our said lords had with them 350 horses, including those of the

---

[2] Charles, duke of Orléans, had been captured by the English at Agincourt in 1415. Conditions for his release were negotiated, albeit unsuccessfully, at Arras. He was finally released in 1440.

[3] The phonetic French spelling of English personal names has been corrected in a number of instances in this document.

ambassadors of the king of Sicily,[4] the duke of Brittany[5] and the duke of Alençon; and there came to meet the said lords the marquis of Suffolk, the earl of Dorset, the lord Scales, the lord of Castillion, the son of Gaston [de Foix], and two other barons, together with more than a hundred knights and esquires, up to a number of about 300 horses, all very richly dressed in cloth of gold, silk, and jewelry, their horses being harnessed in silver, gold and jewelry, some of them, indeed, in cloth of gold.

Afterwards, a league from London, came the bishop of Norwich, with three other prelates in his company, in fine and rich clothes, as churchmen wore.

Then came my lords the duke of Exeter, the earl of Huntingdon, the earl of Warwick, the earl of Salisbury, the lord Talbot, the earl of Ormond, two other earls, together with several other great lords.

They all entered thus together into the city of London. At the end of the bridge by the city was the mayor of London, on foot, carrying a sword before him, accompanied by the other officers and governors of the said city, all dressed in a livery, with furs of marten or squirrel. On both sides of the street, as far as the ambassadors' lodging, were the important burgesses and merchants of this city dressed, in hundreds or fifties, in clothes all like one another; and there could have been about a thousand of these people of importance about. And behind them, in one of the streets and at the windows of the houses, were many ladies, damsels, burgesses' ladies, and ordinary men and women, who numbered fifty thousand persons or more. And they accompanied the princes, prelates and lords above-mentioned to their houses, doing them great reverence and honour.

The next day the dukes of Exeter and Buckingham, the earl of Stafford, the [earl] of Dorset and the marquis of Suffolk, the lord Talbot, the lord Scales, and several other great lords came to fetch the said ambassadors to take them to the king. And they led them to Westminster, where the king was. And they came into a large hall, where the king was seated in a chair covered with cloth of gold; he himself was dressed in a long robe of cloth of gold, trimmed with marten and sable. On his right were the Cardinal of York, the archbishop of Canterbury and several other prelates, while on his left stood the dukes of Gloucester, Exeter, Buckingham and Warwick, and my lords the [earl] of Dorset and the marquis of Suffolk, the earls of Salisbury, Ormond and Shrewsbury, and several other barons and great lords of the kingdom.

The king three times lifted his hat, and got up from his chair to greet

[4] René, nominally king of Sicily and Jerusalem, and duke of Anjou, had very recently become Henry VI's father-in-law, the English king having married his daughter, Margaret, in April 1445. See II.1.E.

[5] Francis I, duke of Brittany, 1442–50.

the said ambassadors. My lord of Rheims offered and presented to him the letters of the king, addressing both him and his company with some very fine words. There also came before the king my lords the earls of Vendôme and Laval, and my lord of Précigny, all dressed in figured crimson velvet, their robes being long; all three were accompanied by several bannerets, knights and esquires, all finely and splendidly clothed and dressed, and their people dressed in their liveries, well and honourably. And after they had made their salutation and their greeting, they were accompanied back to their lodging, which was about half a league distant from the palace, by the dukes of Buckingham and Exeter and the [earl] of Dorset and the marquis of Suffolk.

The following day the said lords came to fetch my lords the ambassadors to go before the king. There they presented and showed the king their instructions; and my lords the ambassadors spoke long in secret with the king. Then my lords the ambassadors were accompanied back to their lodgings by the above-mentioned lords.

VI.1.D Personal interviews between rulers were fairly rare, but were none the less an essential part of diplomatic procedure. Here, Philippe de Commynes, councillor to Louis XI, describes his master's interview with Edward IV on the bridge at Picquigny, near Amiens, in August 1475. Special note should be taken of the elaborate security precautions which had been arranged. (French text in Philippe de Commynes, *Mémoires*, ed. J. Calmette, II, 62–7; also translated in *Memoirs*, trans. M. Jones, pp. 257–9.)

Our barriers thus made, as you have heard, the two kings came the following day, which was the 29th day of August in the year 1475. The king had about eight hundred men-at-arms with him, and he arrived the first. Over on the side where the king of England was, his entire army stood at the ready; and although we did not think that we could see the whole of it, there seemed to us to be a remarkably large number of horsemen all together, so that those whom we had on our side seemed rather puny by comparison, since a quarter of the king's army was not present. It had been decided that with each of the kings there would be twelve men, some of the most important and closest to their king, who had already been ordered to the barriers. On our side we had four of the king of England's men observing what we were up to, and we had as many over on the English king's side. As I have told you, the king had been the first to arrive, and was already at the barriers; and there were twelve of us near him, among whom was the late John, duke of Bourbon, and his brother, the cardinal. It had been the king's will that I should be dressed like him on that day; for he had long been accustomed frequently to have someone who was dressed like him.

The king of England came along the way which I have mentioned, well accompanied and looking very much a king. With him was his brother, the duke of Clarence, the earl of Northumberland, certain other lords, his chamberlain, called lord Hastings, his chancellor and others; there were only three or four dressed in cloth of gold like him. He was wearing a hat of black velvet on his head, on which was a large fleur-de-lis in stones. He was a very fine, tall prince, but he was beginning to put on weight; I had seen him look better before, for I have no memory of ever having seen a finer looking man than he had been when my lord of Warwick made him flee from England.

As he approached to within four or five feet of the barriers, he doffed his hat, and bent his knee to within six inches from the ground. The king, who was already leaning on the barriers, also bowed low to him, and they began to embrace through the holes, the king of England then making an even deeper bow. The king opened the interview by saying: 'My lord cousin, you are most welcome. There is no man in the world whom I so wish to see as you. And blessed be God that we are gathered here with this good intention.' The king of England replied to these remarks in quite good French.

Then the chancellor of England, a prelate called the bishop of Ely,[6] began to speak: he started with a prophecy, in which the English are never lacking, which maintained that in this place of Picquigny a great peace between France and England was to be arranged. After this the letters, which the king had caused to be given to the king of England concerning the treaty which had been made, were brought out. And the said chancellor asked the king whether he had ordered them to be drawn up in this form, and whether their contents were acceptable to him. To which the king replied affirmatively, including in this letters which had been given to him on behalf of the king of England.

And then a missal was brought, and the two kings placed a hand on it, each placing their other hand on the [relic of] the holy, true Cross; and both swore to observe what had been promised between them, namely, a truce of nine years, to include the allies of both sides, and a marriage between their children, as contained in the said treaty.

After the oath had been taken our king, who always had the right phrase, began to say to the king of England, laughing as he did so, that he ought to come to Paris, where he would feast him with the ladies, and would give him my lord the Cardinal of Bourbon as confessor, for he was one who would certainly absolve him from that sin, if he had ever committed it, for he knew well that the said cardinal was an understanding man.[7]

[6] The chancellor of England at this time was actually the bishop of Lincoln: the bishop of Ely was treasurer.

[7] This may be a reference to the fact that Edward IV was well-known to be fond of women.

After this, or a similar, conversation had gone on for a little while, the king, who took charge in the present company, caused us to retire, saying that he wished to speak alone with the king of England. Those with the English king retired, too, without waiting to be told to do so. After the two kings had spoken for a time, the king summoned me and asked the king of England whether he recognised me. 'Yes,' he replied, recalling the places where he had seen me, and that in the past I had been put to much trouble to serve him, at the time I was with the duke of Burgundy.

The king then asked him, in the event of the duke of Burgundy being unwilling to accede to the truce (he had, as you have heard, replied very rudely about it), what he ought to do about it. The king of England replied that he should talk to him about it once more and, if he did not wish to accept it, he would leave it to them both to make a decision. Then the king spoke about the duke of Brittany (which is what had made him begin this conversation), and asked much the same question. The king of England replied by begging him not to make war upon the duke of Brittany for, in the times of his own troubles, he had never found a better friend. The king then said no more; and in the most gracious and friendly phrases possible, after summoning the company, he took leave of the king of England, saying something civil to each of his men. Then both together, or almost so, drew away from the barrier and mounted their horses. The king went off to Amiens, and the king of England to his army, to which was sent from the king [of France's] household everything which it needed, even down to torches and candles.

Neither the duke of Gloucester,[8] brother of the king of England, nor any of those who were displeased about the peace were present at the interview. But a little while later they appeared, and not long afterwards the duke of Gloucester came to Amiens to see the king who gave him some fine presents, such as plate and horses with all their gear.

VI.2   THE PROBLEMS OF PEACE

Of some wars, it could be said that they had been formally ended; a negotiated settlement marked a terminating point. Of others, however, the same could not truthfully be stated. Some were merely halted by means of a truce, while others were only punctuated by a defeat or the retirement of one of the parties, the future being left uncertain. Peace, whether lasting or not, brought its own problems, not the least of which was what ought to be done with the soldiers whom princes were depriving of an occupation by the cessation of hostilities, and how lands taken in war, perhaps long years before, should be restored to their rightful owners once war had effectively ceased.

[8] In 1483 he succeeded to the throne as Richard III.

VI.2.A A truce, however solemn, was not always generally respected, largely for lack of effective means of enforcing it against those who used war as a way of covering up their own illegal activities. As a consequence, men suffered the attentions of the soldiery and of others even in times of peace [1360]. (Text in *The Chronicle of Jean de Venette*, trans. J. Birdsall and ed. R. A. Newhall, 105–6.)

Although, by God's will, peace had been declared, misfortune and suffering did not on that account cease. It is true that the English ceased to oppress and rob the common people, but many Frenchmen did not refrain from doing so. Robbers and thieves grew in power along the highways and roads and in the woods. They attacked wayfarers more fiercely than ever before, not only robbing them, but even cutting their throats without mercy, as they had not been wont to do before. Many of these thieves and murderers were afterwards taken, brought to justice, and hanged. Indeed, the English who were still occupying fortresses, captured some robbers of this sort, judged them, and hanged them from trees, thus showing themselves kinder to the peasants in the villages than were their own natural lords.

At this time, after peace had been made, there arose a violent dispute between John of Artois, who had called himself count of Eu, and the town of Péronne in the diocese of Noyon concerning the fortification of the castle of the town. Since the controversy continued, John laid siege to Péronne, a good town, strong, walled, and populous. He called to his aid many nobles from France, the duke of Orléans, brother of King John, among others, and many English mercenaries. After many assaults upon the town, he finally took it. He then pillaged and burned it, slaying many of the inhabitants, and he burned many neighbouring towns as well. The nobles of France at that time withdrew their protection from many of the good towns and the cities, and inflicted injuries upon the burgesses, to both their bodies and their possessions, if they chanced to venture forth. These nobles destroyed the good town of Chauny-sur-Oise, among others. Thus those who were most bound to defend their country troubled it most at this time. Wherefore the citizens of Paris, for the distrust they felt of the nobles, kept watchmen on duty at night and sentries at the gates by day, as diligently as if they were expecting an English attack. They longed for the return of King John,[9] that at his coming the wicked noblemen who were molesting the land and all other robbers might be brought to justice, the whole land be made safe, and the roads and woods be cleared of the robbers who were lurking in them on every hand in untold numbers. The highways and roads were actually less safe at this time than they had been when the English were waging war on France, except that houses were not set on

[9] The king, captured at Poitiers in 1356, was a prisoner in English hands.

fire nor men taken captive. The fair of Lendit was held as usual near
Saint-Denis in the Île de France this year, but according to reports few
merchants came to buy merchandise, so great was their fear of being
robbed or of being killed for their money by the robbers who infested
the woods and the roads.[10]

VI.2.B A way had to be found of ridding France of the soldiers who had
        no official cause to fight for. Intervention in a conflict in Spain
        might keep them occupied, if only for a time [1365]. (French
        text in *Chronique des Quatre Premiers Valois (1327–1393)*,
        ed. S. Luce, pp. 163–4.)

King Charles [V] of France despatched my lord Bertrand [du
Guesclin],[11] together with certain members of his council, to see the
Holy Father;[12] whereupon the Holy Father commanded that the Companies should be sent out of France. At that moment the Bastard of
Spain[13] sent to the said Holy Father to seek his help against his brother,
king Peter,[14] who, he intimated, was not a good christian. The Holy
Father, who knew of the evil ways of that bad catholic, King Peter,
offered to those sent by Henry, the Bastard of Spain, the option of
leading the Companies against his brother. There and then the said
envoys made an agreement with my lord Bertrand, the Holy Father
contributing the value of a tenth towards the payment of the soldiers.
Then my lord Bertrand went back to France to consult with Sir Hugh
Calveley[15] and the other English captains, and with such success that
they contracted to go with him. So the French king, Charles, made out
large payments to my lord Bertrand and to those captains of the Companies so that they should leave the country. And Henry the Bastard,
count of Trastamara, on his part went to great lengths and took great
pains to attract the soldiers to his service. So much effort was put into
this, in fact, both by the Holy Father and by the king (each with the
financial contribution [which he made]) that the said companies,
English, French, Norman, Picard, Breton, Gascon, Navarrese and
others, [all comprising] men who lived off war, left the kingdom of
France.

VI.2.C Some of the late inhabitants of the county of Maine, obliged to
        leave as the result of an agreement made between the kings of
        France and England, protest to Henry VI that they have been

---

[10] See VI.3.A for later attempts to remedy this unhappy state of affairs.
[11] He was to become Constable of France in 1370. See Ch. 1, n. 1.
[12] Urban V. Pope from 1362 until 1370.
[13] Henry of Trastamara.
[14] Peter, known as 'the Cruel', king of Castile.
[15] One of the leading English captains of the day. See III.7.A.

betrayed by the English crown, in spite of many years of service to it. They foresee the worst for themselves now that defeat has come [1452]. (French text in *Letters and Papers*, ed. J. Stevenson, II, ii, 598–603.)

1. Here follows the sorrowful lamentation for the loss of both the county of Maine and the duchy of Normandy, in spite of the said truces or cessation of hostilities offered at the assembly above-mentioned, in the year 1452, the [16] year of king Henry the sixth.

2. The churchmen, nobles, soldiers and others, your most humble, true and loyal subjects, formerly resident and dwelling in the towns, country and castles of the county of Maine, entreat you most humbly, having each and every one served the king, our lord, your father[17] (whose soul may God receive) and yourself, both in the war and in the conquest of the said county of Maine, which is yours by right and inheritance, belonging to you since the time of king Henry, second after the Conquest of England, as by other claims and titles. On account of those services, and in order that they might have the means by which the better to live and maintain their position honourably in your service, and also to help repopulate, guard and keep the said county in your obedience, by driving off and keeping back your enemies and adversaries, you had granted and given them many benefices, lands, lordships, estates and possessions situated in that county, which they have possessed and enjoyed, employing much of their goods and wealth to repair them, maintain them in state, and derive profit from them. But you nevertheless ordered the said county of Maine, and generally all that was in your possession and in your obedience within the said county, to be handed over into the hands of the most high and powerful prince, your uncle of France,[18] as may appear from the copy of your letters patent thereupon made.

3. As a result of this deliverance you have abandoned a large number of people, your faithful subjects, placing them in the obedience of your said adversaries, which is much to be deplored. If you had been properly and loyally advised on this matter, you would never have allowed it to happen. In your letters patent, among other matters, it is declared that it was your will and wish that, to any of your subjects who forsook anything in the county of Maine, as a result of it being handed over, reasonable compensation should be made by commissioners appointed by you for this purpose.

4. And although the said petitioners, always desiring to be and submitting themselves as your good, true and loyal subjects, have maintained their fealty and allegiance and obeyed your said ordinance

[16] The manuscript is blank at this point.
[17] Henry V.
[18] Charles VII, whose sister, Katherine, was Henry VI's mother.

and commandment, hoping to receive justice from your uprightness; and although they have abandoned all the benefices, lands, lordships and possessions, which thus belonged to them, as it appears, and many of them have abandoned the lands which they had bought and paid for with their own money, or which belonged to their wives by right of succession from their fathers, mothers and other deceased friends; and although a large sum of money was earmarked for the payment of the said compensation, the said petitioners have none the less so far received no compensation at all, of whatever kind it may be, which has been, and is, to their very great disinheritance, loss, prejudice and damage, and that of their heirs, too.

5. And, what is worse, the said petitioners who retreated to Normandy, have, since that time, on account of the recent conquest of the region by your said uncle of France, lost all that remained to them of their movable goods, upon which they, their wives and children depended for their lives; at the moment the majority of them are utterly ruined and in a state of beggary, which is a great shame, in view of the good and proper right which you have to the said county and to the duchy of Normandy. Wherefore in pity, and for the reverence and honour of God, the above things considered, and in order that the said petitioners may have something with which to sustain their lives and those of their wives, children and households; and especially that they may not have reason, nor be compelled, for lack of proper justice being granted to them and of promises unfulfilled, to lead lives other than should be led by Christians and loyal subjects, may it please your most high majesty to order and provide reasonable payments or compensation to the said petitioners, both from the sum appointed for it, as is said above, and from the goods and lands of those who thus falsely and disloyally gave you advice, as is mentioned above; for it would seem only reasonable and just that the said goods and lands should be taken and used to make payment or compensation. And in doing this, you will be acting rightly and doing justice, and giving charity and alms. The said petitioners thus pray God for you and your most high royal majesty.

It is to be remembered that this petition was neither conceded nor carried out. And because of this very many soldiers were reduced to the very greatest poverty; some, for grief, became ill and died; others were imprisoned for theft and were condemned to death by justice; while others still remained, as rebels, in the kingdom of France.[19]

VI.2.D War led, especially in the fifteenth century, to the seizure and confiscation of lands in France by the English. A major problem in the after-war years was the rehabilitation of those deprived of their lands and properties as a result of the English conquest [1450]. (French text in Archives du Calvados, Caen. F. 1640.)

[19] The last paragraph is in Latin.

Charles, by the grace of God king of France, to the bailiff of Caen, or to his lieutenant, greeting.

We have received the humble petition of Jean Bonifant and Perrette, his wife, daughter and heiress of the late Richard Vaultier, showing how, in the past, the said late Richard Vaultier, in fulfilling his loyalty towards us, left our land of Normandy, which the English, our ancient enemies, were occupying and have long occupied, and withdrew into [the land of] our obedience, in which he remained and lived for a long time, working in our service. And then he was captured by our said enemies, taken away and put to death in the town of Caen, his possessions and lands which he had left being taken and put into the hands of our adversary of England; and since then they have been held and occupied by our said enemies and other of their supporters.

For this reason the said petitioners, who are and should be the heirs of the said Richard Vaultier, must not be allowed to lose or be denied their rightful inheritance. None the less they are afraid that, according to what some say, measures may be taken to deny them possession and enjoyment of the lands, rights and property which have come from the decease of the said Richard Vaultier, a fact which would be to their very great loss, prejudice and disinheritance, if we were not to provide them with an adequate remedy, as they very humbly seek.

We, for these reasons, having considered these matters, and wishing that our true and loyal subjects, their heirs and successors, should have and recover their rights, order you that, in so far as the said lands and possessions left as the result of the death of the late Richard Vaultier are situated within your bailiwick, having called upon our proctor and others who should be summoned to witness that the late Richard Vaultier did in fact withdraw into our obedience, that he did live within it, was taken from it and was put to death by our said adversaries, and that his lands were not confiscated by our enemies for other reasons, you should restore to both the petitioners the lands, goods, and possessions left as a result of the death of the said late Richard Vaultier, and shall put them, or cause them to be put, into possession and seisin of them, and enable them to enjoy and use them fully and peacefully as they would their own property and lands; and you shall compel all those who shall need to be compelled on this account by all ways and means which are right and reasonable, so that the said petitioners shall not be vexed, hindered, molested or prevented in any way to the contrary. For it is our will that it should thus be done. And to the said petitioners we have granted and grant, by our special grace and these presents, that, notwithstanding any judgements made by the judges and officers of our adversary, they shall have possession, seisin, tenure and enjoyment such as they should have had since the time that the said late Richard left this region to come into our obedience, and since he was thus put to death by our said adversaries. . . .

Given at Caen, on the 7th of August, in the year of grace 1450, in the year of our reign the twenty-eighth.

VI.2.E   As this letter of Charles VII indicates, the unscrupulous could take advantage of the ending of war between England and France to feather their own nests. The king orders that steps be taken to ensure that justice be done [1459]. (French and Latin text in *Archives Historiques du Département de la Gironde*, 9 (1867), 265.)

Charles, by the grace of God king of France, to our beloved and faithful councillors holding the *Grands Jours*[20] at Bordeaux, salutation and greeting.

We have been informed that several nobles and other of our subjects in our territory around Bordeaux and in the duchy of Guyenne, in the period between the first and second conquests[21] and recoveries which we made of the said lands of Guyenne, did, under cover of the Edict of Compiègne[22] and for other reasons, and without leave or the authority of justice, enter and seize actual possession of properties, estates and goods belonging to certain of our subjects, and are withholding and occupying them wrongfully and without cause, without allowing or permitting any enjoyment of them to those who, before them, held them and were, in some cases, the possessors of them at the time of the first conquest, and in other cases, after it, to their great loss and detriment, as has been shown to us.

We, these things considered, wishing that each and everyone should have right and justice administered to him, as is only proper should be done, order and command you expressly that to all our subjects whom you shall find despoiled or dispossessed of their goods and property, without authority and command of justice, without having been able to secure a hearing on the matter, after they shall have appealed to you, you shall cause good justice to be done to them as quickly as possible. For this is what pleases us should be done.

Given at Razilly, near Chinon, on the 19th day of September, in the year of grace 1459, and of our reign the thirty seventh.

Thus signed: By the king.   J. Burdelot [Secretary]

On the back is written: Read, published and recorded at Bordeaux, on the Days, on the 15th day of October, in the year 1459.

Thus signed: Brunat [Secretary]

---

[20] Two occasions, in 1456 and 1459, on which members of the Paris *parlement*, or supreme court, heard appeals from inferior courts in Gascony.

[21] I.e., between 1451 and 1453. See ch. V, n. 31.

[22] An edict of 1429 by which Charles VII attempted to regulate land tenure in areas reconquered by his armies from the English.

VI.2.F In the months after the conclusion of the treaty of Brétigny, the English justices were given considerable powers to deal with the social problem presented by the presence of discharged soldiers returned from the war in France [1360]. (Anglo–Norman text and translation in C. G. Crump and C. Johnson, 'The Powers of Justices of the Peace', *English Historical Review*, 27 (1912), 227, 234.)

Statute made in the Parliament held at Westminster in the 34th year [of the reign]

These are the things which our lord the king, prelates, lords and the commons have ordained in this present Parliament held at Westminster, the Sunday next before the feast of the Conversion of St Paul,[23] to be kept and published openly throughout the realm, that is to say:

First, that in every county of England there are to be assigned for the keeping of the peace one lord and with him three or four of the best chosen of the county, together with some persons learned in the law, and that they have power to distrain the evil-doers, rioters and all other barrators, and to pursue, arrest, take and chastise them according to their trespass or misprision, and to cause them to be imprisoned and duly punished according to the law and customs of the realm, and according to what in their discretion and good counsel shall seem best to them;

And also to inform themselves and to enquire touching all those who have been plunderers and robbers beyond the sea, and are now returned and go wandering, and will not work as they were used to do before this time, and to take and arrest all those whom they are able to find by indictment or by suspicion, and to put them in prison, and to take of all those who are of good fame, where they shall be found, sufficient security and mainprise for their good bearing towards the king and his people, and the others duly to punish, to the end that the people be not troubled or damaged by such rioters, nor the peace broken, nor merchants or others passing on the high roads of the realm disturbed or put in fear of the peril which may arise from such evil-doers.

VI.2.G The English poet, Thomas Hoccleve, bemoans the sad lot of soldiers who, in years past, had fought for their country in the wars against France [1411–12]. He asks that, in their old age, they be accorded greater respect, especially by young soldiers. (Text in *Hoccleve's Works: III. The Regement of Princes*, ed. F. J. Furnivall, pp. 32–4.)

---

[23] The feast was observed on 25 January.

'O fekil world! allas, thi variaunce!
How many a gentilman may men nowe se,
That *whilom* [formerly] in the werrës olde of fraunce,
Honured were, & holde in grete *cheerte* [respect]
ffor *hire* [their] prowesse in armës, & plente
Of frendës hadde in youthe, & now, for schame,
Allas, hir frendeschipe is croked & lame.

Now age *vnourne* [decrepid] a-wey putteth fauour,
That floury youthe in his seson conquerde;
Now al forgete is the manly labour
Thorgh whiche ful oftë they hire *foos afferde* [foes frightened],
Now be tho worthi men bet with the yerde
Of nede, allas! & non hath of hem routhe;
Pyte, I trowe, is beried, by my trouthe.

If sche be deed, god haue hire soule, I preye;
And so schal mo hereafter preye, I trowe.
He that pretendith him of most nobley,
If he hire lakkë, schal wel wyte & knowe
That crueltee, hire foo, may but a *throwe* [a (short) time]
Hym *suffre* [permit] for to lyue in any welthe;
Hertë petous, to body & soule is helthe.

Ye oldë men of armës that han knowe
By syghte & by report hire worthynesse,
Lat nat mescheef tho men thus ouer-throwe!
Kythe [show] vp-on hem youre manly *gentilesse* [kindness]!
Ye yongë men that entre in-to prowesse
Of armes, eek youre fadres olde *hunurith* [honour];
Helpe hem your self, or sum good hem procurith!

Knyghthode, awakë! thou slepist to longe;
Thy brothir, se, *ny* [nearly] dyeth for myschief;
A-wake, and rewe vp-on his *peynës* [hardships] stronge!
If thou heer-after come vn-to *swych pref* [such distress]
Thow wolt ful sorë *triste* [desire] after releef;
Thou art nat seur what that ye schal be-fall:
Welth is ful *slipir* [uncertain], be ware lest thou fall!

. . .

God willë that the nedy be releeued;
It is *on* [one] of the werkës of mercy;
And syn tho men that ben in armes *preeued* [proved],

Ben in-to *pouert* [poverty] fallë, trewëly
Ye men of armës oghten specialy
Helpe hem: allas! han ye no pitous blood
That may yow stirë for to do hem good?

VI.3 MEASURES FOR ECONOMIC REVIVAL

Wars tended to restrict, discourage and even destroy trade, especially on an international plane. But trade was coming to be seen as one of the chief means of re-establishing a country's stability through economic revival. Two French kings, Charles VII and Louis XI, came to appreciate its value both to their subjects and to themselves; their measures reflect much of the positive advice given to them on this subject.

VI.3.A Charles VII orders that positive measures be taken to stimulate the growth of the old French fairs, affected by the wars of the past [1455]. (French text in *Ordonnances des Rois de France de la Troisième Race*, ed. L. G. de Bréquigny, XIV, 359.)

Charles, by the grace of God king of France, to our well beloved and faithful governors and councillors ordained by us for the matter of the collection of our taxes, and to the assessors in the matter of the taxes ordered for the war in the towns and districts of Paris, Rouen, Troyes, Châlons, Rheims, Provins, Château-Thiéry, Gien, Orléans, Tours, Blois, and to the assessors on the matter of the said taxes in all other towns and districts of our kingdom, or to their deputies, salutation and greeting.

On account of the wars which have lasted for so long time in this kingdom and of the mortality which has occurred in several parts of it, and also because of the taxes and other charges which have been raised on account of it from the subjects of our kingdom, our said kingdom has been greatly depopulated, and certain of its ancient and notable fairs have for long been discontinued, while others have grown less important. We have been informed that several of our predecessors as Kings of France, in times past, in order to attract persons from foreign parts and cause alien merchants to come into our kingdom, have granted exemptions from these taxes and accorded franchises to merchants and others who wished to come, so that helped by these franchises, many merchants have in past time come from many foreign lands to attend these fairs; in this way trade has been well and properly maintained, to the great advantage of the common good of our said kingdom. We, having this in mind and desiring the good of the kingdom and of its trade, have franchised and exempted, [and] franchise and exempt by these presents, from the tax of 12 pence per pound, all commodities and merchandise which are brought to and sold at the fairs that belong to us: [namely] Le

Lendit[24] and St Laurence in Paris; the ancient fairs of Champagne and
Brie; St Romain at Rouen and at Guibray, near Falaise, in our duchy
of Normandy, and to other of our fairs established of old in the towns
and cities of our kingdom, the which tax of 12 pence per pound is
imposed at present the kingdom over, or in most parts of it. We wish
thus that all these merchants who shall sell the above-mentioned commodities and merchandise at the said fairs shall [continue to] bring, or
cause to be brought, goods to be sold there.

Thus we order and solemnly command you, and each of you, as it is
appropriate, that you shall allow and permit the said merchants to enjoy
and use fully and peaceably the said franchises and exemptions, by
allowing them to be quit and free of the said tax of 12 pence per pound,
as is set out above. We also order you who have charge of assessing
taxes that you should cause these presents to be proclaimed and published, each of you on the limits of your jurisdictions, so that none may
claim ignorance of them. And as there may be need of copies of the
above in different places, we wish that the copies of these, issued under
our royal seal, be given full credence as if they were the original.

Given at Bois-Sire-Amé, on the 16th day of June, in the year 1455,
and of our reign the thirty-third.

Thus signed: By the King in his council. H. Chaligaut [Secretary]

VI.3.B   A memorandum addressed to Louis XI in which the writer,
          Regnault Girard, argues the urgent need to open the port of
          Bordeaux to English trade and shipping, in order to restore
          economic prosperity to the region [c. 1465]. (French text in
          Archives Historiques du Département de la Gironde, 56 (1925–6),
          34–5, 37–8.)

The city of Bordeaux is one of the large and well-populated cities of
this kingdom, situated on the river Gironde: the distance between the
town and the place where the river enters the sea is about 26 leagues or
so. The river takes sea ships with keels, and of any size, into the city, into
the harbour which is called La Lune, which is an excellent thing: one
should favour a river which carries sea-going ships so deep into the land.

Item, what are its uses? We may compare it to the stomach of a
person which receives meat which is offered to it, and then distributes
it to the various members. Thus the said town receives ships and
merchandise from all parts and coming from all kingdoms; then it distributes them to many members and to many [outside] places, such as
the kingdoms of Spain, Navarre and Aragon, and elsewhere to the lands
of my lords of Armagnac, Foix, Béarn and Albret, as well as into the
Languedoc and elsewhere, as these members demand it. Thus you may
see the situation of Bordeaux, and how the said city is useful.

[24] See VI.2.A.

Item, the second question is, how to make it as fine and rich as it can be. It can be done through the island of England, and this is how. The island of England is a large and rich kingdom which produces much merchandise, such as fine wools (out of which they make much cloth), lead, tin, metal, coals of different kinds and other goods. They also have many ships and about twice a year, namely about All Saints' Day[25] and in March, the said English come, 100, 120, or 200 ships at a time, carrying the aforementioned goods, and they come to cast anchor at Bordeaux.

Item, when the ships have come from the above-mentioned countries, merchants bring money to buy their goods; and the English, too, bring gold and silver . . . and they convert these into the wines of Gascony; and then all go back to their own country. And in this way the said gold and silver, in the above manner, remain in the said Bordeaux, and [consequently] in this country.

Item, the English leave the goods which they cannot immediately sell with people in Bordeaux, so as to have them sold; and these people make a great profit, for the people from the above-mentioned regions often come to seek and then buy this merchandise. Thus trade is maintained in the town by the fact that people come there. For this reason, it seems that without the relationship with, and the goods of, the kingdom of England, Bordeaux cannot be Bordeaux, for there would be no meeting place nor any congregation of merchants. . . .

Item, as the philosophers say, it is very sensible to extract money from the hands of the enemy by subtle methods; this can be done if the king allows the said English to come for the sake of having the luxury wines of Gascony; for they will bring gold in quantity as well as goods from their country, which could be valued at 100,000 nobles and perhaps more. This would bring much profit to the king and his kingdom.

Item, the said goods will be dispersed into the kingdoms and regions aforementioned, which will bring in much gold and silver, all of which will remain within the lordship of the king. You should know that the king has great interest that his subjects be rich, so that they may help him at the time and in the manner which they are called upon.

And if you say that many merchants, other than English, can come there, Flemings and Normans, for instance, I reply that there is very little trade with these places compared with the English trade which is accustomed to come to Bordeaux. And even if they gave the wine away at Bordeaux for nought, the above-mentioned countries have not enough ships to carry half the wine which is produced. . . .

VI.3.c Louis XI takes active steps to ensure that foreign shipping and merchants shall be able to trade with Bordeaux [1465]. (French text in *Recueil des Privilèges accordés à la ville de Bordeaux par Charles VII et Louis XI*, ed. M. Gouron, pp. 165–6.)

[25] 1 November.

Louis, by the grace of God king of France, to our well beloved
cousin the earl of Comminges, marshal of France, our lieutenant in
Guyenne, to the seneschal of Guyenne, to the mayor of Bordeaux, and
to all our other justices and officers, or to their lieutenants, greetings.

Since we have desired, and desire, the good and prosperity of our
town and city of Bordeaux, and, as has been shown to us on behalf of our
said town, the coming and going of merchandise will be one of the
chief causes for its conservation, prosperity and well-being; and because
of the divisions which have come about and arisen, foreign merchants,
as well as their ships and goods, may be unwilling and reluctant to come
into our said town for fear of being taken, arrested or [otherwise]
molested:

We, desiring the prosperity, profit and well-being of this our town
and of our good subjects dwelling in it, and considering the great love
which they have for us and the loyalty which they have maintained
towards us, have granted and now grant, wish and hold as pleasing that
all merchants, of whatever country or nation they may be, may come
henceforth into our said town to trade, together with their merchant
ships and the goods therein contained, in safety and security; provided
that the ships of the lands of Flanders, Holland, Zeeland, Brittany and
other places and territories in rebellion against us, together with the
merchants and others being in them, may come no closer to our town of
Bordeaux than La Marque, nor may they enter our town without the
permission of him or those who, before now, have been accustomed to
grant it; in addition, the above merchants, ships and goods, and other
ships, merchants and goods, should it happen that their coming and
tarrying in the locality of Bordeaux should not be pleasing to us, shall be
bound to unload and depart, under pain of forfeiting to us their ships,
persons, property and goods, and will have a maximum of fifteen days
within which to do this.

We therefore order you, and each of you as it may concern him,
that, by our present grace, will and grant, you shall allow and permit the
said ships, merchants and other persons being in them, to use and take
advantage of their goods in peace, without causing or allowing anything
to be done to the contrary. And so that none may claim ignorance of
this, we wish that these presents be proclaimed in our said town of
Bordeaux, or elsewhere, where it shall be appropriate.

Given at Montluçon, on the 6th day of July, in the year of grace 1465,
and of our reign the fourth.

Thus signed: By the king, the lord of Montereul being present.

Rollant [Secretary]

FINAL COMMENTS

THE FOREGOING COLLECTION of documents will have given the reader some sense of the number and variety of sources available to the student of late medieval war. One of the subject's characteristics which may have struck him is the apparent difference between the ideals and rules advocated by the theorists and social critics, and the actual ways of making war as men practised them in those times. The contradiction is a notable one, so much so that it makes the historian doubt whether in reality the ideal had much practical validity. How could it be said that the necessary preconditions for a just war, which Aquinas set out (I.1.A), had been properly observed when *routier* captains made war almost as they liked (III.6.A, B; III.7.A), ignoring the directive that a war must be declared officially, by a properly-constituted authority, and must not be motivated by self-advantage, for it to be regarded as just? How is it, as the evidence clearly shows, that the treatment frequently accorded by soldiers to their prisoners did not measure up to the high standards of morality and behaviour described, for example, by Christine de Pisan (III.3.A)?

The answer probably lies in the fact that there was, as the documents will have suggested, more than one way of regarding war, a fact which greatly influenced men in their attitudes as to how it should be fought. Some saw it as a noble cause (the achievement of peace) to be pursued by means which reflected that high ideal, the methods used being as important as the end to be achieved; the two could not be divorced. Such an attitude is rightly associated with the writings of Jean Froissart, the 'Chronicler of European Chivalry',[1] who was probably less interested in the military aims of the war (perhaps because he did not properly understand them) than with recording the opportunities which war gave to individuals, especially to those nobly-born, to perform fine deeds, thereby bringing both honour to their ideal and reputation to themselves. It is with great approval that Froissart tells the story of Edward III, the paragon of chivalric knighthood and virtuous endeavour, founder of the most noble Order of the Garter, reprimanding Sir Godfroy de Charny for acting in a manner which was considered base, a reprimand which, we are told, left de Charny full of shame, and

[1] Taken from G. G. Coulton's study of that name.

then praising Sir Eustace de Ribemont for having fought so valiantly (I.2.B). Similarly, when John II was captured at Poitiers, the Black Prince consoled him with the thought that even in defeat he had brought honour upon himself, an opinion which is reflected in other writings of the period.[2]

But not all, as Froissart himself was ready to admit, lived up to such high ideals[3]. Not all were concerned with glory and reputation: some preferred the more substantial and tangible rewards which lined the pocket or, for instance through the grant of a title, gave the outward appearance of nobility. Such men were rather more concerned with their private interests than with the rights of the king, for the saving of which the war was being officially fought. War gave men opportunities for self-advantage which only the more foolish would not, or could not, seize upon. Self-interest gave them something to fight for: as John Wynter and Nicholas Molyneux clearly demonstrated (I.3.B) men went to war anticipating the possibility, indeed the probability, of achieving some material gain from war and conquest. The attitude of such men, carefully planning the future, was hardheaded and realistic. It was one of the less pleasing but most characteristic attitudes which war produced among those who made a business out of it, whether they served a mercenary captain in fourteenth-century France or Italy, or were in the retinue of an English king in fifteenth century France.

It is in such a context and against such a background that the study of the chivalric ideal and of the laws of war assume so much importance. Chivalry was an attempt to civilize men who went to war. It tried to instill in them not only a sense of honour, but also one of moderation and restraint, a willingness to appreciate that the opponent, especially if he were of the caste which understood chivalry, had rights. Among these was the right to be treated humanely even in the hurly-burly of the battlefield. If the dialogue with which Froissart describes the capture of the king of France at Poitiers in 1356 is probably somewhat exaggerated, the sentiments which it expresses were typical of two knights of the period.[4]

Chivalry could take the worst out of war; it was men's hope that the conventions, or laws, of war would do the same. These laws, part of what medieval warfare owed to ancient tradition and practice, contained a strong chivalric element. Their importance, in practical terms, was that they constituted an attempt to reconcile the ideal practice of war with men's interests. They contain, therefore, no condemnation of the notion that men might expect to derive personal advantage from a war fought over a king's rights, no assertion, for instance, that pillaging, *per se*, was

[2] Froissart, *Chroniques*, V, pp. 461, 463.
[3] Froissart, *Chroniques*, VI, p. 204
[4] Froissart, *Chroniques*, V, pp. 453–4.

wrong. What they did do was to set up standards according to which men's behaviour and activities in war might be judged; they tried to achieve a measure of justice between individuals brought into dispute within the wider context of a general conflict; in brief, they recognised that certain practices could only be carried out at certain times, and thereby cast a restraining hand upon those who might be tempted to feel that force, if successfully applied, was answerable to none.

The decline of chivalric influence upon the practice of war was also, in some measure, a reflection of the declining importance in war of the chivalric class, the nobility. Writing towards the end of the fifteenth century, Caxton could well bemoan the fact that men who, in the past, would have been able to prepare a horse and use armour could no longer do so, preferring the life of ease or the life of law to that of the knight. Disappearing, too, were the days of the great chivalric war leaders, men like the Black Prince or Thomas Montacute, earl of Salisbury (I.2.E), the second killed at the siege of Orléans in 1428 by that least chivalric of weapons, a cannon ball.[5] In England, with few exceptions, the new nobility in the late fourteenth and fifteenth centuries was not recruited from among those who had achieved fame or reputation by great deeds. Such actions were still rewarded, but rather by membership of one of the chivalric orders; that of the Garter, for instance, which included the flower of chivalry among its members, not all of whom possessed the natural advantages of birth, and not all of whom were English or subjects of the English Crown.

The nobility was not superseded but was, to some extent, replaced in the higher echelons of military leadership by men of humbler birth who were able to make a 'full-time' contribution to the pursuits of war, from which they came to derive considerable advantage. On the French side, the prime example is that of the man who became Constable of France, Bertrand du Guesclin who, the chronicler tells us, claimed that his origins were too humble for him to occupy that high military office in a worthy manner.[6] Examples, perhaps in greater number, are found on the English side. The men praised by Caxton—Walter Manny, John Chandos and Hugh Calveley—were men whose reputations were made in war during the fourteenth century (I.2.E); while in the fifteenth century Matthew Goth, a Welshman, won notoriety in France which earned him a place in popular tradition on both sides of the Channel.[7] It was people such as these who did so much towards keeping the

[5] '. . . In this yere was the good Erle of Salesbury, Sere Thomas Mountague, slayn at the sege of Orlyaunce with a gonne, wheche was a noble lord and a worthy werreor among all Crystyn men.' (*The Brut*, II, pp. 450, 454.)

[6] Froissart, *Chroniques*, VIII, pp. 45–7.

[7] A. D. Carr, 'Welshmen and the Hundred Years' War', *Welsh History Review*, 4 (1968), pp. 39–41.

Hundred Years' War going. If, when Henry V first went to France in 1415, he had the active support of most of the English nobility to back him, when he returned on his second expedition two years later, that support had already greatly dwindled, and had been replaced by that of rather lesser men, knights and esquires, who hoped to reap the advantages which foreign war, under a famous king, was likely to bring them.[8]

Such change was significant. Accompanying it went the idea of social advancement, a concept clearly understood by contemporaries.[9] Lack of records prevents one from making satisfactory or complete pronouncements on the progress of such advancement through war in the late middle ages. If membership of a chivalric order provided recognition of military fame and reputation, it is harder to chart the acquisition of material wealth from the activities of war. Some, however, were undoubtedly successful. Sir William de la Pole, a merchant from Hull, was to found a baronial house as a result of his ability to lend Edward III money when that king was in need. Another to benefit in much the same way was Jacques Coeur, who, in the middle years of the fifteenth century, served as a banker to the French king when he most needed support on a large scale. On both sides men continued to derive considerable benefit from the war—or at least hoped to do so, as John Wynter and Nicholas Molyneux plainly hoped to. Sir John Fastolf not only became a Knight of the Garter, but he also held important administrative and military positions in France; and, to cap all these, he was able to bring back wealth for investment in land and building in England, Caister being built with the ransom paid by the duke of Alençon, captured at the battle of Verneuil in 1424. War had undoubtedly helped Fastolf along the road to wealth and position in society.[10]

The theme of war and change may be further illustrated if one observes how institutions were changed by the requirements of war. If, earlier in the Middle Ages, war had been controlled (or perhaps held in check) both by the commonly accepted forms of military obligation and by the lack of an adequate system to pay for war, the late Middle Ages were to see this radically altered. The limitation of military service due for only forty days in the year was effectively swept away, a radical change made likely and possible by the willingness and ability of rulers to pay their soldiers, thus enabling them to raise armies pre-

[8] M. R. Powicke, 'Lancastrian Captains', *Essays in Medieval History presented to Bertie Wilkinson*, pp. 371–82.

[9] K. McRobbie, 'The Concept of Advancement in the Fourteenth Century in the Chroniques of Jean Froissart', *Canadian Journal of History*, 6 (1971) pp. 1–19.

[10] On this question see, for instance, K. B. McFarlane, 'The Investment of Sir John Fastolf's Profits of War', *Transactions of the Royal Historical Society*, 5th series, 7 (1957), pp. 91–116; and E. M. Carus-Wilson, 'Evidences of Industrial Growth on some Fifteenth-Century Manors', *Economic History Review*, 2nd series, 12 (1959–60), pp. 190–205.

pared to serve for as long as financial reward, whether in pay or some other form, was forthcoming. These financial requirements necessitated the active development of financial institutions, above all of the taxation systems, on both sides of the Channel. Such developments were an active recognition, too, of the need to share out the financial responsibilities of war among all the king's subjects, including the clergy, although in France the nobility was exempt from much of this burden. The effects of such change might be considerable. If the French Estates remained fairly docile, the need for the English Parliament to vote the extraordinary taxation which the requirements of war demanded presented the Commons in Parliament with the opportunity to criticise the government of the day or to voice suggestions for the better administration of the nation's business.[11]

Without such changes, the evolution of vital military institutions, notably the indenture, would have proved impossible. The large scale payment of armies was significant in two ways: it made possible the extension of war into more than a local quarrel; it also involved the nations in war because the nation, in providing payment for armies, was investing something of its wealth in war and in war institutions. The effort of the community as a whole is to be observed in parliamentary grants which were, by order of the Commons, on occasions specially ear-marked for use in the French war.

To what extent the community's feeling concerning war was accurately reflected in the assemblies, either in the national Parliament in England or in the local Estates in France, it is difficult to say. But the involvement of the nation may be closely observed in the attempts made, at many levels and by the use of different methods, to make it aware of what war was about and what issues were at stake. We have evidence of the ways used to foster a conscious public opinion by seeking its help in national defence or asking for its moral assistance through prayer and processions, as well as ample illustrations, if we need them, of the very diverse ways by which public sentiment could be urged to rally behind a cause. But opinion sometimes spoke out even when not urged to do so: it did so, especially, in times of anger and despair at the manner in which war was being waged. Thus we see frustrated opinion being justified in the murders of William de la Pole, duke of Suffolk, and of Adam Moleyns, bishop of Chichester, both considered responsible for the humiliations and disappointments of the last years of the Anglo-French war. Such outbursts were characteristic of a crisis in the English

[11] See E. B. Fryde, 'Parliament and the French War, 1336–40', *Essays in Medieval History presented to Bertie Wilkinson*, pp. 250–69; C. C. Bayley, 'The Campaign of 1375 and the Good Parliament', *English Historical Review*, 55 (1940), pp. 370–83; T. F. Tout, 'The English Parliament and Public Opinion, 1376–1388', *Collected Papers of Thomas Frederick Tout*, II, pp. 173–90.

conscience. Their importance lies in the fact that they indicate that men could become so passionately concerned with vital interests at stake in war that they could take the law into their own hands and commit extreme acts of violence against those who betrayed the country's interests. There is a marked contrast between such action and the relatively docile position adopted by the Commons in 1383 when they refused to give advice concerning foreign enterprises, leaving the resolution of such issues to the superior wisdom of the lords and the king. Less marked, but no less indicative, is a tract such as the *Libelle of English Polycye* (c. 1436), which attempted to persuade the government to take certain, active steps to defend English maritime interests in the Channel and in Calais. Public opinion did not always need to be stimulated by the methods of propaganda; it sometimes knew what it wanted, and was not always afraid to tell the government so.

It is from roots of this kind that nationalism was to spring. Far from being an abstract concept to which lip service might be paid, nationalism was becoming an increasingly positive sentiment which thrived upon war, and upon the feeling of common commitment which war could generate. Seen in the context which we have been describing, the growth of national sentiment is practical evidence of the fact that nations were coming to realise that an increasingly large number of their constituent elements was becoming caught up, in some way or other, in war. Nationalism, as the product of a war-situation, was the mark of cohesion within a nation, commonly united against an enemy. It was in this spirit that the Norman 'patriot', Alain Chartier, when reflecting upon the evils and difficulties of war in the fifteenth century, wrote of himself and of others like him as the sons of a common Mother, France.[12] With his country as his mother, his relationship with those who spoke the same language was clearly established. Those who spoke no French, or poor French, were foreigners, exploiting the country for their own end. These were the enemy.

Finally, attention is also drawn to another important development which was closely related to war. The need for communication between states (a task often given to heralds) and, above all, the need for means to negotiate between independent rulers over a long period of war led to a greater use of formal diplomatic exchanges. This resulted in a considerable increase in the numbers of persons involved in diplomacy, especially since the size of embassies, which, on really important international occasions, might reach the number of fifteen or twenty formally-appointed ambassadors on each side, could be quite large. The personnel of embassies was often varied: a king had to be represented by someone of the blood royal, or at least by a great nobleman; and the experts, too, were needed to carry out and supervise the real business of the embassy,

[12] Alain Chartier, *Le Quadrilogue Invectif*, p. 20.

the negotiation of terms. Such men provided not only the expertise required, but the experience of a particular problem (such as the legal difficulties underlying Anglo–French differences), since they were, with increasing frequency, appointed to a succession of missions aimed at resolving the same diplomatic problem. Diplomacy, therefore, was another aspect of war which was gradually taken over by the men of skill and experience. In this respect, as the French were obliged to admit in the fifteenth century, the English had established a long lead. By the first years of the fourteenth century, they had already created an office, the Keeper of the Processes, whose holder was responsible for maintaining the documentation and legal evidence required for the successful pursuit of precise political ends. Responding to the exigencies of war, English diplomacy was to develop during the course of the next century or so, even though it was not always successful in avoiding or postponing war. In England, as well as abroad, it was to provide men with an academic legal training, the graduates in canon and civil law from Oxford and Cambridge, with an opportunity to serve the king with their experience of these codes which were the nearest the middle ages came to the concept of international law. In this way, diplomacy became increasingly professionalised. The next step, not quite yet reached in northern Europe, although beginning to be known in Italy, was the resident ambassador. However, with their expertise and experience, the ambassadors of England and France were moving in the direction which would before so very long witness the appointment of permanent diplomats resident in foreign courts.

The study of war in the late middle ages is, generally speaking, beginning to take on new approaches to the subject. On the one hand there is a need for a considerable amount of detailed study about the administration of war: H. J. Hewitt (*The Organization of War under Edward III, 1338–1362*) has led the way for England. Philippe Contamine (*Guerre, État et Société à la fin du Moyen Age*) has now done fine work of a similar nature for France, although his work is altogether more massive in volume and more far-reaching in conception, scope and time-span covered. But the subject is far from exhausted. We require to know more, for instance, about defence systems in both England and France; about navies and their methods of organisation and recruitment; about English armies which went to France; taxation and its relationship to war, too, could be fruitfully investigated, so that we may have a clearer understanding how the sums actually voted in Parliament or by the Estates came to be spent—or, as was sometimes the case, misspent.

There is, therefore, a whole field of military organisation to be studied, the emphasis being placed upon the work and organisation of the quartermaster and the pioneer who deserve greater attention than they have been given hitherto. But in addition to this there is a need to study wars in terms of the societies in which they were fought, to underline the fact that wars not only affected the historic development of societies and social groups, but were often less affected by the principles over which they were fought than by the needs of people who became involved in them. Thus even the best conceived plans of diplomats could be brought to nought if those whose personal interests they manipulated were opposed to them,[13] (e.g. VI.2.c). There is therefore a need to emphasise the important fact that men, either as individuals or collectively, were not willing to be used as pawns in a game between kings. The public rights of subjects were of greater importance than the private rights of kings:[14] so those who negotiated peace terms between France and England in 1439 were reminded. It brings home to us the increasing awareness that dawned during the period that a monarch's legal rights were not worth fighting for if the material interests of his people were to suffer as a direct consequence of a war fought in his name. Attitudes to war were undergoing a change.

It is thus chiefly the study of the effects of war upon society that will be of the greatest value in future historical enquiry. In England, the way has to some extent already been shown. But we need to know more than we do at present of the impact of war upon the English population. That impact was probably not felt in the same way in all parts of the country. If in the north, the threat and, all too often, the reality of invasion from Scotland was an ever-present feature of life (V.2.c), to be used as a good excuse for refusing to contribute financially to the French war, in the south a form of defensive system likewise existed to keep the enemy at bay, chiefly at times of crisis. It is not unlikely that the inland shires felt the invasion threat less: were they therefore tapped for a greater contribution, especially in manpower, towards armies being sent abroad? A regional approach to this problem might perhaps prove the most rewarding. Such information is not normally contained in the better-known sources such as the chronicles. The future here must be in the thorough investigation of private collections—such as the Fastolf Papers at Magdalen College, Oxford, used by the late K. B. McFarlane and others—the contents of some local record offices (including ecclesiastical archives), and, above all, the great national manuscript collections of the British Museum, the Public Record Office and the National Libraries of Scotland and Wales. Much as these have yielded

[13] J. J. N. Palmer, *England, France and Christendom, 1377–99*, Chs. 8 and 9; C. T. Allmand, 'La Normandie devant l'opinion anglaise à la fin de la Guerre de Cent Ans', *Bibliothèque de l'École des Chartes*, 128 (1970), pp. 345–68.
[14] 'Documents relating to the Anglo-French Negotiations of 1439', ed. C. T. Allmand, *Camden Miscellany*, XXIV, p. 149.

in the past, they still have much to reveal, so that a fuller and consequently truer picture of society at war may emerge.

In France, the picture is one of light and hope. The way was shown, a quarter of a century ago, by the publication of Robert Boutruche's classic study, *La crise d'une société: seigneurs et paysans du Bordelais pendant la Guerre de Cent Ans*. If few can hope to measure up to the standards reflected in that now famous study, the approach may at least be emulated. Like so many French studies of value, it is essentially regional: it employs methods borrowed from statistics and sociology which have much to teach us; and, not least, it is firmly based upon the material of archives, both local and national. Among these last the most likely to yield much knowledge are legal records, notarial registers of accords and settlements, 'transcripts' of the proceedings of the *parlement de Paris* and, for a period, that of Poitiers, both forms of documentation which, in spite of the difficulties which they pose to the researcher (these are as much practical as anything) allow him to gain a picture of a society living out its problems and coming to terms with itself, both in time of peace and of war. Sources of this kind are becoming increasingly appreciated as very valuable evidence for the study of society—and especially of litigious society—and have been used with great effect by a number of historians.[15]

Such, one may venture to suggest, may be some of the main lines of approach for future study. The geographical scope must be limited: the approach should be modern, and the materials used, whether accounts or legal records, should be those which enable the historian to study war in analytical terms. The possibilities, not least of comparison with other societies, whether they be those of Italy, Germany or Spain, are considerable—and exciting.

[15] For example by P-C. Timbal (*La Guerre de Cent Ans vue à travers le registres du Parlement, 1337–1369*) and A. Bossuat (for whose work see the select bibliography).

SELECT BIBLIOGRAPHY

ABBREVIATIONS

AB	Annales de Bourgogne	MA	Le Moyen Age
ABret	Annales de Bretagne	MM	Mariner's Mirror
AE	Annales de l'Est	MSAN	Mémoires de la Société
AM	Annales du Midi		des Antiquaires de
AN	Annales de Normandie		Normandie
BEC	Bibliothèque de l'École	OHE	Oxford History of
	des Chartes		England
BIHR	Bulletin of the Institute	PBA	Proceedings of the British
	of Historical Research		Academy
BJRL	Bulletin of the John	RH	Revue Historique
	Ryland's Library	RHD	Revue d'Histoire
CHJ	Cambridge Historical		diplomatique
	Journal	RHDFÉ	Revue historique de droit
CJH	Canadian Journal of		français et étranger
	History	RHE	Revue d'Histoire
CYS	Canterbury and York		ecclésiastique
	Society	RHS	Royal Historical Society
EconHR	Economic History Review	RS	Rolls Series
EETS	Early English Text	SATF	Société des Anciens
	Society		Textes Français
EHR	English Historical Review	SHF	Société de l'Histoire de
HMC	Historical Manuscripts		France
	Commission	SHN	Société de l'Histoire de
HJ	Historical Journal		Normandie
HT	History Today	SHP	Société de l'Histoire de
JSA	Journal of the Society of		Paris
	Archivists	STS	Scottish Text Society
JWCI	Journal of the Warburg	TRHS	Transactions of the Royal
	and Courtauld Institutes		Historical Society

General—Complete Texts

AQUINAS, THOMAS. *Summa Theologiae* (numerous editions).
L'Art de Chevalerie. Traduction du De Re Militari de Végèce par Jean de Meun. Ed. U. ROBERT. SATF. Paris 1897. [Indicates the growing popularity of Vegetius. See *Knyghthode and Bataile*, below.]

BARBOUR, JOHN. *The Bruce; or the Book of the most excellent and noble prince, Robert de Broyss, King of Scots.* Ed. W. W. SKEAT. EETS. Extra Series 11, 21, 29, 55. 2 vols. London 1870–89. STS. 2 vols. Edinburgh–London 1894. [A vivid verse chronicle.]

BASIN, THOMAS. *Histoire des Règnes de Charles VII et de Louis XI.* Ed. J. QUICHERAT. SHF. 4 vols. Paris 1855–9. [Latin text translated into French as *Histoire de Charles VII.* Ed. and trans. C. Samaran. 2 vols. Paris 1964. Les Chroniques de l'Histoire de France au Moyen Age.]

The Black Prince. An Historical Poem, written in French, by Chandos Herald. Ed. H. O. COXE. Roxburghe Club. London 1842.

The Boke of Noblesse : addressed to King Edward the Fourth on his invasion of France in 1475. Ed. JOHN G. NICHOLS. Roxburghe Club. London 1860. [One man's view of war and peace.]

The Book of the Ordre of Chyualry [William Caxton]. Ed. A. T. P. BYLES. EETS. Original Series 168. London 1926. [Important as an indicator of practices and values.]

BROMYARD, JOHN. *Summa Predicantium.* Basle 1484.

The Brut; or The Chronicles of England. Ed. FRIEDRICH W. D. BRIE. EETS. 2 vols. Original Series 131, 136. London 1906, 1908.

BUEIL, JEAN DE. *Le Jouvencel.* Ed. L. LECESTRE. 2 vols. SHF. Paris 1887–9. [Important.]

CHARTIER, ALAIN. *Le Quadrilogue Invectif.* Ed. E. DROZ. 2nd. rev. ed. Paris 1950.

The Chronicle of Jean de Venette. Trans. JEAN BIRDSALL. Ed. RICHARD A. NEWHALL. New York 1953.

Chronicon Galfridi le Baker de Swynebroke. Ed. E. MAUNDE THOMPSON. Oxford 1889.

Chronique de Mathieu d'Escouchy. Ed. G. DU FRESNE DE BEAUCOURT. SHF. 3. vols. Paris 1863–4. [Useful for the study of war.]

Chronique de Richard Lescot. Ed. JEAN LEMOINE. SHF. Paris 1896.

Chronique des Quatre Premiers Valois (1327–1393). Ed. SIMÉON LUCE. SHF. Paris 1862.

COMMYNES, PHILIPPE DE. *Mémoires.* Eds. J. CALMETTE and G. DURVILLE. 3 vols. Paris 1924–5. Repr. 1964. [A classic work.]

— *Memoirs. The Reign of Louis XI 1461–83.* Trans M. JONES. Harmondsworth 1972.

The Coventry Leet Book; or Mayor's Register. Ed. M. D. HARRIS. EETS. 2 vols. Original Series 134, 138. London 1907, 1909.

Le Débat des Hérauts d'Armes de France et d'Angleterre, suivi de The Debate between the Heralds of England end France, by John Coke. Eds. L. PANNIER and P. MEYER. SATF. Paris 1877.

The essential portions of Nicholas Upton's De Studio Militari, before 1446, translated by John Blount, Fellow of All Souls (c. 1500). Ed. F. P. BARNARD. Oxford 1931. [Useful for the formal and procedural aspects of war.]

FROISSART, JEAN. *Oeuvres: Chroniques.* Ed. KERVYN DE LETTENHOVE.

25 vols. Brussels 1870–77. [The greatest of the war-chroniclers of the fourteenth century.]

The Great Chronicle of London. Eds. A. H. THOMAS and I. D. THORNLEY. London 1938.

'William Gregory's Chronicle of London'. In *The Historical Collections of a Citizen of London in the Fifteenth Century.* Ed. JAMES GAIRDNER. Camden Society. London 1876.

Histoire de Gaston IV, comte de Foix, par Guillaume Leseur. Ed. HENRI COURTEAULT. SHF. 2 vols. Paris 1896. [A valuable chronicle for military affairs.]

Historie of the Arrivall of Edward IV in England and the finall Recouerye of his Kingdomes from Henry VI, A.D. MCCCCLXXI. Ed. J. BRUCE. Camden Society. London 1838. [A professional view of military events.]

Hoccleve's Works: III. The Regement of Princes. Ed. F. J. FURNIVALL. EETS. Extra Series 72. London 1897.

Journal d'un Bourgeois de Paris 1405–1449. Ed. A. TUETEY. SHP. Paris 1881. Trans. J. SHIRLEY: *A Parisian Journal 1405–1449.* Oxford 1968. [A view of war by a non-combatant.]

Knyghthode and Bataile. A XVth century verse paraphrase of Flavius Vegetius Renatus' treatise 'De Re Militari'. Eds. R. DYBOSKI and Z. M. AREND. EETS. Original Series 201. London 1935. [See *L'Art de Chevalerie*, above.]

LEGNANO, JOHN OF. *Tractatus de Bello, de Represaliis et de Duello.* Ed. T. E. HOLLAND. Trans J. L. BRIERLY. Oxford 1917. [A legal work of great influence.]

The Libelle of Englyshe Polycye. A Poem on the use of Sea-Power, 1436. Ed. GEORGE WARNER. Oxford 1926. Also printed in *Political Poems and Songs.* Ed. T. WRIGHT. RS. London 1861. II, pp. 157–206.

Le Livre des faicts du bon messire Jean le Maingre, dit Boucicaut, maréchal de France et gouverneur de Gennes. Eds. J. F. MICHAUD and J. J. F. POUJOULAT. In *Nouvelle Collection des Mémoires pour servir à l'Histoire de France.* Vol. II. Paris 1836.

Ordonnances des Roys de France de la Troisième Race. Various editors. 21 vols. Paris 1723–1849. Repr. 1967–8. [Contains many basic texts.]

PISAN, CHRISTINE DE. *The Book of Fayttes of Armes and of Chyualrye.* Trans. WILLIAM CAXTON, Ed. A. T. P. BYLES, EETS. Original Series 189. London 1932. Corrected reissue 1937. [Fundamental for an understanding of war in the late Middle Ages.]

— *Le Livre des Fais et Bonnes Meurs du Sage Roy Charles V.* Eds. J. F. MICHAUD and J. J. F. POUJOULAT. In *Nouvelle Collection des Mémoires pour servir à l'Histoire de France.* Vol II. Paris 1836. [Useful information on the techniques of war.]

The Register of John Trefnant, Bishop of Hereford (A.D.1389–1404). Ed. W. W. CAPES. Cantilupe Society. Hereford 1914. Also published by CYS, London 1916, under the title *Registrum Johannis Trefnant, Episcopi Herefordensis, A.D. MCCCLXXXIX–MCCCCIV.*

The Register of Thomas Spofford, Bishop of Hereford (A.D. 1422–1448). Ed. A. T. BANNISTER. Cantilupe Society. Hereford 1917. Also published by CYS, London 1919, under the title *Registrum Thome Spofford, Episcopi Herefordensis, A.D. MCCCCXXII–MCCCCXLVIII*.

Registre Criminel du Châtelet de Paris du 6 septembre 1389 au 18 mai 1392. Publié pour la Société des Bibliophiles François. 2 vols. Paris 1861, 1864. [Much evidence of the nefarious influence of war upon society.]

Rotuli Parliamentorum. 6 vols. London 1767–77.

Le Songe du Vieil Pèlerin of Philippe de Mézières, Chancellor of Cyprus. Ed. GEORGE W. COOPLAND. 2 vols. Cambridge 1969. [An important work of reform of the late fourteenth century.]

Statutes of the Realm. 11 vols. London 1810–28.

The Tree of Battles of Honoré Bonet. Trans. GEORGE W. COOPLAND. Liverpool 1949. [Fundamental and influential.]

El Victorial. Crónica de Don Pero Niño, conde de Buelna, por su alférez, Gutierre Diez de Games. Ed. JUAN DE MATA CARRIAZO. Madrid 1940. Trans. JOAN EVANS: *The Unconquered Knight. A Chronicle of the Deeds of Don Pero Niño, Count of Buelna*. London 1928.

WAURIN, JEAN DE. *Recueil des Croniques et Anchiennes Istories de la Grant Bretaigne, à present nommé Engleterre*. Eds. W. and E. L. C. P. HARDY. RS. 5 vols. London 1864–91. [The first three volumes are translated into English in the same series.]

General—Collections of Texts

Aquinas: Selected Political Writings. Ed. A. P. D'ENTRÈVES. Trans. J. G. DAWSON. Oxford 1948.

Archives historiques du département de la Gironde. Paris–Bordeaux: 9 (1867); 65 (1925–6).

Choix de pièces inédites relatives au règne de Charles VI. Ed. L. DOUËT-D'ARCQ. SHF. 2 vols. Paris 1863–4. [Contains many interesting documents.]

Chronique du Mont-Saint-Michel (1343–1468). Ed. SIMÉON LUCE. SATF. 2 vols. Paris 1879, 1883. [Not a chronicle, but a most interesting collection of documents drawn from archives.]

CONTAMINE, PHILIPPE. *Azincourt*. Paris 1964.

La désolation des églises, monastères et hôpitaux en France pendant la Guerre de Cent Ans. Ed. HENRI DENIFLE. 2 vols. Paris, 1897, 1899. [Useful, but essentially one-sided evidence.]

Documents inédits sur l'invasion anglaise et les États au temps de Philippe VI et de Jean le Bon. Ed. A. GUESNON. Paris 1898.

'Documents relating to the Anglo–French Negotiations of 1439'. Ed. C. T. ALLMAND. *Camden Miscellany XXIV*. RHS. London 1972, pp. 79–149.

English Historical Documents: IV. 1327–1485. Ed. A. R. MYERS. London 1969.

English History in Contemporary Poetry:
   I. The Fourteenth Century. Ed. H. BRUCE. London 1928.
   II. Lancaster and York, 1399–1485. Ed. C. L. KINGSFORD. London
   1913. Reissued 1933.
Foedera, conventiones, literae et cujuscunque generis acta publica. Ed.
   T. RYMER. 10 vols. The Hague 1745. [A major source.]
La Guerre de Cent Ans vue à travers les registres du Parlement 1337–1369.
   Ed. P.-C. TIMBAL. Paris 1961. [A valuable collection of original legal
   documents illustrating many aspects of war and its effects.]
*History of the Battle of Agincourt and of the Expedition of Henry the Fifth
   into France in 1415.* Ed. N. H. NICOLAS. 2nd ed. London 1832.
   Repr. 1970.
'Indentures of Retinue with John of Gaunt, Duke of Lancaster, enrolled
   in Chancery 1367–1399'. Ed. N. B. LEWIS. *Camden Miscellany XXII.*
   RHS. London 1964. Pp. 77–112.
*Letters and Papers illustrative of the Wars of the English in France during
   the Reign of Henry the Sixth, King of England.* Ed. JOSEPH STEVENSON.
   RS. 2 vols in 3. London, 1861, 1864. [A veritable mine of informa-
   tion.]
*Lettres de Rois, Reines et autres Personnages des Cours de France et
   d'Angleterre depuis Louis VII jusqu'à Henri IV, tirées des archives
   de Londres par Bréquigny.* Ed. J. J. CHAMPOLLION-FIGEAC. Collection
   de documents inédits sur l'histoire de France. Vol. II (1301–1515).
   Paris 1847. [A valuable source of information.]
*Memorials of London and London Life in the XIIIth, XIVth and XVth
   Centuries, A.D. 1276–1419.* Trans. H. T. RILEY. London 1868.
Paris pendant la domination anglaise (1420–1436). Ed. A. LONGNON.
   SHP. Paris 1878. [Useful evidence of the effects of war.]
*Recueil des privilèges accordés à la ville de Bordeaux par Charles VII et
   Louis XI.* Ed. M. GOURON. Bordeaux 1937.
Report on the Manuscripts of the Corporation of Beverley. HMC. London
   1900.
*Rouen au temps de Jeanne d'Arc et pendant l'occupation anglaise (1419–
   1449).* Ed. PAUL LECACHEUX. SHN. Rouen–Paris 1931. [Evidence
   of how an enemy-occupied city lived.]
Selected English Works of John Wyclif. Ed. T. ARNOLD. 3 vols. Oxford
   1869–71.
Twenty-Six Political and other Poems. Ed. J. KAIL. EETS. Original Series
   124. London 1904.

Attitudes to War

BARBER, RICHARD. *The Knight and Chivalry.* London 1970.
BOND, BRIAN. 'The "Just War" in Historical Perspective'. *HT*, 16 (1966),
   pp. 111–19.
COULTON, G. G. *The Chronicler of European Chivalry.* In *The Studio.*
   Special Winter Number. London 1930. [A full-length study of
   Froissart's Chronicle.]

FERGUSON, ALBERT B. *The Indian Summer of English Chivalry: Studies in the Decline and Transformation of Chivalric Idealism.* Durham, North Carolina 1960.

HUIZINGA, JOHAN. *The Waning of the Middle Ages.* Trans. F. Hopman. London 1924. Reprinted Harmondsworth 1972. [A classic work.]

— 'La valeur politique et militaire des idées de chevalerie à la fin du moyen âge'. *RHD*, 35 (1921), pp. 126–38.

JARRETT, BEDE. *Social Theories of the Middle Ages, 1200–1500.* London 1926.

KEEN, MAURICE H. *The Laws of War in the Late Middle Ages.* London 1965. [A study of importance and significance.]

— 'Brotherhood in Arms'. *History*, 47 (1962), pp. 1–17.

KILGOUR, R. L. *The Decline of Chivalry as shown in the French Literature of the Late Middle Ages.* Cambridge, Mass. 1937.

LEWIS, PETER S. 'Une devise de chevalerie inconnue, crée par le comte de Foix? Le Dragon'. *AM*, 76 (1964), pp. 77–84.

MCFARLANE, K. B. 'An Indenture of Agreement between two English Knights for Mutual Aid and Counsel in Peace and War, 5 December 1298'. *BIHR*, 38 (1965), pp. 200–10.

— 'A Business-partnership in War and Administration, 1421–1445'. *EHR*, 78 (1963), pp. 290–310. [A highly suggestive article.]

MCKISACK, MAY. *The Fourteenth Century.* OHE. Oxford 1959. [Contains a chapter on chivalry.]

MATHEW, GERVASE. 'Ideals of Knighthood in late Fourteenth-Century England'. In *Studies in Medieval History presented to Frederick Maurice Powicke.* Eds. R. W. HUNT, W. A. PANTIN, and R. W. SOUTHERN. Oxford 1948. Pp. 354–62.

— *The Court of Richard II.* London 1968.

PRESTAGE, E. (Ed.). *Chivalry. Its Historical Significance and Civilizing Influence.* London 1928.

RENOUARD, YVES. 'L'Ordre de la Jarretière et l'Ordre de l'Étoile'. *MA*, 55 (1949), pp. 281–300.

SQUIBB, G. D. *The High Court of Chivalry. A Study of the Civil Law in England.* Oxford 1959.

VALE, M. G. A. 'A Fourteenth-Century Order of Chivalry: the "Tiercelet"'. *EHR*, 82 (1967), pp. 332–41.

VANDERPOL, ALFRED M. *Le droit de guerre d'après les théologiens et les canonistes du moyen-âge.* Paris–Brussels 1911.

— *La doctrine scolastique du droit de guerre.* Paris 1925.

WILMOTTE, MAURICE. *Froissart.* Brussels 1948.

Causes of the Hundred Years' War

CUTTINO, G. P. 'Historical Revision: The Causes of the Hundred Years' War'. *Speculum*, 31 (1956), pp. 463–77. [A useful survey of the literature up to 1956.]

DÉPREZ, E. *Les Préliminaires de la Guerre de Cent Ans.* Paris 1902. [Still very valuable.]

LE PATOUREL, JOHN. 'Edward III and the Kingdom of France'. *History*, 43 (1958), pp. 173–89. [Important.]
— 'The Origins of the War'. In *The Hundred Years' War*. Ed. K. A. FOWLER. London 1971. Pp. 28–50. [The latest—and perhaps the best.]
LIEBMAN, C. J. 'Un sermon de Philippe de Villette, abbé de Saint-Denis, pour la levée de l'Oriflamme (1414)'. *Romania*, 68 (1944–45), pp. 444–70.
LUCAS, HENRY S. *The Low Countries and the Hundred Years' War, 1326–1347*. Ann Arbor 1929. [A well-known study.]
TEMPLEMAN, G. 'Edward III and the Beginnings of the Hundred Years' War'. *TRHS*, 5th series, 2 (1952), pp. 69–88. [A useful survey of the literature up to 1952.]
WOLFF, PHILIPPE. 'Un problème d'origines: La Guerre de Cent Ans'. In *Éventail de l'histoire vivante: homage à Lucien Febvre* II. 1953, pp. 141–8.

Narrative Histories of the War

CALMETTE, J. and PÉRINELLE, G. *Louis XI et l'Angleterre*. Paris 1930.
CALMETTE, J. and DÉPREZ, E. *Histoire Générale: Histoire du Moyen Age. La France et l'Angleterre en conflit*. Ed. G. GLOTZ. Vol. VII (i). Paris 1937.
CONTAMINE, PHILIPPE. *La Guerre de Cent Ans*. Paris 1968. [Short, recent narrative account.]
COVILLE, A. *Les premiers Valois et la Guerre de Cent Ans 1328–1422*. Histoire de France. Ed. E. LAVISSE. Vol. IV (i). Paris 1902.
CRUICKSHANK, C. G. *The English Occupation of Tournai, 1513–1519*. Oxford 1971. [Shows how the Anglo–French conflict continued into the sixteenth century.]
FOWLER, KENNETH A. *The Age of Plantagenet and Valois*. London 1967. [The best recent survey, taking into account modern approaches to the history of war.]
JACOB. E. F. *Henry V and the Invasion of France*. London 1947.
— *The Fifteenth Century*. OHE. Oxford 1961.
KEEN, MAURICE H. *England in the Later Middle Ages*. London 1972. [Stresses the influence of wars upon late medieval England.]
PERROY, ÉDOUARD. *The Hundred Years' War*. Trans. W. B. WELLS. London 1951. [The classic account: essential reading.]
— *L'expansion de l'Orient et la naissance de la civilisation occidentale*. (Histoire générale des Civilisations: III. Le Moyen Age) 5th rev. ed. Paris 1967. [A good chapter on war.]
PETIT-DUTAILLIS, C. *Charles VII, Louis XI et les premières années de Charles VIII 1422–1492*. Histoire de France. Ed. E. LAVISSE. Vol. IV (ii). Paris 1902.
RUSSELL, PETER E. L. R. *The English Intervention in Spain and Portugal in the Time of Edward III and Richard II*. Oxford 1955.
THIELEMANS, MARIE-ROSE. *Bourgogne et Angleterre. Relations politiques et*

économiques entre les Pays-Bas bourguignons et l'Angleterre, 1435–1467. Brussels 1966.

Campaigns

BURNE, ALFRED H. *The Crécy War. A Military History of the Hundred Years' War from 1337 to the peace of Brétigny, 1360*. London 1955. [A modern soldier's view of medieval warfare.]
— *The Agincourt War. A Military History of the latter part of the Hundred Years' War from 1369 to 1453*. London 1956.
— 'John of Gaunt's Grande Chevauchée'. *HT*, 9 (1959), pp. 113–21.
HEWITT, H. J. *The Black Prince's Expedition of 1355–1357*. Manchester 1958. [An excellent example of military history of the modern kind.]
LANDER, J. R. 'The Hundred Years' War and Edward IV's 1475 Campaign in France'. In *Tudor Men and Statesmen: Studies in English Law and Government*. Ed. A. J. SLAVIN. Baton Rouge 1972, pp. 70–100.
MILLER, EDWARD. *War in the North*. Hull 1960. [On border warfare.]
MORRIS, JOHN E. *The Welsh Wars of Edward I*. Oxford 1901. [A pioneering work.]
— 'The Archers at Crécy'. *EHR*, 12 (1897), pp. 427–36.
NEWHALL, RICHARD A. *The English Conquest of Normandy, 1416–1424. A Study in Fifteenth-Century Warfare*. New Haven and London 1924. [Important.]
NICHOLSON, RANALD. *Edward III and the Scots. The Formative Years of a Military Career, 1327–1335*. Oxford 1965.

Armies and their Organisation

BELLIER-DUMAINE, C. 'L'administration du duché de Bretagne sous le règne de Jean V: les institutions militaires'. *ABret*, 16 (1900–1901), pp. 112–29.
BRUSTEN, CHARLES. *L'Armée Bourguignonne de 1465 à 1468*. Brussels 1953.
CONTAMINE, PHILIPPE. *Guerre, État et Société à la fin du Moyen Age. Études sur les armées des rois de France, 1337–1494*. Paris and The Hague 1972. [A study of fundamental importance.]
— 'Batailles: Bannières: Compagnies. Aspects de l'organisation militaire française pendant la première partie de la Guerre de Cent Ans'. *Cahiers Vernonnais*, 4 (1964), pp. 19–32. [Important.]
— 'Les armées française et anglaise à l'époque de Jeanne d'Arc'. *Revue des Sociétés Savantes de la Haute Normandie: Lettres et Sciences Humaines*, 57 (1970), pp. 5–33. [Useful comparative analysis.]
— 'The French Nobility and the War'. In *The Hundred Years' War*. Ed. K. A. FOWLER. London 1971, pp. 135–62.
CRUICKSHANK, C. G. *Army Royal. Henry VIII's Invasion of France, 1513*. Oxford 1969.
HEWITT, H. J. *The Organization of War under Edward III, 1338–62*. Manchester and New York 1966. [A book of the greatest importance.]
— 'The Organisation of War'. In *The Hundred Years' War*. Ed. K. A. FOWLER. London 1971, pp. 75–95.

JONES, MICHAEL. 'An Indenture between Robert, lord Mohaut, and Sir John de Bracebridge for life service in peace and war, 1310'. *JSA*, 4 (1972), pp. 384–94.

JUSSELIN, M. 'Comment la France se préparait à la Guerre de Cent Ans'. *BEC*, 73 (1912), pp. 209–36.

LEWIS, N. B. 'An early indenture of military service, 27 July 1287'. *BIHR*, 13 (1935–6), pp. 85–9. [Professor Lewis' articles are essential reading.]

— 'The English Forces in Flanders, August–November 1297'. In *Studies in Medieval History presented to Frederick Maurice Powicke*. Eds. R. W. HUNT, W. A. PANTIN and R. W. SOUTHERN. Oxford 1948, pp. 310–18.

— 'The Summons of the English Feudal Levy: 5 April 1327'. In *Essays in Medieval History presented to Bertie Wilkinson*. Eds. T. A. SANDQUIST and M. R. POWICKE. Toronto 1969, p. 236–49.

— 'The Recruitment and Organization of a Contract Army, May to November 1337'. *BIHR*, 37 (1964), pp. 1–19.

— 'The Last Medieval Summons of the English Feudal Levy, 13 June 1385'. *EHR*, 73 (1958), pp. 1–26.

— 'The Organisation of Indentured Retinues in Fourteenth-Century England'. *TRHS*, 4th series, 27 (1945), pp. 29–39. Repr. in *Essays in Medieval History*. Ed. R. W. SOUTHERN. London 1968, pp. 200–12.

LOT, FERDINAND and FAWTIER, ROBERT. *Histoire des Institutions françaises au Moyen Age: II. Institutions royales*. Paris 1958. [Contains two useful chapters on the French army and navy.]

LYON, BRYCE D. *From Fief to Indenture. The Transition from Feudal to Non-Feudal Contract in Western Europe*. Cambridge, Mass. 1957. [Important; includes a chapter on 'The Military Role of the Fief-Rente'.]

NEWHALL, R. A. *Muster and Review*. Harvard 1940. [Important for English military developments in the fifteenth century.]

PALMER, JOHN J. N. 'The last summons of the feudal army in England (1385)'. *EHR*, 83 (1968), pp. 771–5. [Reply to N. B. Lewis, *EHR*, 1958.]

POWICKE, MICHAEL R. *Military Obligation in Medieval England. A Study in Liberty and Duty*. Oxford 1962. [A valuable study.]

— 'Lancastrian Captains'. In *Essays in Medieval History presented to Bertie Wilkinson*. Eds. T. A. SANDQUIST and M. R. POWICKE. Toronto 1969, pp. 371–82.

— 'The English Aristocracy and the War'. In *The Hundred Years' War*. Ed. K. A. FOWLER. London 1971, pp. 122–34.

PRINCE, ALBERT E. 'The Army and Navy'. In *The English Government at Work, 1327–1336: I. Central and Prerogative Administration*. Eds. JAMES F. WILLARD and WILLIAM A. MORRIS. Mediaeval Academy of America. Cambridge, Mass. 1940, pp. 332–93. [Clear outline of English military and naval administration at the start of the Hundred Years' War.]

— 'The Indenture System under Edward III'. In *Historical Essays in*

Honour of James Tait. Eds. J. G. EDWARDS, V. H. GALBRAITH and
E. F. JACOB. Manchester 1933, pp. 283–97. [Important.]
— 'The Payment of Army Wages in Edward III's Reign'. *Speculum*,
19 (1944), pp. 137–60.
— 'The Strength of English Armies in the Reign of Edward III'.
EHR, 46 (1931), pp. 353–71.
RAMSAY, JAMES H. 'The Strength of English Armies in the Middle Ages'.
EHR, 29 (1914), pp. 221–7.
REEVES, A. COMPTON. 'Some of Humphrey Stafford's Military Indentures'.
Nottingham Mediaeval Studies, 16 (1972), pp. 80–91.
SHERBORNE, JAMES W. 'Indentured Retinues and English Expeditions to
France, 1369–1380'. *EHR*, 79 (1964), pp. 718–46. [A useful
contribution.]
VALLET DE VIRIVILLE, A. 'Notices et extraits de chartes et de manuscrits
appartenant au British Museum de Londres'. *BEC*, 2nd series,
3 (1846), pp. 110–47.

Captains and their Companies

BOSSUAT, ANDRÉ. *Perrinet Gressart et François de Surienne, agents de
l'Angleterre*. Paris 1936. [A fine study.]
— *Jeanne d'Arc*. Paris 1968. [A short but balanced 'life'.]
BUCHAN, ALICE. *Joan of Arc and the Recovery of France*. London 1948.
[The best short 'life' in English.]
CHAMPION, PIERRE. *Guillaume de Flavy, capitaine de Compiègne. Contri-
bution à l'histoire de Jeanne d'Arc, et à l'étude de la vie militaire et
privée au XVe siècle*. Paris 1906. [A useful study of a fifteenth-
century military leader, with good documentation.]
COSNEAU, E. *Le Connétable de Richemont (Artur de Bretagne, 1393–1458)*.
Paris 1886. [Detailed study of an important military and political
personality.]
FOWLER, KENNETH A. *The King's Lieutenant. Henry of Grosmont, first Duke
of Lancaster, 1310–1361*. London 1969. [Good on military affairs.]
QUICHERAT, J. *Rodrigue de Villandrando*. Paris 1879. [A famous leader of
'irregular' troops.]
TUETEY, A. *Les Écorcheurs sous Charles VII*. 2 vols. Montbéliard 1874.
[Basic study: good documentation.]

Navies

KEPLER, J. S. 'The Effects of the Battle of Sluys upon the Administration
of English Naval Impressment 1340–1343'. *Speculum*, 48 (1973) pp.
70–7.
LA RONCIÈRE, C. DE. *Histoire de la Marine française*. 6 vols. Paris 1899–
1934. [Basic study of the French navy.]
NICOLAS, N. H. *A History of the Royal Navy*. 2 vols. London 1847. [Still
the best study of the English navy of this period.]
OPPENHEIM, M. *A History of the Administration of the Royal Navy and of*

Merchant Shipping in relation to the Navy. Vol. I. London and New York 1896. [Includes an interesting first chapter.]

REID, W. STANFORD. 'Sea-Power in the Anglo–Scottish War, 1296–1328'. *MM*, 46 (1960), pp. 7–23.

RICHMOND, COLIN F. 'The Keeping of the Seas during the Hundred Years' War: 1422–1440'. *History*, 49 (1964), pp. 283–98. [Important.]

— 'English Naval Power in the Fifteenth Century'. *History*, 52 (1967), pp. 1–15. [Important.]

— 'The War at Sea'. In *The Hundred Years' War*. Ed. K. A. FOWLER. London 1971, pp. 96–121. [A valuable survey.]

SHERBORNE, JAMES W. 'The Hundred Years' War. The English Navy, Shipping and Manpower, 1369–1389'. *Past and Present*, 37 (1967), pp. 163–75. [Places the war at sea in its proper perspective.]

— 'The Battle of La Rochelle and the War at Sea, 1372–5'. *BIHR*, 42 (1969), pp. 17–29.

WAITES, BRYAN. 'The Fighting Galley'. *HT*, 18 (1968), pp. 337–43.

Personnel, Weapons and Supplies

BURLEY, S. J. 'The Victualling of Calais, 1347–65'. *BIHR*, 31 (1958), pp. 49 ff.

GAIER, C. 'L'approvisionnement et le régime alimentaire des troupes dans le duché de Limbourg et les terres d'Outre-Meuse vers 1400'. *MA*, 74 (1968), pp. 551–75.

GASK, G. E. 'The Medical Staff of Edward III'. In *Sidelights on the History of Medicine*. Ed. Z. COPE. London 1957, pp. 47–56.

HOOKER, J. R. 'Notes on the organisation and supply of the Tudor military under Henry VII'. *Huntington Library Quarterly*, 23 (1959–60), pp. 19–31.

PRESTWICH, MICHAEL. 'Victualling estimates for the English garrisons in Scotland during the early fourteenth century'. *EHR*, 82 (1967), pp. 536–43.

WOLFF, PHILIPPE. 'Achats d'armes pour Philippe le Bel dans la région toulousaine (1295)'. *AM*, 61 (1948), pp. 84–91.

Prisoners and Ransoms

BOSSUAT, ANDRÉ. 'Les prisonniers de guerre au XVe siècle: la rançon de Jean, seigneur de Rodemack'. *AE*, 5th series, 3 (1951), pp. 145–62.

— 'Les prisonniers de guerre au XVe siècle: la rançon de Guillaume, seigneur de Châteauvillain'. *AB*, 23 (1951), pp. 7–35.

— 'Les prisonniers de Beauvais et la rançon du poète Jean Regnier, bailli d'Auxerre'. In *Mélanges d'histoire du Moyen Age dédiés à la mémoire de Louis Halphen*. Paris 1951, pp. 27–32.

PERROY, ÉDOUARD. 'Gras profits et rançons pendant la Guerre de Cent Ans: l'affaire du comte de Denia'. In *Mélanges d'histoire du Moyen Age dédiés à la mémoire de Louis Halphen*. Paris 1951, pp. 573–80. [This article, with the three previous ones, is fundamental for the study of prisoners and ransoms.]

'The Ransom of John II, King of France, 1360–1370'. Ed. DOROTHY M. BROOME. *Camden Miscellany XIV*. RHS. London 1926.

ROGERS, A. 'Hoten versus Shakell: a ransom case in the Court of Chivalry, 1390–95'. *Nottingham Mediaeval Studies*, 6 (1962), pp. 74–108; 7 (1963), pp. 53–78. [More on the comte de Denia.]

TISSET, P. 'Capture et rançon de Jeanne d'Arc'. *RHDFÉ*, 4th series, 46 (1968), pp. 63–9.

Booty and Profit

ALLMAND, C. T. 'War and Profit in the Late Middle Ages'. *HT*, 15 (1965), pp. 762–9.

HAY, DENYS. 'The Division of the Spoils of War in Fourteenth-Century England'. *TRHS*, 5th series, 4 (1954), pp. 91–109.

— 'Booty in Border Warfare'. *Transactions of the Dumfriesshire and Galloway Natural History and Antiquarian Society*, 3rd series, 31 (1954), pp. 145–66.

MCFARLANE, K. B. *The Nobility of Later Medieval England*. Oxford, 1973. [Contains a valuable section on the nobility and war.]

Rewards in Land and Offices

ALLMAND, C. T. 'The Lancastrian Land Settlement in Normandy, 1417–50'. *EconHR*, 2nd series, 21 (1968), pp. 461–79.

— 'Alan Kirketon: a clerical royal Councillor in Normandy during the English occupation in the fifteenth century'. *JEH*, 15 (1964), pp. 33–9.

CHARMA, A. 'Partie des dons faits par Henri V, roi d'Angleterre, lorsqu'il se fut rendu maître de la Normandie'. *MSAN*, 23 (1858), pp. 1–23.

PUISEUX, L. *L'émigration normande et la colonisation anglaise en Normandie au XVe siècle*. Paris 1865.

Discipline

FOWLER, KENNETH A. 'Les finances et la discipline dans les armées anglaises en France au XIVe siècle'. *Les Cahiers Vernonnais*, 4 (1964), pp. 55–84.

NEWHALL, R. A. 'Discipline in an English army of the Fifteenth Century'. *The Military Historian and Economist*, 2 (1917), pp. 141–51.

ROWE, B. J. H. 'Discipline in the Norman Garrisons under Bedford'. *EHR*, 46 (1931), pp. 194–208.

The Art of War

LOT, FERDINAND. *L'art militaire et les armées au moyen âge, en Europe et dans le Proche Orient*. 2 vols. Paris 1946.

OMAN, CHARLES W. *A History of the Art of War in the Middle Ages: II. 1278–1485*. London 1924. Reissued 1959. [Still supreme in English.]

TAYLOR, F. L. *The Art of War in Italy, 1494–1529*. Cambridge 1921.

I

Weapons and Fortifications

*Bibliotheca Phillippica. Medieval Manuscripts: New Series. Part VII·
21 November 1972.* [Sotheby's sale catalogue: useful for the war
machines of Conrad Kyeser.]

BLAIR, C. *European Armour, c. 1066–c. 1700.* London 1958.

Conrad Kyeser aus Eichstätt: Bellifortis. Ed. GÖTZ QUARG. Düsseldorf
1967.

CONTAMINE, PHILIPPE. 'L'artillerie royale française à la veille des guerres
d'Italie'. *ABret,* 71 (1964), pp. 221–61.

FAWTIER, ROBERT. 'Documents inédits sur l'organisation de l'artillerie
royale au temps de Louis XI'. In *Essays in Medieval History
presented to Thomas Frederick Tout.* Eds. A. G. LITTLE and F. M.
POWICKE. Manchester 1925, pp. 367–77.

FFOULKES, C. J. *The Gun-Founders of England.* Cambridge 1937.

— *Arms and Armament. An historical Survey of the Weapons of the
British Army.* London 1945. Reprinted 1947.

GARDNER, J. STARKIE. *Armour in England from the earliest times to the
seventeenth century.* London and New York 1898.

HALE, JOHN R. 'The Development of the Bastion, 1440–1534'. In *Europe
in the Late Middle Ages.* Eds. J. R. HALE, J. R. L. HIGHFIELD and
B. SMALLEY. London 1965, pp. 466–94.

The History of the King's Works. Eds. R. ALLEN BROWN, H. M. COLVIN
and A. J. TAYLOR. 3 vols. London 1963. [Important and useful.]

LACABANE, L. 'De la poudre à canon et de son introduction en France au
XIVe siècle'. *BEC,* 6 (1844), pp. 28–57.

MACKLIN, H. W. *Monumental Brasses.* 7th ed. London 1953. [Useful for
armour.]

MANN, J. G. *Catalogue of European Arms and Armour in the Wallace
Collection.* 2 vols. 2nd rev. ed. London 1962.

MCGUFFIE, T. H. 'The long-bow as a decisive weapon'. *HT,* 5 (1955),
pp. 737–41.

O'NEIL, B. H. ST. J. *Castles and Cannon. A Study of Early Artillery Fortifications in England.* Oxford 1960. [An important study, relating
developments in both military architecture and artillery.]

PAYNE-GALLWEY, R. *The Crossbow . . . Its Construction, History and
Management.* London 1958.

THOMPSON, A. HAMILTON. *Military Architecture in England during the
Middle Ages.* Oxford 1912.

TOUT, T. F. 'Firearms in England in the Fourteenth Century'. *EHR,* 26
(1911), pp. 666–702. Repr. in *The Collected Papers of Thomas
Frederick Tout.* Manchester 1934. Vol. II, pp. 233–75.

TOY, SIDNEY. *A History of Fortification from 3000 B.C. to A.D. 1700.*
London 1955.

TURNER, HILARY L. *Town Defences in England and Wales. An Architectural
and Documentary Study. A.D. 900–1500.* London 1971.

VIARD, J. 'Le siège de Calais, 4 septembre 1346–4 août 1347'. *MA*, 2nd series, 30 (1929), pp. 129–89.

VICTORIA AND ALBERT MUSEUM, LONDON. *Catalogue of Rubbings of Brasses and Incised Slabs.* Ed. MURIEL CLAYTON. 2nd ed. London 1968. [Useful illustrative matter.]

WARNER, PHILIP. *Sieges of the Middle Ages.* London 1968.

— *The Medieval Castle. Life in a Fortress in Peace and War.* London 1971.

The Non-Combatant and the War

ALLMAND, C. T. 'The War and the Non-Combatant'. In *The Hundred Years' War.* Ed. K. A. FOWLER. London 1971, pp. 163–83.

BOUTRUCHE, ROBERT. *La crise d'une société; seigneurs et paysans du Bordelais pendant la Guerre de Cent Ans.* Paris 1947. Repr. 1963. [A famous study of a society gripped by war.]

JOUET, ROGER. *La résistance à l'occupation anglaise en Basse-Normandie, (1418–1450).* Cahier des Annales de Normandie, 5. Caen 1969.

LUCE, SIMÉON. *La France pendant la Guerre de Cent Ans. Épisodes historiques et vie privée aux XIVe et XVe siècles.* 2 vols. Paris 1890, 1893.

RICHARDSON, H. G. 'Illustrations of English History in the Medieval Registers of the Parlement of Paris'. *TRHS*, 4th series, 10 (1927), pp. 55–85.

VERGER, JACQUES. 'The University of Paris at the End of the Hundred Years' War'. In *Universities in Politics. Case Studies from the Late Middle Ages and Early Modern Period.* Eds. JOHN W. BALDWIN and RICHARD A. GOLDTHWAITE. Baltimore and London 1972, pp. 47–78.

Propaganda and Public Opinion

BOSSUAT, ANDRÉ. 'La littérature de propagande au XVe siècle. La mémoire de Jean de Rinel, secrétaire du roi d'Angleterre, contre le duc de Bourgogne (1435)'. *Cahiers d'Histoire*, 1 (1956), pp. 131–46.

COVILLE, ALFRED. 'Poèmes historiques de l'avènement de Philippe de Valois au traité de Calais (1328–1360)'. In *Histoire littéraire de la France*, 38. Paris 1949, pp. 259–333.

GUENÉE, BERNARD and LEHOUX, F. *Les entrées royales françaises de 1328 à 1515.* Paris 1968.

Historical Poems of the XIVth and XVth Centuries. Ed. ROSSELL HOPE ROBBINS. New York 1959. [A valuable collection.]

LEWIS, PETER S. 'Two Pieces of Fifteenth-Century Political Iconography'. *JWCI*, 27 (1964), pp. 317–20.

— 'War Propaganda and Historiography in Fifteenth-Century France and England'. *TRHS*, 5th series, 15 (1965), pp. 1–21.

MCFARLANE, K. B. 'William Worcester: a Preliminary Survey'. In *Studies presented to Sir Hilary Jenkinson.* Ed. J. CONWAY DAVIES. London 1957, pp. 196–221.

MCKENNA, J. W. 'Henry VI of England and the Dual Monarchy: Aspects of Royal Political Propaganda, 1422–1432'. *JWCI*, 28 (1965), pp. 145–62. [Valuable.]

OWST. G. R. *Preaching in Medieval England. An Introduction to Sermon Manuscripts of the period c. 1350–1450*. Cambridge 1926. Reprinted New York 1965. [Important.]

— *Literature and the Pulpit in medieval England*. Cambridge 1933. Reprinted Oxford 1961.

The Poems of Laurence Minot. Ed. J. HALL. 3rd ed. Oxford 1914.

Political Poems and Songs, relating to English History, composed during the period from the Accession of Edward III to that of Richard III. Ed. T. WRIGHT. RS. 2 vols. London 1859–61.

PRINCE, ALBERT E. 'A Letter of Edward the Black Prince describing the Battle of Nájera in 1367'. *EHR*, 41 (1926), pp. 415–8.

ROSKELL, J. S. and TAYLOR, F. 'The Authorship and Purpose of the *Gesta Henrici Quinti*: II'. *BJRL*, 54 (1971), pp. 223–40. [On the relationship between propaganda and history.]

ROWE, B. J. H. 'King Henry VI's Claim to France in Picture and Poem'. *The Library: Transactions of the Bibliographical Society*, 4th series, 13 (1933), pp. 77–88.

The War Ballads of Laurence Minot. Ed. D. C. STEDMAN. Dublin 1917.

Representation and Finance

BAYLEY, C. C. 'The Campaign of 1375 and the Good Parliament'. *EHR*, 55 (1940), pp. 370–83.

BEAUREPAIRE, C. DE. *Les états de Normandie sous la domination anglaise*. Evreux 1859.

BRYANT, W. N. 'The financial dealings of Edward III with the county communities, 1330–1360'. *EHR*, 83 (1968), pp. 760–71.

COVILLE, A. *Les états de Normandie: leurs origines et leur développement au XIVe siècle*. Paris 1894.

DOUCET, R. 'Les finances anglaises en France à la fin de la Guerre de Cent Ans, 1413–1435'. *MA*, 2nd series, 27 (1926), pp. 265–332.

The English Government at Work, 1327–1336: II. Fiscal Administration. Eds. W. A. MORRIS and J. R. STRAYER. Cambridge, Mass. 1947.

FRYDE, EDMUND B. 'Parliament and the French War, 1336–40'. In *Essays in Medieval History presented to Bertie Wilkinson*. Eds. T. A. SANDQUIST and M. R. POWICKE. Toronto 1969, pp. 250–69.

HARRISS, GERALD L. 'Aids, Loans and Benevolences'. *HJ*, 6 (1963), pp. 1–19.

HENNEMAN, J. B. 'Financing the Hundred Years' War: Royal Taxation in France in 1340'. *Speculum*, 42 (1967), pp. 275–98.

— *Royal Taxation in Fourteenth Century France. The Development of War Financing 1322–1356*. Princeton 1971.

MCFARLANE, K. B. 'Loans to the Lancastrian Kings: the Problem of Inducement'. *CHJ*, 9 (1947), pp. 51–68. [A fine study of one method of raising money.]

NEWHALL, R. A. 'The War Finances of Henry V and the Duke of Bedford'. *EHR*, 36 (1921), pp. 172–98.

PRESTWICH, MICHAEL. *War, Politics and Finance under Edward I*. London 1972.

REY, M. *Les finances royales sous Charles VI. Les causes du déficit 1388–1413*. Paris 1965. [Especially pp. 355–435.]

— *Le domaine du roi et les finances extraordinaires sous Charles VI, 1388–1413*. Paris 1965.

ROWE, B. J. H. 'The Estates of Normandy under the Duke of Bedford, 1422–1435'. *EHR*, 46 (1931), pp. 551–78.

TAYLOR, CHARLES H. 'Assemblies of Towns and War Subsidy, 1318–1319'. In JOSEPH R. STRAYER and CHARLES H. TAYLOR, *Studies in Early French Taxation*. Cambridge, Mass. and London 1939, pp. 107–200.

— 'French Assemblies and Subsidy in 1321'. *Speculum*, 43 (1968), pp. 217–44.

Private War

MAS-LATRIE, R. DE. 'Du droit de Marque ou droit de Représailles au moyen âge'. *BEC*, 27 (1866), pp. 529–77.

Nationalism

ASCOLI, G. *La Grande Bretagne devant l'opinion française. I : depuis la Guerre de Cent Ans jusqu'à la fin du XVIe siècle*. Paris 1927. [Contains much useful information.]

BOSSUAT, ANDRÉ. 'Les origines troyennes. Leur rôle dans la littérature historique au XVe siècle'. *AN*, 8 (1958), pp. 187–97.

GROSJEAN, G. *Le sentiment national dans la Guerre de Cent Ans*. Paris 1928. [The basic work on the subject.]

KEENY, B. C. 'Military Service and the Development of Nationalism in England, 1272–1327'. *Speculum*, 22 (1947), pp. 534–49.

KIRKLAND, DOROTHY. 'The Growth of National Sentiment in France before the Fifteenth Century'. *History*, 23 (1938–39), pp. 12–24.

LANGLOIS, C.-V. 'Les Anglais du moyen âge d'après les sources françaises'. *RH*, 52 (1893), pp. 298–315.

Peace-making

ALLMAND, C. T. 'Diplomacy in late-medieval England'. *HT*, 17 (1967)' pp. 546–53.

— 'The Anglo-French Negotiations, 1439'. *BIHR*, 40 (1967), pp. 1–33.

CHAPLAIS, P. T. V. M. 'Règlement des conflits internationaux franco-anglais au XIVe siècle (1293–1377)'. *MA*, 57 (1951), pp. 269–302.

CUTTINO, G. P. *English Diplomatic Administration, 1259–1339*. Oxford. 2nd rev. ed. 1971. [An important work on English diplomatic administration and history in the early fourteenth century.]

— 'The Process of Agen'. *Speculum*, 19 (1944), pp. 161–78.

DÉPREZ, E. 'La conférence d'Avignon (1344). L'arbitrage pontificale entre la France et l'Angleterre'. In *Essays in Medieval History presented to T. F. Tout*. Eds. A. G. LITTLE and F. M. POWICKE. Manchester 1925, pp. 301–20.

DICKINSON, JOYCELYNE G. *The Congress of Arras 1435. A Study of Medieval Diplomacy*. Oxford 1955. [A fine study.]

DUFOURNET, P. *La destruction des mythes dans les Mémoires de Philippe de Commynes*. Geneva 1966. [Chapter VII on war and diplomacy.]

FOWLER, KENNETH A. 'Truces'. In *The Hundred Years' War*. Ed. K. A. FOWLER. London 1971. Pp. 184–215.

GANSHOF, FRANÇOIS L. *Histoire des relations internationales. I: Le Moyen Age*. 3rd rev. ed. Paris 1964. [A basic work on the diplomacy of the Middle Ages.]

GUILLEMAIN B. 'Les tentatives pontificales de médiation dans le litige franco–anglais de Guyenne au XIVe siècle'. *Bulletin historique et philologique du comité des travaux historiques et scientifiques (1957)*, pp. 423–32.

LUCAS, HENRY S. 'The Machinery of Diplomatic Intercourse'. In *The English Government at Work 1327–1336. I: Central and Prerogative Administration*. Eds. JAMES F. WILLARD and WILLIAM A. MORRIS. Mediaeval Academy of America. Cambridge, Mass. 1940, pp. 300–31.

MOLLAT, GUILLAUME. 'Innocent VI et les tentatives de paix entre la France et l'Angleterre (1353–1355)'. *RHE*, 10 (1909), pp. 729–43.

PALMER, JOHN J. N. 'The Anglo–French Peace Negotiations, 1390–1396'. *TRHS*, 5th series, 16 (1966), pp. 81–94.

— 'The War Aims of the Protagonists and the Negotiations for Peace'. In *The Hundred Years' War*. Ed. K. A. FOWLER. London 1971, pp. 51–74.

QUELLER, D. *The Office of Ambassador in the Late Middle Ages*. Princeton 1967. [The best work on the subject.]

WAGNER, ANTHONY. *Heralds of England. A History of the Office and College of Arms*. London 1967. [On the role of the herald in diplomacy.]

The Effects of Peace

ALLMAND, C. T. 'La Normandie devant l'opinion anglaise à la fin de la Guerre de Cent Ans'. *BEC*, 128 (1970), pp. 345–68. [Emphasises opposition to peace.]

BOSSUAT, ANDRÉ 'Le rétablissement de la paix sociale sous le règne de Charles VII'. *MA*, 60 (1954), pp. 137–62. Reprinted as 'The Re-establishment of Peace in Society during the Reign of Charles VII'. In *The Recovery of France in the Fifteenth Century*. Ed. P. S. LEWIS. London 1971, pp. 60–81. [An important article suggestive of new approaches of study.]

BOUTRUCHE, ROBERT. *Bordeaux de 1453 à 1715*. (*Histoire de Bordeaux*. Ed. C. HIGOUNET. Vol. 4.) Bordeaux 1966.

CARUS-WILSON, E. M. 'The Effects of the Acquisition and of the Loss of Gascony on the English Wine Trade'. *BIHR*, 21 (1947), pp. 145–54. Repr. in CARUS-WILSON, E. M., *Medieval Merchant Venturers*. London 1954. 2nd edn. 1967.

CRUMP, C. G. and JOHNSON, C. 'The Powers of Justices of the Peace'. *EHR*, 27 (1912), pp. 226–38. [On some social effects of peace.]

JAMES, MARGERY K. *Studies in the Medieval Wine Trade*. Ed. E. M. VEALE. Oxford 1971. [Contains two important essays on the wine trade.]

LEWIS, PETER S. (Ed.). *The Recovery of France in the Fifteenth Century*. London 1971. [Contains some valuable essays translated into English.]

POSTAN, M. M. 'Some Social Consequences of the Hundred Years' War'. *EconHR*, 12 (1942), pp. 1–12.

RENOUARD, YVES. 'Les conséquences de la conquête de Guienne par le roi de France pour le commerce des vins'. *AM*, 61 (1948), pp. 15–31.

'Some Documents regarding the Fulfilment and Interpretation of the Treaty of Brétigny, 1361–1369'. Ed. PIERRE CHAPLAIS. *Camden Miscellany XIX*. RHS. London 1952. [On the practical difficulties of interpreting a peace settlement.]

War and Development in Society

BEELER, JOHN. 'Military Developments from Prehistoric Times in 1485'. In *A Guide to the Sources of British Military History*. Ed. R. HIGHAM. London 1972, pp. 43–64.

BELLAMY, J. G. *The Law of Treason in England in the Late Middle Ages*. Cambridge 1970.

BERESFORD, MAURICE W. *New Towns of the Middle Ages. Town Plantation in England, Wales and Gascony*. London 1967.

CARUS-WILSON, E. M. 'Evidences of industrial growth in some fifteenth-century manors'. *EconHR*, 2nd series, 12 (1959–60), pp. 190–205. [On war as a stimulus to economic growth.]

CAZELLES, R. *La société politique et la crise de la royauté sous Philippe de Valois*. Paris 1958.

FOWLER, KENNETH A. 'War and Change in Late Medieval France and England'. In *The Hundred Years' War*. Ed. K. A. FOWLER. London 1971, pp. 1–27. [A useful survey article.]

LEWIS, PETER S. 'Decayed and Non-Feudalism in Later Medieval France'. *BIHR*, 37 (1964), pp. 157–84. [On changing social and military relationships, chiefly in south-western France.]

— *Later Medieval France. The Polity*. London and New York 1968. [A valuable survey of late medieval French society.]

MCFARLANE, K. B. 'Bastard Feudalism'. *BIHR*, 20 (1943–5), pp. 161–80. [A classic study.]

— 'War and Society, 1300–1600. England and the Hundred Years' War'. *Past and Present*, 22 (1962), pp. 3–13. [A short but important contribution.]

MCROBBIE, KENNETH. 'The Concept of Advancement in the Fourteenth

Century in the Chroniques of Jean Froissart'. *CJH*, 6 (1971), pp. 1–19.

MOREL, HENRI. 'Une association de seigneurs gascons au XIVe siècle'. In *Mélanges d'histoire du Moyen Age dédiés à la mémoire de Louis Halphen*. Paris 1951, pp. 523–34.

PERROY, ÉDOUARD. 'Social Mobility among the French *Noblesse* in the Later Middle Ages'. *Past and Present*, 21 (1962), pp. 25–38.

POSTAN, M. M. 'The Costs of the Hundred Years' War'. *Past and Present*, 27 (1964), pp. 34–53. [A reply to 'War and Society 1300–1600' by K. B. McFarlane listed above.]

WHITE, LYNN, JR. *Medieval Technology and Social Change*. Oxford 1962. Reprinted 1971. [A now well-known study.]

INDEX